THE CALIFORNIA WORLD HISTORY LIBRARY

Edited by Edmund Burke III, Kenneth Pomeranz, and Patricia Seed

Imperial Connections

Imperial Connections

India in the Indian Ocean Arena,
1860–1920

Thomas R. Metcalf

UNIVERSITY OF CALIFORNIA PRESS

Berkeley / Los Angeles / London

University of California Press, one of the most distinguished university presses in the United States, enriches lives around the world by advancing scholarship in the humanities, social sciences, and natural sciences. Its activities are supported by the UC Press Foundation and by philanthropic contributions from individuals and institutions. For more information, visit www.ucpress.edu.

An earlier version of chapter 5 appeared as "Hard Hands and Sound Healthy Bodies: Recruiting 'Coolies' for Natal, 1860–1911" in *Journal of Imperial and Commonwealth History*, vol. 30 (2002): 1–26. Reproduced by permission of Taylor and Francis, www.tandf.co.uk.

Frontispiece: Sikh sentry, Fort Johnston, Nyasaland, by Harry Johnston. Courtesy of the Royal Geographical Society, London.

University of California Press
Berkeley and Los Angeles, California

University of California Press, Ltd.
London, England

Library of Congress Cataloging-in-Publication Data

Metcalf, Thomas R., 1934–.
    Imperial connections : India in the Indian Ocean arena, 1860–1920 / Thomas R. Metcalf.
        p.   cm. — (The California world history library ; 4)
    Includes bibliographical references and index.
    ISBN 978-0-520-24946-2 (cloth : alk. paper)
        1. Indian Ocean Region — Colonization — History.   2. East Indians — Indian Ocean Region — Colonization — History.   3. East Indians — Employment — Indian Ocean Region — History.   4. Great Britain — Colonies — Africa — Administration.   5. Great Britain — Colonies — Asia — Administration.   6. India. Army — Colonial forces — Indian Ocean Region.   I. Title.
    DS340.M48   2007
    909'.09824081 — dc22   2006021611

15   14   13   12   11   10   09   08   07
10   9   8   7   6   5   4   3   2   1

The publisher gratefully acknowledges the generous contribution to this book provided by the Ahmanson Foundation Humanities Endowment Fund of the University of California Press Foundation.

Contents

Illustrations

Maps

Figures

Preface

This volume originated during the course of two trips, one to South Africa and the other to Malaya, devoted to a project undertaken some years ago on British colonial architecture. During the first, to South Africa in 1982, although I had long known of the existence of overseas Indian communities across the empire, I came to experience at first hand the situation of Indians as a group uneasily placed between black and white in the apartheid era. How, I wondered, had an Indian community, by then some three-quarters of a million in number, been induced to migrate to South Africa, and what did this migration tell us about the ties between India and South Africa under British colonialism? During a month in the Pietermaritzburg archives, I began the research on recruitment of Indian indentured labor that forms chapter 5 of this volume. Some years later, while touring Malaya and Singapore, I was startled to discover, primarily in Kuala Lumpur but across the peninsula as well, an array of "Saracenic"-styled buildings erected by the British and by the Malay sultans. How, I wondered, had this architectural style, developed in India as the British sought to portray themselves in Mughal garb, and discussed in my book *An Imperial Vision*, been taken up in Malaya, where the Mughals had never ruled and the indigenous architectural forms possessed nothing in common with those of India?

From India — I soon came to realize as I reflected on these initial encounters — ideas, peoples, and even the sinews of power flowed outward during the heyday of empire across the Indian Ocean to the west, to Africa, and to the east, to Malaya and East Asia. This message was driven home as I was writing this work by the American invasion of Iraq in 2003. Prompted by that quasi-imperial military operation, with the long drawn out "insurgency" that it precipitated, I turned back to examine the earlier British occupation of Mesopotamia during the First World War. Here I found that — from the 1914 occupation of Basra on through the 1916 disaster at Kut to the 1920 rebellion — the subjugation of Iraq was the work of the Indian army, and its subsequent colonial governance, until 1921, was undertaken by Indians and by British officials from India. The India of the Raj clearly, then, had to be seen as a "colonizing" as well as a "colonized" land. Such ambiguity is not comfortably incorporated into nationalist historiography, whether Indian or African. Nor have historians of the British Empire, whether proud of its accomplishments or critical, thought to place India, rather than Britain, at its center. This book is an attempt to assess the consequences, alike for India and the empire, of looking at both from the perspective of the Indian Ocean.

To avoid confusion, it is essential at the outset to make clear that certain terms used in this book are subject to varying meanings. The most important of these is "colonial." In current scholarly writing the term "colonial" — as in "colonial discourse," or "post-colonial theory" — refers to the subjugation of one people by another. In this work general references to "colonial governance" or "colonial rule" usually carry the same connotation. The term, however, carries a separate, more restrictive, usage in the administration of the British Empire. In this usage Britain's "colonies," both those of conquest and of settlement, are grouped together and are set apart from India. This distinction took administrative form in the distinction between the Colonial Office, responsible for the governance of "colonies," and the India Office, charged with responsibility for the government of India. Phrases such as "Indian recruitment for 'colonial' police forces" or "Indian migration to the 'colonies,'" adopt this more restrictive usage. A further distinction must be made between two uses of the administrative title "colonial secretary." This term denotes both the Secretary of State for the Colonies, at the Colonial Office in London, and the chief administrative officer under the governor of a colony, such as the Colonial Secretary of the Straits Settlements. The terms "India" and "Indian" are also subject to varied usage. They can mean the British-controlled government of India as in "the Indian government," the territory under the jurisdiction of the Raj as in "British India," or the residents of that country as in "Indians" or "the Indian people." It is hoped that context will make clear which of these various referents is meant in particular instances.

I have carried out research for this project in a wide range of archives. I should like to acknowledge and thank the directors and staff of the following: the Oriental and India Office Collections of the British Library; the Public Record Office (now the National Archives), Kew; the National Archives of India, New Delhi; the Kwazulu-Natal Record Office, Pietermaritzburg; the library of the National University, Singapore; and the libraries of the University of California, Berkeley, and of the University of Michigan, Ann Arbor. I made brief visits as well to the Singapore Archives; the Malaysian Archives, Kuala Lumpur; and the Zanzibar Archives.

I am deeply indebted to Katherine Prior for research assistance in the British Library and the National Archives (Kew), where she located and transcribed documents for me both when I was in England and when I was back in the United States. For research assistance in Berkeley I am indebted to several of my then graduate students, most notably Ariana De Rochefort-Reynolds, Priya Satia, and Deana Heath. While I was in London in 2004, Caroline Shaw located relevant files at Kew from the online index and e-mailed the citations to me so that I might immediately consult the original documents. Robin Mitchell compiled material for me on the Gurkhas, while Corrie Decker showed me around Zanzibar in January 2005. In Zanzibar, Abdul Sheriff, in several talks at the palace museum and through his writings, introduced me to the history of Zanzibar, while Amyn Bapoo of the Aga Khan Development Network enabled me to tour the conservation projects currently under way in that city. I am grateful to Ali Asani of Harvard for arranging these meetings. In Ann Arbor, Nafisa Sheik helped with the time-consuming task of preparing the manuscript for publication.

Research for this study was supported by Clare Hall, Cambridge, where I was a visiting fellow during spring 1996; by the National University of Singapore and its Institute for Southeast Asian Studies during January–February 1997; by the American Institute of Indian Studies for research in New Delhi in 1997 and again in January 2005; by the Rockefeller Study Center, Bellagio, Italy, where I was a fellow during May–June 1999; and by the Mellon Foundation, which generously awarded me an Emeritus Fellowship for the years 2004–05 and 2005–06. The Mellon Fellowship made possible travel to England, India, Zanzibar, and Kenya, as well as research assistance during those two years. In addition, the University of California awarded me a President's Fellowship in 1997, with additional support from its faculty research funds over the following years.

Several of my colleagues and friends have encouraged me with their advice and suggestions as the project has proceeded. Thomas Laqueur, from the very outset, helped me frame ways of thinking about India as an imperial "center" and invited me to present my work at the National Humanities Center while he was in residence there. James Vernon shared with me the teaching of a stimulating graduate seminar on Britain and the empire at Berkeley. Chris Bayly, over the course of several visits to Cambridge, with pints of beer at his favorite pub, provided continuing encouragement and suggestions. Radhika Singha, in conversations in both Delhi and Ann Arbor, and by sharing her unpublished work with me, enabled me to get a much fuller sense of India's role in the First World War. Dane Kennedy, who subsequently revealed himself to be one of the University of California Press's anonymous readers, gave me a number of valuable suggestions for revision and urged me to push the project forward. In Ann Arbor, the South Asian *kitabmandal* group, especially Will Glover and Farina Mir, have provided me with consistent friendship, encouragement, and suggestions. In the fall of 2005 the History Department of the University of Michigan appointed me a visiting professor to teach a course incorporating my research within the larger history of the Indian Ocean. I am grateful to the then chair, Sonya Rose, for arranging this appointment and to the students in this seminar, both undergraduate and graduate, for the energy and ideas they shared with me. Lynne Withey at the University of California Press encouraged me from the outset to publish this work with the press; and even when she took up the onerous duties of press director, she continued to act as my editor. It is a rare treat to work with such an individual.

Several institutions, over the course of a number of years, invited me to give talks or seminars on the subject of this volume. The critical comments of the listeners at these sessions were indispensable in helping me develop my ideas and sharpen my focus. These institutions include Cambridge University (at the invitation of C. A. Bayly); Oxford University (at the invitation of David Washbrook); the Jawaharlal Nehru University, New Delhi (at the invitation of Kunal Chakrabarti and with the encouragement of Majid Siddiqi); the National Humanities Center, Research Triangle Park, North Carolina; Bowdoin College (at the invitation of Rachel Sturman); the University of Washington, Seattle; and the World History Association, which invited me to be a plenary speaker at its 1999 meeting in Victoria, BC. The talk I gave in Victoria was subsequently published as "Empire Recentered: India in the Indian Ocean Arena," in Gregory Blue, Martin Bunton, and Ralph Croizier, eds.,

Colonialism and the Modern World: Selected Studies (Armonk, NY: M. E. Sharpe, 2002). I am grateful to Clive Dewey for inviting me to present an early draft of my study of colonial policing at the "New Military History" conference at Cambridge in 1997, and to the Berkeley and Davis history departments for the invitation to be guest speaker at their annual joint dinner in 2003. As the project was nearing its end, an invitation as visiting scholar at the Institute for International Integration Studies, Dublin, Ireland, in February–March 2006 gave me an opportunity to discuss my work with students and faculty at Trinity College and at the National University of Ireland, Galway. Especially stimulating were our discussions of parallels between colonialism in India and in Ireland. I am grateful to Deana Heath at Trinity and Tadhg Foley at Galway for arranging this visit.

It is impossible for me to acknowledge how much this project owes to Barbara Metcalf. She time and again took time out from her own busy life of research and teaching to think with me about the project, and then to go through every chapter with a sharp pencil. She never allowed me to rest content with lazy thinking or unexamined assumptions. Her presence and support throughout the course of this project, indeed during forty-some years of marriage, have alone made it possible for me to thrive and flourish. To her this book is dedicated.

Introduction

Empire Recentered

As he descended from the first ascent of Mt. Kenya in 1899 and marched toward Nairobi, then still little more than a railroad encampment, having had a number of uneasy encounters with the indigenous people, Halford Mackinder imagined himself crossing an invisible border. "Suddenly," he wrote, "one passed out of Africa into Asia, out of *Bwana* country into *Sahib* country! There was a bazaar. . . . There I found a man paying wages. . . . I came back to civilization."[1]

Mackinder's experience was like that of many others during the scramble for empire from the 1870s to the First World War. For the explorer and the early colonial administrator in the "wilds" of Africa, India, which had been brought under British rule a century before, represented a reassuring center of order, of civilization, of empire. The existence of the Raj, this study argues, made possible British imperial conquest, control, and governance across a wide arc of territory stretching from Africa to eastern Asia. Further, with India placed at its center, the British Empire has to be imagined differently. In this vision, India is not just one among many British colonies, or a "periphery" of the capitalist system, or a land of "subalterns" struggling to be free. It is in addition a nodal point from which peoples, ideas, goods, and institutions — everything that enables an empire to exist — radiated outward. For much of South Africa, especially Natal, for Central and East Africa, for the Arabian and Gulf coasts, for the islands of the Indian Ocean, for the Malayan peninsula and beyond, the ties of empire ran not only to London but also to Calcutta, Bombay, and Madras.

I

To be sure, the British established and directed this vast imperial enterprise, and they did so to secure wealth and advantage for themselves. The Union Jack and no other banner fluttered from a thousand flagstaffs from Cape Town to Shanghai. But, as we shall see, the initial conquests on the ground were the work of Indians, the sepoy soldiers of the Indian Army; and the policing of the conquered territories fell to Indian, usually Sikh, troopers. Exploitation of the resources of the new colonial empire was the work of Indians. Some were recruited as indentured laborers for cane fields from Natal to Fiji and the Caribbean, and for the Uganda Railway. Others were drawn by the trading opportunities held out to Indians who had money and entrepreneurial skills, men who migrated, commonly from Gujarat or Tamilnadu to colonial towns such as Durban, Nairobi, Singapore, and Kuala Lumpur. Further, with the exception of a few top-ranked civil servants recruited in Britain, the professional and clerical staff employed in the new colonial territories — including those of British ancestry — was largely drawn from India and from the Indian administrative services. In effect, the late Victorian and Edwardian empire in Africa and Southeast Asia was run by Indians and by Britons trained in India. The practice of empire was, as well, shaped by structures of governance devised in British India. From Macaulay's law codes to the paired creation of the Collector in the district and the Resident at the princely court, from the classifying of ethnic groups to the working of "divide and rule," the India of the Raj was the touchstone around which colonial administrative systems were put together. Sometimes Indian precedents were defiantly rejected, as we will see, but India was too powerful a presence in the empire simply to be ignored.

As they flocked to the new colonial territories and took up positions within them, Indians increasingly came to imagine their own identities in new ways. Above all, they conceived of themselves not merely as colonial subjects but as imperial citizens. Both those who settled overseas and those who stayed behind conceived of the British Empire as an arena open to talents, where all, Indian and British alike, might flourish. They envisaged an empire that, as V. S. Srinivasa Sastri wrote, upheld "equality not discrimination" as its principle, "brotherhood not domination" as its motto, and "uplift not exploitation" as its aim.[2] To a considerable extent, all of the early or "moderate" nationalists, including those who led the Indian National Congress, subscribed to this view. Keenly aware of India's role as an imperial center, men like Govind Ranade and Dadabhai Naoroji saw the empire, at its best, as providing shared opportunities, on the basis of a shared loyalty to the Crown, for the spread of wealth and knowledge to all.

Participation in the overseas empire also helped to create a sense of a distinctive "Indian" nationality. In part, this arose from the painful experience of discrimination, especially at the hands of white settler colonists. The promised ideals, and expectations of equal treatment, all too frequently evaporated in the reality of lived experience. In India, contact with whites was, for most, infrequent and was mediated by established rules of conduct. In the settler and plantation colonies, by contrast, Indians experienced firsthand a harsh and virulent racism. Indenture, above all, which reduced Indians to the status of "coolies," and especially the abuse of Indian women at the hands of plantation managers evoked an abhorrence among those who sought recognition of their respectability, and hence their right to equal treatment, in the larger empire. The campaign to end indenture was to channel much Indian resentment against the broken promises of "imperial citizenship."

Surely the best known of these colonial racial encounters is that of Mohandas Gandhi. A young English-trained lawyer, Gandhi went to Natal in search of employment when he could not succeed at the Bombay bar. For him, as with so many others, the empire was a place of opportunity and evoked a loyalty that he endeavored to repay on such occasions as the formation of an ambulance corps during the 1899–1902 South African War. Yet — as the movie *Gandhi* so vividly recounts — despite being well educated, well dressed, and in possession of a first-class ticket, Gandhi found himself unceremoniously ejected from his train carriage and left to ponder the meaning of the British Empire on the station platform at Pietermaritzburg.

Residence overseas, whether in England or in the colonies, also, by its very nature, encouraged Indians to conceive of themselves as Indian. Life within the India of the Raj was confined by a colonial sociology that placed all its inhabitants in a set of boxes — of caste, community, region — and vigorously denied the existence of any larger entity. More to the point perhaps, daily life in colonial India — as in most countries — caught people up in a swirl of loyalties and commitments that intersected and interacted with each other. Kin and family, caste and clan, these loyalties overshadowed and pushed to the margin conscious enunciation of a larger sense of belonging to a nation. Abroad, however, Indians came face-to-face with their nationality. Indian students in London, for instance, sought out the company of each other in Indian students' associations. In South Africa, although Gandhi was first hired by Indian merchants who were, though Muslim, like himself members of Gujarati trading castes, he soon discovered that discrimination affected all Indians. Hence he placed himself at the head of protest movements that in time included, among others, the oppressed laborers in the cane fields. The Natal Indian Congress and the newspaper *Indian Opinion,* both of which Gandhi founded, made visible this newly formulated sense of Indian identity and opened the way to Gandhi's mobilization of a larger Indian community when he returned home.[3]

Such a nationality came at a price. Gandhi was unable in South Africa to include black Africans in his political activities. In India, he could only partially and with difficulty incorporate Muslims into a conception of India embedded in a deeply Hindu worldview. Furthermore, the growth of a sense of nationality and the nationalist enthusiasms it unleashed helped undercut the very opportunities the British Empire had provided for men like Gandhi. The British Empire depended for its success as much upon a free flow of people across frontiers as upon its vaunted "free trade" policy. Until 1914 passports did not exist, and where similar documents did exist, their use was often not enforced. Within the empire, however, colonial nationalism began putting up barriers to migration. Restrictive immigration policies were first enunciated by Natal in the mid-1890s, and these in turn inspired similar restrictions in Australia and Canada after 1900. A reluctant government of India, fearful of who might enter the country, began, during the First World War, imposing its own restraints on mobility. By the 1920s the passport officially signified that its holder was "Indian." Its possession might gain a "respectable" Indian temporary entry into Australia, but the imperial citizen was no more.[4]

It is often forgotten that, like Indians, resident Britons ("Anglo-Indians," as they were called in the nineteenth century) also hastened to take advantage of the opportunities provided by the growth of the colonial empire. To be sure, officials at the top of the administrative hierarchy disdained service outside India. Viceroys, appointed for short periods of five years, might move from place to place, but the members of the "heaven-born" Indian Civil Service, with rare exceptions such as Bartle Frere in the later nineteenth century and Malcolm Hailey in the twentieth, saw no advantage for themselves in transfers to small colonies with uncertain prospects. Matters were different lower down the scale. Technically trained personnel and military officers readily grasped at tours of duty in the new colonies. For military officers, tired of endless garrison duty on dusty parade grounds or, like Frederick Lugard, chafing under the constraints of scandal, colonial service opened up opportunities for combat and even for fame. Midlevel officials trained in such fields as engineering, forestry, and architecture too saw in colonial service a way to carve out for themselves positions of greater responsibility than existed in the bureaucratic India of the Raj.

Typical perhaps is the career of William Willcocks (1852–1932). Born "in a tent in the Dehra Doon" to a father employed in the Irrigation Branch of the Public Works Department, Willcocks attended a boarding school in the Mussoorie hills together with mixed-race children and then went to Roorkee Engineering College. He preferred it, he said, to Cambridge because it "stood on the Ganges Canal." After graduation, he was himself employed on the Ganges canal works. In 1884, recommended by his former superior the engineer Sir Colin Scott-Moncrieff, who had gone on ahead, he joined the Egyptian Irrigation Service. There, in addition to developing plans for several barrages and canals, Willcocks was placed in charge of the initial surveys preparatory to the construction of the first Aswan Dam. In 1897 he took up the position of manager of the Cairo Water Company, at double his government salary, and that was followed by employment with an Egyptian land development company laying out subdivision plots. In 1908 Willcocks was summoned to Mesopotamia by the Ottoman authorities to prepare plans for the Hindia barrage on the Tigris. After three years there, frustrated by official interference, he handed over his project reports and returned to Egypt, where he lived in retirement until his death.[5]

Willcocks was, to be sure, English in nationality, and he took advantage of the privileges and professional associations which that status secured to him; but his career, spanning the empire from India to Egypt and Mesopotamia, was nevertheless not so far removed from that of a senior engineer of Indian origin. He never at any time lived in England and indeed traveled there only twice for short visits. As he wrote of his first visit, in the autumn of 1898, speaking like the colonial he was, "The short days, the foggy atmosphere, and the universal gloom so depressed me that I understood why so many Egyptians who were sent to England [for study] . . . came back to Egypt hating everything English." To like the English climate, he said with feeling, "you must be born and bred in it."[6] Like so many others "born and bred" in the Raj, Indian and English alike, Willcocks made of Indian service a springboard to professional success beyond its shores. At the same time, he helped spread British Indian irrigation techniques and knowledge, formulated in such places as Roorkee College and the Ganges Canal, to river systems in Africa, the Middle East, and elsewhere. Indian ideas and practices, as we will see, moved with Indian trained personnel from the Indian center to colonial peripheries around the Indian Ocean.

The British in India also imagined themselves at the center of a vast sphere of influence controlled from India's mountaintop capital of Simla. The institutional embodiment of this "subimperial" diplomacy, which one recent author has called the "empire of the Raj," was the Foreign Department of the government of India. H. M. Durand (1850–1924), foreign secretary from 1885 to 1894 and author of the "Durand line" separating India and Afghanistan, vividly imagined India's role in Asia in his 1885 "Memorandum on the External Relations of the Government of India." He proposed that the government of India ought to control England's relations with "all the purely Asiatic continental powers" from Persia and Siam to China and Korea. If "all the reins" of Asian diplomacy could be gathered into the hands of "one controlling authority" centered in India, then "Englishmen all over Asia" would gain and the empire would be stronger and more secure.[7] Although this grandiose vision was never implemented, nevertheless the bureaucrats at Simla exercised a controlling authority across much of the Middle East, where they appointed residents at the Gulf and Persian courts and, through the agency of the Bombay presidency, at the outposts of Aden and Zanzibar. Relations with Afghanistan and Central Asia too, as part of Kipling's "Great Game," fell under the control of the Indian Foreign Department.

Larger Contexts: Imperial, Oceanic, Global

In practice, whatever its protagonists might claim, the historiography of imperialism over the years has been hardly less Eurocentric than the traditional accounts of Western civilization. The scholar simply adds to the European narrative the voyages of Vasco da Gama and the exploits of Clive, or else, following Immanuel Wallerstein, constructs a "world system" emanating from the European "core." At their best such histories, most influentially in the case of Robinson and Gallagher, help explain the patterns of conquest and rule — why here? why then? — in particular times and places. Once the historian sets foot on the colonial shore, however, the focus of attention abruptly narrows. In most accounts of colonialism, each colony is assumed to exist only in its relationship to the imperial center. These studies in effect conceive of the British Empire as a set of strings — or better yet, as lines of telegraph wire through which information flows up and policy directives flow down — running from each colony to the metropole in London. The history of each colony is thus written in isolation from those of its neighbors. Not surprisingly, this historiography is itself embedded in the archive. The records of the Colonial Office in Kew are organized colony by colony, so that, for instance, CO237 contains files relating to Malaya, while CO533 contains those that deal with Kenya. Furthermore, consulting materials related to the India of the Raj requires traveling to the far opposite side of London, to the British Library, and learning a wholly different cataloging system devoid of references to the Colonial Office records.

In recent years, much has been done to combat the inadequacies of traditional imperial history. We have seen an outpouring of works that show how British history, far from being a wholly domestic saga of parties, politics, and classes, was shaped by possession of the empire. In other words, as a number of scholars have amply demonstrated, the empire did not just exist "out there," but also "at home," where, as an "imperial social formation," it made its presence felt in institutions and values that lay at the heart of British society.[8] Although much of this work contains more of assertion than of demonstration and is now being challenged on the ground that it exaggerates the influence of the empire, nevertheless this new imperial historiography, suggestive and provocative, is a striking advance over the old and provides us with fresh ways to think about the history of Britain, the empire, and the nation. I do not propose here to participate in that historiography. What the empire meant for Britain is not my concern. This study remains "out there," in the empire. My task is to break away from the old notion of each colony dangling separately at the end of its own string. In so doing, I endeavor to look, as it were, horizontally, from one colony to another, not vertically, along the telegraph lines up and down to London.

The most useful conceptual frame for such an enterprise may be that of the web. As the scholar Tony Ballantyne, who has written on the spread of Aryan ideology from India to Maori New Zealand, has recently argued, "I believe it is productive to conceive of the empire not in terms of a spoked wheel with London as the 'hub,' where the various spokes (whether flows of finance, lines of communication, or the movement of people and objects) from the periphery meet, but rather in terms of a complex web consisting of horizontal filaments that run among various colonies in addition to 'vertical' connections between the metropole and individual colonies." Ballantyne goes on to acknowledge that India was a "subimperial center in its own right."[9] While accepting the utility of the web metaphor as a way of providing a structural coherence for the empire — as a "complex system of overlapping and interwoven institutions, organizations, ideologies, and discourses," in Ballantyne's words —

I emphasize the subimperial role of India within it. If not quite a "spider" sitting at the heart of the web, India is, I argue, more than just one of the many colonial "knots" that may be said to constitute that web.

In addition to the metaphor of the web, it is perhaps useful to consider our study within the framework of what may be called oceanic history. Traditional historiography takes as its focus a bounded spatial territory, usually of the nation —"France" or the "United States," say — or else of some large geographical entity, such as "Europe" or "South Asia." Within recent years, however, scholarship shaped around the study of oceans has grown dramatically. This approach was, of course, pioneered by Fernand Braudel, who looked at the Mediterranean Sea not as a barrier separating Europe from Africa, or Christendom from Islam, but rather as comprising a set of linked pathways for ideas, trade, and migration around its shores. Venice, Alexandria, Beirut, Salonica — all flourished within this larger Mediterranean world in which the ties that bound them together mattered more than their individual subjugation to doge or vizier.

In recent years, other oceans have come into view. We now have studies of the "black Atlantic" and the "Pacific rim." The Indian Ocean, for the early modern period, can be said to have had its Braudel in K. N. Chaudhuri, author of, among other major studies, *The Trading World of Asia and the English East India Company, 1660–1760* (1978), *Trade and Civilisation in the Indian Ocean to 1750* (1985), and *Asia before Europe: Economy and Civilisation of the Indian Ocean from the Rise of Islam to 1750* (1990). Chaudhuri's work has been complemented and extended by more specialized studies, among them the several volumes by Michael Pearson on the Portuguese, by Om Prakash on the Dutch, and by Sanjay Subrahmanyam on southern India. From the East African side, we have the work of Edward Alpers, and from the perspective of Southeast Asia, that of Anthony Reid. More general accounts of the ocean have now begun to appear as well, from those by Kenneth McPherson and Michael Pearson entitled *The Indian Ocean*, to L. Fawaz and C. A. Bayly's edited volume, *Modernity and Culture: From the Mediterranean to the Indian Ocean* (2002). In addition, there is Amitav Ghosh's fascinating semi-autobiographical account of the medieval Indian Ocean trading network, *In an Antique Land* (1992). Within the past few years the coherence of the Indian Ocean as a region has been made dramatically visible by the tsunami of December 26, 2004. Triggered by an undersea earthquake off the Indonesian coast, this great wall of water wreaked devastation across the breadth of the Indian Ocean from Kenya to Thailand.

The most striking feature of these various histories, taken together, is their almost unvarying focus on international trade and on the 250 years from the 1498 arrival of the Portuguese in Indian waters to the rise of British power in India after the 1757 battle of Plassey. With the coming of the colonial era, the historiography of the Indian Ocean fades away to almost nothing. It is as if a bustling sea full of vessels and people had suddenly been emptied, its waters drained away. As a mere "British lake," the Indian Ocean no longer commanded the attention of historians. To some degree, this dramatic shift in interest was a product of the archive. The records of the various European trading companies, with their immense holdings, made possible the writing of a richly textured history of the early modern Indian Ocean. There was also, of course, the sheer excitement generated by trade rivalries, combat at sea, and the growth of the spice and textile industries, not to mention the establishment of European enclaves on the Asian continent from Goa to Malacca. With the abolition of the European companies in the years around 1800, this rich archive for the study of oceanic history comes to an abrupt end. Not surprisingly, historians of the nineteenth century turned elsewhere, above all to the great land empire that makes up the British Raj in India. Sailing ships and trading voyages are replaced in the archive, and hence in the history books as well, by discussions of land revenue, property rights, and the organization of Indian society. So far as the ocean does engage historians, it is simply as an arena in which Britain demonstrated its imperial hegemony at the expense of "millennia-old indigenous maritime activities" that "crumbled" as they were "overwhelmed."[10]

The "British lake" of the nineteenth century was, however, far from empty.[11] Flows of people, ideas, and institutions, not to mention a vigorous trade, traversed its waters throughout the century. This study intends to use the notion of an Indian Ocean arena to help us navigate our way through the web of empire. As is shown throughout this volume, from Zanzibar to Singapore, from Durban to Basra to Penang, the port cities of the Indian Ocean rim, with their hinterlands, defined the India-centered imperial web of the nineteenth century. The Raj comprehended the sea as well as the land.

The Indian Ocean did not exist by itself in space. Always it was linked to and part of a larger world order. How far and in what ways, we might ask, can the Indian Ocean arena of the nineteenth century usefully be described in terms of the currently fashionable theories of globalization? The globalization literature takes as its central concern economic questions, those of markets, commodities, patterns of trade, price convergences, and the like. Above all, it asks how and when did the entire globe

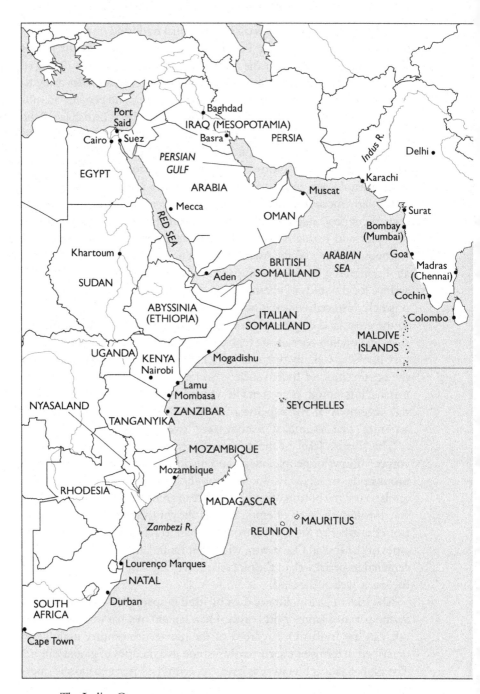

MAP I. The Indian Ocean, c. 1900

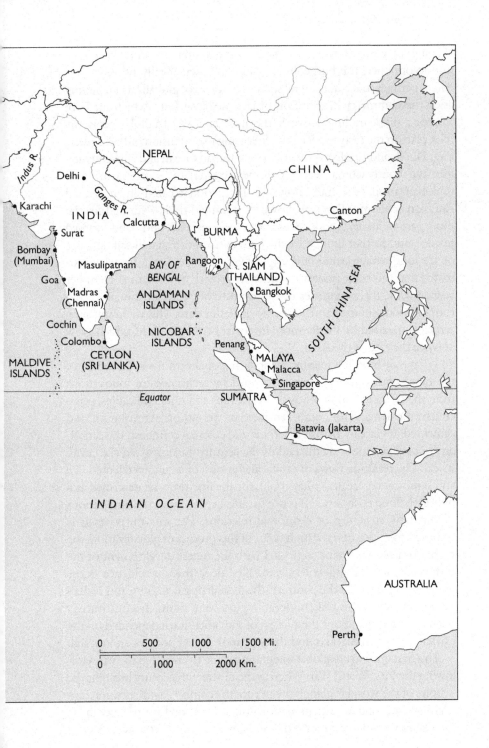

Indus R.

NEPAL

Delhi

Ganges R.

Karachi

INDIA

Calcutta

CHINA

Canton

Surat

BURMA

Bombay
(Mumbai)

Masulipatnam

Rangoon

SIAM
(THAILAND)

BAY OF
BENGAL

Goa

Madras
(Chennai)

ANDAMAN
ISLANDS

Bangkok

SOUTH CHINA SEA

Cochin

NICOBAR
ISLANDS

Colombo

Penang

CEYLON
(SRI LANKA)

MALAYA

MALDIVE
ISLANDS

Malacca

Singapore

Equator

SUMATRA

Batavia (Jakarta)

INDIAN OCEAN

AUSTRALIA

Perth

0   500   1000   1500 Mi.

0   1000   2000 Km.

become integrated into one unified trading system? I cannot take fully into account here this burgeoning literature. Schematically, however, one could, perhaps, trace out several successive waves of globalization. Setting aside the commercial revolution of late medieval Italy, which made of Europe a single trading network, the first step toward a global economy took place in the early modern era, following the extension of Portuguese, then Dutch and English, power into the Indian Ocean and subsequently into the South China Sea. Sometimes referred to as an era of "protoglobalization," the trade flows of this period created an integrated Eurasian economy. This was, however, a limited trade — limited for the most part to luxury goods including spices, tea, silk, and hand-loomed textiles, and further limited by the high costs of carriage in sailing ships on the long voyage around the Cape of Good Hope. Jan deVries has estimated that this trade underwent a steady growth of some 1.1 percent per year over the three centuries from 1500 to 1800, with an annual 50,000 tons of goods shipped to Europe by the latter date. This trade was nevertheless dwarfed by the far more important Atlantic trade, which grew at twice the rate of the Asian.[12]

What may be called mature or modern globalization was a product of the nineteenth century. Pushed forward by technological innovations from the telegraph and railway to steamships and undersea cables, powered by the demand for goods generated by the industrial revolution, and cemented in place by British free trade and colonial conquest, this "modern" global economy by the end of the century encompassed the entire world. The resulting flows of capital and goods, of an unprecedented size and significance, created what could, for the first time, be described as a fully globalized economy.[13] It is not feasible here to assess the implications of this new structure of economic relations. For our purposes it is sufficient to notice that the high point of this process of globalization, the years from 1890 to 1920, coincided with the fullest development of the India-centered subimperial system. Nor does this coincidence occur wholly by chance. To the contrary, the globalizing economy and India's predominance in the Indian Ocean region were mutually constitutive. Each helped bring about the success of the other. Each depended on the existence of open markets and the easy mobility of peoples and capital.

This first era of truly global integration came to an end in the years following the First World War. Whereas the nineteenth century brought the peoples of the world together, the twentieth century — with its wars, economic crises, and resurgent nationalisms, both in Europe and in its increasingly restive colonies — drove them apart. This economic reversal went hand in hand with the decline and ultimate collapse of the India-centered system this book describes. From the 1920s, and even more so from the 1930s, with the coming of the Great Depression, free trade gave way to tariff barriers, and the free movement of peoples to immigration restrictions. The nation-state alone remained. Caught up in its struggle for freedom, and seeking prosperity from within its own resources, India endeavored, so far as it could, to cut itself loose from a larger, "global" world order. For a full fifty years, from the 1930s to the 1980s, an insistent search for self-sufficiency defined India's politics and drove its state-oriented development activities. Change came only in the late 1980s with Rajiv Gandhi's hesitant neoliberal reforms. These, in turn, at once mirrored and helped bring about a new worldwide era of globalization at the end of the twentieth century. Only at the turn of the current century did levels of international trade and investment as a proportion of economic output approach those of a hundred years before. "To me as an economic historian," Alan Taylor of Northwestern University noted in 1999, "it was really the nineteenth century that represented the birth of the global economy. . . . These days it's just getting back to where it was 100 years ago."[14]

Themes and Topics

The structure of this work is not that of a conventional narrative history. The individual chapters, organized around selected topics, move backward and forward in time within the larger chronological limits of the volume, approximately 1870 to 1920. Furthermore, the work closely analyzes certain subjects but neglects others that may appear equally relevant to the larger argument. The work, in sum, makes no attempt to be comprehensive. It is best considered as a set of essays that together offer us a view into the working of the British Empire from the perspective of the India of the Raj.

Some may ask why the volume does not examine the era of East India Company rule, from the 1760s to 1858. A case can certainly be made that important elements of the India-centered empire that I examine here existed in the days of the company. To an even greater extent than was the case for the Raj, the East India Company exercised authority outside the Indian subcontinent. Penang (from 1786), Singapore (from 1819), and Malacca (from 1825), for instance, were under the direct jurisdiction of the company and remained so until the formation of the separate colony of the Straits Settlements in 1867. Units of the company's sepoy army were on several occasions dispatched overseas in support of its trading activities and to meet the threat posed by the Dutch and other hostile powers. For a time too the company held enclaves, such as Fort Marlborough, on the coast of Sumatra.

In addition, transportation of convicts took place from India to Mauritius — some fifteen hundred between 1814 and 1837 — as well as to Singapore, which received convicts after 1825 until the creation of the Andaman prison colony in 1858. Most important, of course, the China trade from its beginning depended upon the existence of a secure base in the company-controlled territories of India. Opium grown in India, marketed through country traders operating in Calcutta, and smuggled into China was indispensable in the righting of Britain's unfavorable balance of trade with China and testified to India's pre-eminence in the Asian trading system. Outside the company's control but facilitated by its naval pre-eminence in the Indian Ocean, the dhow trade endured between India and eastern Africa and the Gulf, as did the annual passage of Muslim pilgrims from India to Mecca for the hajj.

These developments, though consequential and worthy of study on their own terms, can, for our purposes, perhaps most usefully be considered as precedents, or more accurately, as the beginnings of what later was to become the India-centered empire of the Raj. The 1858 shift from company to Crown rule accompanied and helped precipitate a transformed relationship — alike political and economic — of India with the larger Indian Ocean region. As the globalization literature makes abundantly clear, the intensification of world trade and communication in the steamship era inaugurated new and heightened levels of commodity production, migration, and overseas investment. India stood at the heart of this newly globalized world and was one of its major beneficiaries. Equally important, the expansion of the British Empire after 1875, as it came to encompass much of Africa and Southeast Asia, took place on a scale vastly greater than any imperial conquest that had gone before, save only that of India itself. This extension of the empire opened up opportunities for Indians and for the British in India never previously imagined. The half century from the 1870s to 1920 must be considered as a period set apart from the years that went before, as well as from the years that followed.

The volume examines in successive chapters the institutions of colonial governance; the construction of ethnic and racial identities among colonial peoples; the Indian Army's role in extending and securing the empire; the employment of Indians, especially Sikhs, in colonial police forces; the working of indentured labor recruitment, through an on-the-ground study of Natal's agencies in India; and the transformation of East Africa during the early years of colonial rule into something of an extension of India, with a close examination of the building of the Uganda Railway and the nature of Indian settlement in the region. The conclusion explores the reasons for the decline of these interregional networks after 1920 and addresses the elusive question of whether and in what ways Indians may have benefited from their incorporation into the Indian Ocean–centered empire.

CHAPTER I

Governing Colonial Peoples

As new colonial territories around the Indian Ocean were brought under British rule, the varied governing strategies formulated in the India of the Raj made their way across the sea. This is not surprising. By the late nineteenth century the India of the Raj, first under the East India Company and then under the Crown, had existed for a century and had developed an array of administrative practices, well known and easily accessible, that provided exemplars of how an empire might be organized and run. The legal and administrative structures of the Raj were the most predominant and visible such export, but the influence of the Raj extended as well to such disparate matters as landholding, forest management, and the design of irrigation systems. These institutions and practices traveled across the ocean in several different guises. One was the diffusion and adoption of "Indian" ideas of governance with little avowed acknowledgement of their Indian origin. Among these were such administrative constructs as "indirect rule" through princes and the notion of "martial races." On occasion, as we will see, Indian precedents were acknowledged only to be contested or, more commonly, to be taken as a jumping-off point for a transformed administrative structure in the new colonial context. A second mode of transmission was the movement of Indian officials, bringing Indian strategies of governance with them, to places as different as Egypt, Iraq, and the Straits. Finally, newly appointed colonial officials who had no experience of India frequently looked to the India of the Raj as a reservoir of useful practices and precedents as they struggled to set up their own governments.

Constructing Colonial Legal Systems

Two fundamental concerns shaped all discussion of law in the colonies. One was a belief that imperial rule could be justified only by a commitment to the rule of law. An avowed "despotism," which the British saw as a mark of the regimes they had supplanted, had at all costs to be avoided. At the same time, the law had to take into account and in some degree respect those customs and traditions that the British saw as central to the peoples over whom they ruled. These two objectives were not wholly compatible, nor did they by themselves dictate any particular legal strategy. Fitting the law to the people ruled out any wholesale adoption, in India or elsewhere, of the case-based English system with its precedents coming down from the Middle Ages; yet to a very large degree, the English prided themselves on possessing a rule of law surpassing in its perfection that of other peoples. The result of this extended struggle was the establishment throughout the colonial world of complex and varied regimes of legal pluralism. It is not possible here to investigate the working even of the colonial Indian legal order, much less that of colonies elsewhere. My objective is to show how colonial "Indian" law, as well as "indigenous" and "English" law, could shape colonial legal systems. Following the suggestive insights of Lauren Benton, I argue that "the law worked both to tie disparate parts of empires [together] and to lay the basis for exchanges of all sorts between political and culturally separate imperial or colonial powers."[1]

In India, from the time of Warren Hastings (governor-general, 1772–84) onward, the British determined that the substantive civil law should incorporate what they regarded as the traditional personal rights of the people; these they defined as embodied in the ancient texts of the two religions of Hinduism and Islam. In civil suits regarding marriage, inheritance, and the like, Hastings wrote, "the laws of the Koran with respect to Mahomedans, and those of the Shaster with respect to the Gentoos [Hindus] shall be invariably adhered to." The British thus began the practice, subsequently extended throughout the empire, of defining "tradition" so as to create bounded self-contained communities, and then enforcing these definitions upon those who were subject to them. The British recoiled, however, from enforcing the criminal laws of their Mughal predecessors. Many of these punishments they found abhorrent, while too much, in their view as they sought a rule of law, was left to the discretion of individual officials. Punishment for serious criminal acts had also to be taken out of the hands of aggrieved individuals and made crimes against the state. The result was the creation of what became known as "Anglo-Muhammadan" law blending elements of British and of Mughal legal cultures. The British endeavored to restrict the use of English law to British subjects, who were placed under the jurisdiction of a Supreme Court created in 1772. But the separation of jurisdictions could not be strictly maintained as Indians appealed to the Supreme Court and the Anglo-Muhammadan law became infused with the English practice of citing cases and precedents in decision making.[2]

By the 1830s the British had determined to create by codification an alternative basis both for the substantive criminal law and for procedure more generally, and to make all residents of India subject to these codes. (The substantive civil law, with its distinction between Hindu and Muslim, was not codified.) The impetus for change came from the utilitarian philosophers in Britain, most notably Jeremy Bentham, who sought to make the law simple, uniform, and rigorous in its application in place of the complexity and arbitrariness that characterized so much of the English legal system in the late eighteenth century. Bentham's influence on the English legal system was to be negligible, with only occasional and piecemeal reforms enacted during the early Victorian era. In India, however, where powerful vested interests did not cumber the stage, codification could be brought to a successful conclusion. Even so, this was to be a contentious and extended process. Thomas Macaulay, as law member of the governor-general's council in the 1830s, took the first step with the drafting of the Indian Penal Code. Inspired by Bentham, Macaulay set out to create a code marked by "uniformity where you can have it; diversity where you must have it; but in all cases certainty." He explicitly rejected as a model the English criminal law as administered by the Indian Supreme Court. The result, as Eric Stokes described it, was "a code of law drawn not from existing practice or from foreign law systems, but created *ex nihilo* by the disinterested philosophic intelligence."[3]

Bureaucratic inertia, with the decline of utilitarian enthusiasm, delayed enactment of the penal code until 1860. The process of codification spurred by the upheaval of the 1857 revolt, the penal code was joined by the enactment in 1859 of the civil procedure code and in 1861 of the criminal procedure code. Although less rigorously based on Benthamite principles than Macaulay's penal code, the two codes of procedure still showed the effects of Bentham's conviction that the law must be made simple, efficient, and certain. As John Stuart Mill wrote of the draft code of civil procedure, it promised to secure "so far as judicial institutions can secure that blessing, as good and accessible an administration of civil justice as the lights of the age are capable of conferring on it."[4]

The Indian codes, then, as enacted were not in principle compilations of existing, and for the most part still unreformed, English law. Indeed, Bentham and his followers, as we have seen, repudiated the law of England as the basis on which Indian law should be constructed. Nor were these codes "Indian" in any obvious fashion. Although adapted to Indian conditions in part and drafted for use in India, they were not designed to embody Indian legal practices, either those of the Mughal Empire or its successor state of the Company Raj. Rather, especially with Macaulay's penal code, they were founded upon universal principles of jurisprudence, which took legislative form in India only because of the opportunities provided by British colonialism. That colonialism provided an unparalleled opportunity to introduce such a reform was not lost on Benthamite legal scholars. As Macaulay told the House of Commons in 1833, "A Code is almost the only blessing — perhaps it is the only blessing — which absolute governments are better fitted to confer on a nation than popular governments."[5]

Given the character of the new codes, how can they be said in any way to be the product of an Indian legal culture? These codes were, after all, drafted by Englishmen, and Macaulay notwithstanding, much of their substance was, in practice, as David Skuy has argued, derived from English legal usage and embodied in English legal precepts.[6] Yet whether in Kenya or the Straits, Iraq or Nigeria, the attempt to enact these codes into law outside India, as we will see, triggered immense controversy. Time and again these codes were perceived by local colonial officials and not least by white settlers as fundamentally different from and at odds with English law. They were, in appearance if not reality, incontestably Indian. In sum, whatever the content of the codes, their adoption overseas visibly involved the export to Britain's colonies of a legislative culture crafted in India, and by the Raj for India. Macaulay might describe the Indian Penal Code as the work of a disinterested philosophic intelligence, and scholars like Skuy might find "English legal principles" embedded in it. For many in Britain's colonies at the time, however, these codes, because they were not the familiar common law of England, embodied "Indian" jurisprudence and were scorned or embraced accordingly.

One might start with the Straits Settlements. Singapore, with its ancillary outposts of Penang and Malacca, had been placed under the rule of the East India Company from its founding in 1819. The enactment of the Indian Penal Code by the Raj therefore provoked a flurry of discussion as to whether it ought appropriately be extended to the Straits as well. These initial discussions in 1861 promptly precipitated antagonism between, on one hand, the members of the Straits executive government, all of whom from the governor down to the local magistrates favored the use of the code, and, on the other, the local legal community, which opposed it. In the face of this divided opinion, together with an ongoing reconsideration of the status of the Straits Settlement following the abolition of the East India Company, no action was then taken. In 1867 the Straits Settlements become a Crown colony under the Colonial Office. No longer tied to India, the Straits government was now free to chart its own legal course.

The very next year, in 1868, T. Braddell, the colony's attorney general, raised the question of whether the Straits criminal law ought to be reformed. As he pointed out in a memorandum for the legislative council, without the "advantage of the improvements introduced by the penal code," the Straits criminal law remained frozen where it had been in 1829, when the last Indian act prior to codification had been enacted. As a first step toward reform, Braddell recommended extending to the colony some half-dozen 1861 English acts amending and consolidating the criminal law. These, he pointed out, had been brought into force in Hong Kong in 1865.[7]

Emboldened by Braddell's proposal, a group of private attorneys, advocates at the Singapore Supreme Court, endeavored to quash at the outset any effort to introduce the Indian code into the Straits. As their spokesman, R. C. Woods, argued, the Indian codes were simply not suited for a colony possessing an established bar and professional legal practitioners. The Indian code, he wrote, "was originally intended for the guidance of mofussil [district] judges and magistrates who had not the advantage of a professional training in legal sciences, and who did not possess more than an elementary knowledge of law." By contrast, "the judges in the Straits Settlements are chosen from the Bar, and doubtless all future magistrates will be also." Hence, the government ought to introduce into the colony the "improved criminal acts of England," for they offered the "advantage of a continued series of decisions of the most eminent judges who have made law the study of their lives." Criminal legislation, Woods concluded, "is progressive; it cannot be confined within the limits of any code."[8] Speaking on behalf of this proposal in the legislative council, the chief justice of the Singapore court insisted that "our criminal law is in general very accurate and well defined and perfectly understood" by the lawyers and judges from England who practiced in the colonial courts; hence no purpose would be served by substituting for that "familiar" system one to which the English lawyer was "a stranger."[9] In short, the Straits Settlements, in their legal culture, should be a colony of

England, not of India. With these remarks, battle was joined in an enduring contest — pitting the Indian codes against the common law — for control of the legal system in Britain's new colonies.

Woods's argument did not evoke much enthusiasm either in the Straits government or in the Colonial Office. Concisely capturing the self-interested motives of Woods and his fellow petitioners, one official wrote simply, "I presume lawyers, like other people, do not like to make useless knowledge which they possess, and create a necessity for knowledge which they have not."[10] Larger issues were, nevertheless, at stake. As Braddell, now converted to the Indian code, told the legislative council, to adopt the 1861 English acts would leave untouched all the heads of law not included in those acts. By contrast, enacting the Indian Penal Code would have, he said (in words that echoed Bentham), the "great advantage of having the whole body of our criminal law in a shape easy of access, easily to be comprehended, and in his opinion more efficient than the criminal law of England."[11] The code was enacted as Straits Ordinance 5 of 1870.

Braddell, with the other members of the legislative council, had no doubt as to the radical departure from English practice that use of the Indian code entailed. Indeed, for this very reason, he refused to accept any alteration of the Indian act. "We were," he wrote, looking back on the debate, "about to cast off from the English law and in consequence lose the guide to interpret the law which we had in English text books and law reports, and to adopt a new system for the interpretation of which we must rely on Indian text books and law reports and it seemed desirable that we should alter the form of the new law as little as possible from the form used in India." The Straits government should do no more than "follow in the footsteps of the Indian legislature as to amendments."[12] From 1870 onward, in its legal culture the Straits Settlements were, to extend Braddell's metaphor, firmly moored in Indian waters.

Enactment of the Indian Penal Code was followed almost at once by enactment of the Indian Code of Criminal Procedure. This ordinance (20 of 1870) was, so the governor told the Colonial Office, "rendered necessary by the enactment in this colony of the Indian Penal Code" and was "virtually a copy" of the Indian act.[13] These acts did not end Indian influence on the process of legal reform in the Straits. To the contrary, Indian enactments remained both models to be emulated and examples of what ought to be avoided. Revision of the criminal procedure code in 1892, for instance, provided an occasion to consider afresh whether Indian precedent ought to be adhered to. In this case, controversy revolved around whether the drafting committee had introduced too many "departures from Indian practice." Grumbling that none of the commit-tee members had ever seen the criminal procedure code "in practical working in India," W. E. Maxwell, the colonial secretary, charged that the revised code unduly restricted magistrates' powers, while multiplying "needless formalities" and opportunities for appeal. In particular, he insisted, while ostensibly "imitating Indian procedures," the committee "have apparently ignored the Indian practice of allowing magistrates to try summarily a very numerous class of cases." The Straits civil service, he pointed out, "is recruited from the very class of men who as judicial officers in India have very extended powers"; hence, "it is in my opinion a distinct waste of power to refuse to employ them in this Colony as freely as is done in India." One detects in this discussion an echo of the endur-ing tension between the colonial executive, which saw in adoption of Indian practices opportunities for a more unfettered exercise of power, and judges and lawyers committed to a more English conception of the rule of law, with its rules, regulations, and appeals. As Maxwell described the members of the drafting committee, they exhibited a "natural perhaps unconscious dislike on the part of a body of lawyers to cheap law."[14]

Meanwhile the British had been, since 1875, extending their control into the states of the Malay Peninsula. Although these states remained under the technical sovereignty of their Malay sultans, their day-to-day governance, as will be discussed presently, was gradually taken over by the states' newly appointed British residents and magistrates. Not surpris-ingly, given the novel situation in which they found themselves — under the Malay sultans but not subject to their authority — these British officials were uncertain as to the principles on which they should admin-ister justice. Hugh Low, as resident in Perak, reported in 1877 that "the law administered in the courts is the law prevalent in Mahomedan coun-tries, supplemented, when necessary, by the laws of Great Britain." By contrast, T. C. S. Speedy, assistant resident in Durian Sabatang, said that, as he had been "up to the present [1877] furnished with no code as definitely applicable in the Malay States," he had "endeavoured as nearly as possible in consonance with Malay custom to follow the Indian Penal Code." In similar fashion, the residents in Selangor and Sungei Ujong reported having brought into force in their states the Straits Penal Code and other ordinances in force in the Straits, but "without the lawyers."[15] So far as procedure was concerned, as a later legal adviser observed of Perak, "except in cases of trial by jury, there was no criminal procedure code of any kind. So far as I can ascertain, the magistrates followed either the English or the Indian procedure, each according to his own taste and fancy."[16]

Over time the government endeavored to bring some order out of this legal jumble. In 1884 the Straits Penal Code was placed in force in Perak, and from there it was extended to the remaining protected Malay states in the subsequent five years. In 1893 the Straits Criminal Procedure Code of the previous year was adopted as law in Selangor, along with a number of other related Straits and Indian acts. But the magistrates in several other states still continued with "no legalized system of criminal procedure of any kind." Hence, in 1896, with the coming into force of the Federated Malay States as a unified government, it was decided to enforce throughout the federation the Straits Criminal Procedure Code. As in the case of the Straits itself, however, Indian practice was not scrupulously followed. As the federation's legal adviser wrote, although this code "would form the best basis for criminal procedure," it needed to be simplified and adapted to fit the circumstances of the Malay states. Most important of these alterations, perhaps, was the decision to adopt neither that most cherished of English institutions — trial by jury — nor the Indian system of unfettered magisterial authority for which Maxwell had argued so strenuously. Instead, the code provided for trial with assessors. As the legal adviser made clear, this procedure was "wholly different" from that in force in India, for there "the judge is not bound to conform to the opinions of the assessors, while here the assessors are actually judges."[17] Despite such modifications as these, by the end of the century the Indian-derived Straits codes had made their way to all the protected states of the Malay Peninsula.

The Straits Settlements and Malaya were not the only colonial territories to which Indian codes and legislative enactments found their way in the later nineteenth century. In July 1897, by the East Africa Order in Council, the major Indian codes, together with some twenty Indian legislative enactments, were put in force throughout the extensive territories of the newly established East African Protectorate. "Her Majesty's criminal and civil jurisdiction in the Protectorate," the government proclaimed, "shall, so far as circumstances admit, be exercised on the principle of, and in conformity with, the enactments hereafter mentioned of the Governor General of India in Council, and the Governor of Bombay in Council, and according to the course of procedure and practice observed by and before the courts in the Presidency of Bombay." Indeed, the order announced, the codes of civil and criminal procedure would have effect "as if the Protectorate were a district of a presidency of India."[18]

This sweeping introduction of seemingly the entire Indian legal system into East Africa marked the culmination of a process that had begun on a small scale some years earlier. In Zanzibar, as that island state fell under

British influence from the late 1840s onward, the British consul, following the Ottoman precedent of extraterritoriality, claimed jurisdiction over British subjects and British protected persons in the sultan's domains. The 1866 Zanzibar Order in Council formalized this jurisdiction and provided for appeals from the consular court to the Bombay high court. The following year the consul promulgated the Indian Penal Code as the criminal law for those subject to his jurisdiction; in 1884 an order in council extended to Zanzibar a number of further Indian acts, including the codes of civil and criminal procedure and the evidence and succession acts. By these acts, as one commentator wrote, Zanzibar was made, "so far as concerns the administration of justice to British subjects, a part of Her Majesty's Indian Empire."[19]

That Zanzibar was so treated is perhaps not surprising. As I discuss elsewhere, Indian traders and merchants, most of whom were British subjects, flocked to Zanzibar during the last half of the nineteenth century, and were followed by bankers and professionals of all kinds, as well as laborers. The further extension of Indian law onto continental Africa was in large measure a logical outcome of the extension of British power from Zanzibar into the interior. In 1890 the Imperial British East Africa Company, as the British government's chosen agent in East Africa, established a consular court in Mombasa, and in 1891, when it took over Witu from the Germans following the Heligoland settlement, the company introduced the Indian codes into that coastal district. Yet British opinion was by no means united. Inaugurating a conflict of legal systems that would unsettle the working of Britain's colonial courts in Africa for decades to come, the imperial authorities, by the Africa Order in Council of 1889, ruled that jurisdiction within continental Africa was to be exercised "upon the principles of, and in conformity with, the substance of the law for the time being in force in England."

In 1895 the imperial government took over East Africa from the bankrupt company. Convinced that it was "urgent" to establish "a simple and uniform" legal system throughout the new protectorate, Sir A. Hardinge as commissioner determined to substitute the Indian codes for the English law prescribed by the 1889 order in council. "The Indian codes," he told the Foreign Office, echoing views held by many colonial officials both then and later, "are a good deal simpler than English law, and present fewer difficulties to an administrator possessing no special legal training." Further, he pointed out, inasmuch as Zanzibar had already adopted the Indian codes, it was "very desirable" to have "identical" treatment of the same offenses in these two "sister protectorates." The Foreign Office, to which the East Africa Protectorate was then subject, raised no objection to the change.[20] The result was the 1897 order in council.

The 1897 order opened the way for an influx into East Africa of Indian laws. Some twenty Indian acts were introduced by the order itself; others followed in subsequent years. In 1900, furthermore, with the construction of the railway from Mombasa into the interior, the Indian codes were extended to include the Uganda Protectorate as well. The extent of this wholesale adoption of Indian legislative practice surprised even some Indian officials. As one secretariat official wrote, on receiving a copy of the 1897 order, "Various Indian acts are applied by both Orders [for East Africa and Zanzibar], the most remarkable of which is the Transfer of Property Act. Though deemed too advanced for the Indian Punjab, this Act is apparently considered suitable for the wilds of East Africa!"[21] In one critical way, however, the tie with India was cut with the establishment of a high court at Zanzibar to which appeals were to be taken from local courts throughout the protectorates. No longer did an appeal lie to the Bombay high court.

As in the Malay States, however, introduction of these codes was no easy matter. Few of the officials scattered across the protectorate in the late 1890s even possessed copies of the codes; moreover, from the outset the British had committed themselves to respecting "native customs" and, on the coast, Islamic law. Hence, as Hardinge wrote to J. Ainsworth, posted in remote Ukamba, in March 1896, although "you should be guided by the general principles of the Indian Penal and Criminal Procedure codes," it "may not be possible to apply them in every detail." As a kind of awkward compromise, Hardinge told Ainsworth that, "though a copy of it [the Indian Civil Procedure Code] will be sent to you," it was "inapplicable to a savage community" and therefore need not be "strictly" adhered to. Rather "you will have in settling native cases to be guided by common sense . . . and native law and custom."[22] Even as they were brought more fully into effect, however, Indian laws and procedures were intricately interwoven with "native custom" and with Islamic law. The Protectorate Court, sitting at Mombasa with an appeal to Zanzibar, and its subordinate courts exercised jurisdiction over all British and British-protected subjects, including Indians, as well as the nationals of foreign countries. The law administered by it, both civil and criminal, was that of British India. At the same time, on the coast, district-level courts presided over by *qazis* recognized Muslim personal law and administered justice, under British supervision, to the local Muslim population.

The most difficult question was that of integrating the native African population into this system. Hardinge in 1895 had envisaged a day when, "as the progress of civilization makes the change possible," the Indian codes "might gradually take the place of native laws and usages."[23] The 1897 order in council nevertheless stated explicitly that "every criminal charge against a Native, and every civil proceeding against a Native . . . shall be heard and determined in the proper Native Court, and the Protectorate Court shall not exercise any jurisdiction therein." The order further reserved to the British the authority to "make rules and orders for such courts" as necessary and to establish or abolish these courts. But what was to be the jurisdiction of these "Native Courts," and what "rules" were they to follow? These questions were to bedevil the British throughout their years of rule over East Africa. What is important for our purposes is that the tension visible in Hardinge's 1896 instructions to Ainsworth was never wholly resolved. The Native Courts, whether presided over by tribal chiefs, headmen, or British officials, were meant to enforce "native custom," yet at the same time they were to participate in the establishment of a colonial rule of law. For the most part, as Ainsworth himself reported in 1905, law in the native tribunals was in the end "administered by the Collectors and Assistant Collectors," following "nominally" the procedures of the Indian codes; "the practice in these courts, however, is to exercise common sense." Where "common sense" did not suffice, assessors were brought in to assist the British judges in ascertaining local "custom."[24]

As time went on, this Indian-derived legal system came increasingly under attack. Initially, during the first two decades of the twentieth century, a number of the Indian acts were replaced by local ordinances. These local enactments, however, were largely re-enactments of the Indian legislation and made no substantive change in the law. Up to the 1920s, as H. F. Morris has written in his authoritative account of East African law, "the bulk of the criminal work was carried out under Indian law and according to the criminal procedure of India, while important branches of the civil law were Indian, as was the procedure applicable for civil cases." Indian cases, as well as English, were looked to for precedents.[25] From the outset, however, the white settler community, rapidly growing in numbers by the 1920s, adamantly opposed the use of Indian law in East Africa. In its view, the Indian codes, as the products of an authoritarian colonialism, were not fit vehicles for the adjudication of disputes among free Englishmen. As the colonists' association wrote in a petition to the secretary of state as early as 1905, "there is the strongest objection in principle to placing white men under laws intended for a coloured population despotically governed." By the "law of England," the association insisted, "every Englishman carries the common law of England into every new country settled by him over which the King has proclaimed sovereignty."[26]

The Colonial Office turned aside this early petition with the argument that Indian law was codified, whereas English law was not. Hence it could be administered, in East Africa as in India, by ordinary magistrates having no legal training. To introduce English law would require, as Lord Elgin pointed out, the appointment of "a number of legally trained magistrates at greatly increased salaries to take over the judicial duties of the Collectors."[27] Nevertheless it soon became clear that the Colonial Office had little sympathy for the use of the Indian codes in Africa. By the 1920s, it had determined to replace them, and not simply by local enactments but by the introduction of the English common law itself. The Colonial Office was of course always more responsive than the Foreign Office to home opinion and, whether in East or South Africa, was notoriously reluctant to antagonize white settler communities. Hence, it came as no surprise that, as one official in Uganda put it, the Colonial Office would endeavor to "break away from anything savouring of connection with India."[28]

Yet, in the end, the decision to press forward had ostensibly nothing to do with settler pressure. To the contrary, the Colonial Office sought to punish the Kenyan judiciary for what it saw as undue leniency in cases involving settler assaults on native Africans. When one settler was convicted only of inflicting "grievous hurt" and sentenced to two years' imprisonment for killing an African servant, the Colonial Office argued that the problem lay in part with the provisions of the Indian Penal Code. As one Colonial Office official, H. G. Bushe, wrote, "If all this had happened in this country I have no doubt that the accused would have been charged with murder. . . . The position in Kenya is governed by the Indian penal code and this is so technical and so incoherent a document that it is very difficult to understand. If anything, it seems to be inclined to limit the offence of murder rather more than does English law." In reviewing a similar case in Tanganyika, the colonial secretary told the governor that "the procedure at and conduct of the trial point strongly to the desirability of adopting a criminal code in accordance with English law and procedure." As the Indian codes had long been praised for their clarity and conciseness, an argument for repeal based on a presumed lack of coherence is hard to fathom. One can only speculate that these murder cases provided a justification, acceptable to British liberal opinion, for the Colonial Office to do what it wanted to do in any case. In 1923 the colonial secretary told the governor of Kenya to substitute a local ordinance based on English criminal law for the Indian Penal Code; the following year the governor was instructed to replace the existing criminal procedure code with one based on that of a colony such as Nigeria or the Gold Coast where the Indian codes had not been introduced.[29]

Elements of the ensuing controversy resembled that in the Straits Settlements a half century before. Here, however, the sides were reversed. Whereas in Singapore the legal community had advocated the use of English law, in East Africa the bar and bench, with the local governments, all sought to retain the Indian codes. The chief judge of the Nyasaland high court even sought to use the occasion to introduce into his colony not the proposed new code but one based on the Indian model.[30] So intense, in fact, was the local opposition that the draft code was prepared not in East Africa but in the Colonial Office itself. In part, no doubt, self-interested motives were at work in this stubborn refusal to accept a new jurisprudence, for East African lawyers and judges had no desire to abandon a system with which, after several decades' use, they were familiar.

But the arguments that had brought about the use of the Indian codes in the first place still remained compelling to colonial administrators. The Kenya chief justice, pleading for retention of the Indian code, insisted that "the Indian Penal Code and the local Criminal Procedure Ordinance, which is based on the Indian Criminal Procedure Code, are admirably suited for administration by lay magistrates." From neighboring Uganda the chief secretary in 1927 further pointed out that the "Indian Penal Code is a clear and concise statement of English law," which had "the supreme merit of being easily understood by the layman and has been administered in India and elsewhere by laymen with great success for many years." Adverting to the code's origins, he sighed, "It seems a pity that we should be embarrassed because certain people in Kenya apparently have never heard of Lord Macaulay."[31] The penal code, he seemed to imply, inasmuch as it was drafted by an eminent Englishman and embodied, correctly as we have seen, the substance of English law, should not be condemned for its "Indian-ness."

Pressed to defend their decision, officials at the Colonial Office insisted that, as the colonial secretary wrote the three East African governors jointly in 1927, "officers will find it easier to apply a code which employs the terms and principles with which they are familiar in England than one in which these terms and principles have been discarded for others of doubtful import."[32] But more surely was at stake. Some hint of this can be seen in Bushe's response to a Uganda barrister who had come to

London to protest the change. If, Bushe said, "you have magistrates and judges who have been trained in this country, it is far more satisfactory that they should administer English law than Indian law; that the Indian law was not really applicable nowadays in East Africa; and that in any event the great British territories in East Africa ought to come into line with British colonies generally and base themselves upon English law."[33] A uniform legal system with standardized codes of procedure derived from English practice was, in the eyes of the bureaucrats in Whitehall, clearly essential to the effective functioning of a "modernized" British Empire.

As a result, new codes were put in place in all of the East African colonies during the early 1930s. From then onward the region's legal ties with India rapidly became attenuated, while judicial officers trained in England increasingly took over the magisterial work previously undertaken by district officers. During the 1950s, as independence approached, H. F. Morris has written, "English law and procedure were now applied with even more rigidity than before; the legacy of Indian legislation was steadily eroded; and ever increasing attention and authority were accorded to the decisions of the English courts."[34]

East Africa and Malaya did not stand alone in their adoption of Indian legal forms. As the British Empire expanded during the later nineteenth century and the early years of the twentieth, the Indian codes found receptive soil around the rim of the Indian Ocean. A number of Indian acts were brought into operation in neighboring Tanganyika after the British took over responsibility for it in 1920, while to the north of Kenya, in British Somaliland, the Somaliland Order in Council of 1899 extended the principles of the 1897 East Africa order to that territory. As in East Africa, civil and criminal jurisdiction was to be exercised "on the principles of, and in conformity with," Indian legislative enactments. The Sudan Penal Code too was based in part on Indian precedents. Across the Red Sea on the Arabian coast, Aden, controlled by India since its 1839 conquest, was, as Lord Northbrook wrote in 1875, "practically an Indian town, . . . the population is wholly Indian, or is engaged in Indian trade; the capital invested in the place is Indian; the laws and modes of government are Indian, and the officers whose duty it has hitherto been to administer them have been selected from the Indian service."[35] During the First World War, as we will see, Indian officials introduced Indian laws into the newly conquered Ottoman province of Basra in Mesopotamia.

Yet there were clear limits to the reach of Indian legislation. One was set by the legal structure in existence at the time of conquest. Perhaps the most instructive case is that of Egypt. Much has been made by scholars of the "Indianization" of the Egyptian administration under British rule. But on the legal side, the British were tightly constrained as they set out to reform that country's institutions. To some degree, this was a product of their own reluctance to interfere too deeply in a country that they had not legally annexed and from which, they regularly insisted, their departure was imminent. More important, however, Egypt at the time of its occupation in 1882 already possessed a rich structure of laws and institutions; and these, as Robert Tignor has noted, incorporated a range of Ottoman, French, and purely Egyptian influences. Indeed, as Tignor wrote, Egypt's problems "stemmed, not from a lack, but from a super-abundance of courts and judicial systems." Thus, much as Egypt's incoming rulers, many of whom, like Lord Cromer, were drawn from Indian service, may have wished to reconstruct the Egyptian legal system along Indian lines, they could not simply wish out of existence the existing codes and courts. These were not, after all, remnants of some ancient tradition, but rather the products of the French-inspired reforming enthusiasms of such rulers as Muhammad Ali and Khedive Ismail. Ultimately, in the 1890s, a certain amount of Anglo-Indian procedure was grafted onto the existing structure. But the Code Napoleon and related legislation of necessity remained the foundation of the Egyptian legal system.[36]

Distance from India mattered too. The further a colony was from India, the less likely were the Indian codes to be seen as appropriate for its governance. Hong Kong, off the China coast, despite its close ties with Singapore, never adopted the Indian codes. The Central African colonies of Nyasaland and Northern Rhodesia briefly considered adoption only to reject them. In South Africa the enduring Roman-Dutch legal tradition, together with white settler self-government, in the Cape from the 1850s and Natal from the 1890s, and then in the Union of South Africa after 1910, meant that the imperial government had little opportunity to enforce Indian legal forms. In one West African colony — Nigeria — the Indian codes secured a hearing, but the ensuing controversy showed how little support could be expected for them on so distant a coast of Africa.

The opening round took place in 1904, when the chief justice of Frederick Lugard's newly established Northern Nigeria reached to Australia for a model code, which he found in the Queensland Criminal Code of 1899, based on English law. At the same time, the high commissioner of Southern Nigeria, Sir Walter Egerton, proposed introducing into his colony the Straits Settlements Penal Code, based (as we have seen) on the Indian code. In terms almost identical to those used by officials in Kenya,

Egerton argued that the Indian code "has stood the test of time" and was "far simpler and better suited to the needs of an uncivilized or semi-civilized population." In support of this proposal, he cited his own twenty years' experience as a magistrate working the Indian code in the Straits.[37]

At the Colonial Office, Egerton's proposal evoked nothing but fierce hostility. As one official noted in the margin of Egerton's dispatch, "The law of England should be good enough for West Africa." The Queensland code, approved for Northern Nigeria, was, the official added, "practically the law of England," of which "the vast majority of West African judicial officers have (it is to be hoped) some 'experience'!" Bowing to this unanimous sentiment on the part of his legal advisers, the colonial secretary, Lord Elgin, turned aside Egerton's request and left Southern Nigeria's criminal law uncodified. Ten years after the initial discussions, in 1914, Northern and Southern Nigeria were amalgamated into one colony under Lugard's governor-generalship. Now in charge of the whole, Lugard wasted no time securing the extension of the Queensland code from the north of Nigeria to the south. With its enactment in 1916, the effort to introduce the Indian codes into West Africa came to an end.

Clearly, an enduring tension existed between local officials, whose experience working the Indian codes generated sympathy for their use, and the officials of the Colonial Office, who adamantly opposed any adoption of Indian codes outside the immediate arc of Indian influence and even, as in East Africa, sought their repeal. To be sure, at a great distance from India, as the colonial secretary wrote to the East African governors in 1927, it might appear to be "easier" for English-trained officials to employ legal "terms and principles" with which they were "familiar" from home. But even in West Africa, colonial career patterns frequently brought to the region officials familiar with the Indian codes, such as Egerton, as well as W. E. Maxwell, appointed governor of the Gold Coast in 1895 after thirty years service in the Straits. And of course, so far as geography was concerned, Queensland was hardly closer to West Africa than was India.

But one can perhaps go further. The problem, especially for those at home in England, may be said to have resided in the codes themselves. Despite the acknowledged "effectiveness" of the Indian codes as instruments for colonial rule, especially where magistrates untrained in the law were responsible for administering justice, their Indian origin, in effect, "tainted" them. Not only white settlers but also the Colonial Office itself, one might argue, found in these codes a too visible assertion of the role of India as an imperial center. The Colonial Office, one must remember, had no responsibility for India's governance, and often little sympathy for the pleas on behalf of Indians put forward by the viceroy and the India Office. From their London-centered perspective, the Indian codes, no matter how much of the substance of English law they may have contained, were insufficiently "English." The rule of law on which the British prided themselves could, in this vision, appropriately take only one form — the rule of "English" law. As English law was itself reformed, though never codified, during the later nineteenth century, these sentiments can only have grown more intense. The arc carved out for an India-centered legal culture, while vast in its reach across thousands of miles of ocean to East Africa and Southeast Asia, could never be made to encompass the entire British Empire.

Strategies of Governance

With its vast size; its early date of conquest, in the late eighteenth and early nineteenth centuries; and its array of administrative forms, India offered to administrators elsewhere in the empire models for many styles of colonial governance. In practice, these are often collapsed into the two opposed strategies of "direct" and "indirect" rule. While convenient, this division is inevitably arbitrary and, as will be seen, often misleading when applied to particular cases. Still, it may be helpful as we look at India's role in shaping the administrative structure of the empire to use these constructs as a lens to help sharpen our vision of what the British *thought* they were doing, as well as what they were doing, in their colonial empire. It is important too to remember that these administrative ideas found expression not only in the "ideology" of empire but also in the lives of those many officials who took their Indian experience with them to posts in Britain's newly acquired territories.

One might begin with the notion of indirect rule. Central to the practice of this form of colonial governance was the restoration to their thrones of rulers who had been defeated in battle or had otherwise accepted the suzerainty of the British. Such rulers, as "protected princes," were secured from hostile enemies but were now obliged to accept British residents at their courts and to follow the resident's "advice." For the most part, the protected prince retained the internal governance of his former state, but he could not wage war, and he had to acknowledge the British as "paramount power," with the right to intervene as they chose in his state's internal affairs. The prince was frequently obliged as well to pay a "subsidy" in return for military support and protection. This system took shape in India in the 1760s as the British, from their coastal bases, sought allies, or "buffers," against enemies in the interior. The initial appointment of residents, at the courts of the Nizam of Hyderabad and the Nawab of Awadh at Lucknow after 1764, announced Britain's intent to push its influence forward beyond the territories it ruled directly. Wellesley's conquests as governor-general, from 1798 to 1805, vastly extended the reach of what may be called the residency system and changed its objectives. As rulers of the entire Indian subcontinent, with a powerful army at their command, the British no longer required allies against foreign enemies. Instead, the subordination of the country's princes by posting residents at their courts became a device to secure British hegemony over India.

It is needless here to trace out the extended history of Britain's relations with the Indian princely states, whose territories by 1860 encompassed some 40 percent of the subcontinent's area and over a quarter of its population.[38] Sufficient to note is that, as they practiced indirect rule, the British were caught in a contradiction that could never be resolved. On one hand, they sought by sustaining princes in power to take advantage of the legitimacy these men possessed as "traditional" rulers, and thus to present their own Raj as "Indian"; at the same time, by leaving day-to-day governance in the hands of docile princes, they could reduce their own administrative costs. On the other hand, the British were committed to the rule of law, to certain precepts of morality, and to the larger liberal vision of an India transformed by Western education and the creation of a modern state. His throne secured at once from invaders and rebels, the protected prince had little incentive to govern according to British precepts or indeed to interest himself at all in the administration of his state. In the years up to the 1857 revolt, but most especially during Dalhousie's governor-generalship (1849–56), the British commonly endeavored to resolve this dilemma by a policy of active intervention, which, when frustration overcame patience, led to the annexation of princely states on the grounds of failure of heirs, or of simple "misgovernment." But of course annexation extinguished princely governance altogether and with it indirect rule. After the upheaval of the Mutiny, the British reversed course, eschewed annexation, and sought to reassure India's remaining princes, now seen as "bulwarks against the storm which otherwise would have swept over us in one great wave," that their thrones were secure. To be sure, the threat of deposition remained as an instrument for the chastisement of unruly princes, and the British took advantage of princely minorities to introduce reforms. Nevertheless, with the princes now central players in a grand imperial pageant meant to evoke a glittering "traditional" India, the British, for the most part, left them to rule as they wished.

As Britain's colonial empire expanded around the Indian Ocean, the Indian practice of indirect rule through pliant princes exercised a powerful attraction for officials concerned to keep expenses down and avoid needlessly disrupting functioning indigenous systems of governance. As Michael Fisher has written, the Indian "residency system" implied "limited British involvement, fewer potentially embarrassing entanglements, . . . and a subordinate, loyal, traditional, and therefore 'natural' rule." Hence it "proved persuasive for Britons throughout the Empire."[39] In assessing the growth of indirect rule outside India, it is essential to keep in view the distinction between those occasions when Indian precedents were explicitly cited, either approvingly or otherwise, and those when the introduction of indirect rule, though similar in its operation to that of India, owed nothing to direct Indian influence, but rather was a product of similar circumstances. Of the latter, perhaps the most important, setting precedents of its own, was the system of Zulu reserves established by Theophilus Shepstone (1817–1893) in Natal between 1845 and 1875.

Shepstone, a South African and son of a Wesleyan missionary, with no experience of India, began his career as a diplomatic agent to the tribes of the Eastern Cape and then, following its 1843 annexation, moved into Natal as Crown agent and subsequently as Secretary for Native Affairs. In part to allay white settler fears of the still powerful Zulu kingdom, Shepstone set aside large reserves for the Zulus in the colony's hinterland, but at the same time brought them under British suzerainty. Insistent that they be ruled "according to their own laws, customs, and usages," he nevertheless established himself as a Zulu chief under the colony's lieutenant-governor, installed in turn, by a contorted adaptation of tribal custom, as "supreme chief." Shepstone's position as tribal adviser, with his solicitous paternalism, approximated that of a resident at an Indian princely court, while the Natal lieutenant-governor's role at the apex of the system resembled, on a much reduced scale, that of India's viceroy, who as the queen's representative to the princes, stood forth as the visible embodiment of British "paramountcy." Indian precedents, however, played no role in shaping the outcome in South Africa. Rather, Shepstone's system, with its "native reserves" and separation of white from black, laid the institutional foundation for the subsequent South African policy of apartheid.

Only in the last quarter of the nineteenth century did India become an exemplar of indirect rule. From 1875 onward, the British Empire grew rapidly both in Africa and in Southeast Asia, with the result that, from

Northern Nigeria to remote Fiji, as colonial officials cast about for eco-nomical and minimally intrusive forms of colonial governance, they looked toward India and Indian models. It is essential, however, to avoid jumping to conclusions about how indirect rule functioned in this array of colonial territories. Nowhere was there any simple or straightforward adoption of Indian precedents. For our purposes, perhaps the most sug-gestive instance is that of Malaya. There, local British officials, many of whom had previously served in India or Ceylon, set out initially to put in place a variant of the Indian princely system but ended up establishing almost its exact opposite, a system approaching that of "direct rule." Hence developments in Malaya are worth looking at in some detail.

In January 1874 the Pangkor Engagement established a British resident at the court of Perak; before the year was out, neighboring Selangor and Sungei Ujong had also accepted British residents. With this act the British initiated a process of imperial expansion that ultimately extended from Johore, across the causeway from Singapore, north to the Siamese (Thai) border. Enthusiasm among local officials for such a move ante-dated by several years the signing of this treaty. An 1871 committee appointed by A. E. H. Anson, acting governor of the Straits Settlements, first proposed posting residents, to be called political agents, at the courts of the Malay sultans. As one member of the committee, colonial engineer Major J. F. A. McNair, formerly of the Madras Artillery, later wrote on behalf of this proposal, "Many of the Malay chiefs have repre-sented to me that what they want is an officer acquainted with their lan-guage, who would reside near them to give them countenance and sup-port, who would teach them to collect and spend their revenues to the best advantage, to administer a better form of justice, and to maintain order in their country." Anson, forwarding the report to London, acknowledged that the appointment of residents would be desirable, but said that "the time had not yet arrived" for such a step, "having regard to the present barbarous state of the territories."[40]

The next year, 1872, G. W. R. Campbell, serving as acting lieutenant-governor of Penang after many years service in the Ceylon police, took up the cudgels on behalf of the residential system. "I think it is worth con-sideration," he wrote, "whether the appointment under the British Gov-ernment of a British Resident or Political Agent for certain of the Malay States would not, as in India, have a markedly beneficial effect." In "many a native ruled State in India, it is marvellous what work a single well-selected British officer has effected in such matters as roads, schools, and police — even within the compass of a few years." In 1873 Campbell renewed his call for a "friendly intervention" in the Malay states along the lines of that in princely India. Calling for the appointment in Perak of a "carefully chosen discreet man with a good knowledge of the people and their language," Campbell pointed out that "most native states in and around India have such officers and the value of their influence is unquestionable."[41]

In this early phase of the scramble for empire, the Colonial Office was reluctant to encourage what it saw as costly and unnecessary extensions of British power. As the Liberal Gladstone government's colonial secretary Lord Kimberley wrote to the incoming Straits governor Sir Andrew Clarke in 1873, "Her Majesty's Government has no desire to interfere in the internal affairs of the Malay States." Yet at this same time events on the ground in Malaya were prompting a reconsideration of this policy. The state of Perak was the site of rich tin mines whose ore was being worked by immigrant Chinese laborers. Factional contests among these miners, who were caught up in disputes between contenders for the throne of Perak, provoked "disturbances" that in turn threatened the profitability of the mines and also offered, or so the British feared, opportunities for intervention by foreign powers. Hence Kimberley, who had previously been undersecretary of state for India, went on to authorize Clarke to use his influence with the native princes to "rescue, if possible, these fertile and productive countries from the ruin which must befall them if the present disorders continue." He especially asked Clarke to consider "whether it would be advisable to appoint a British officer to reside in any of the States."[42]

On receipt of these instructions, Clarke summoned the Perak chieftains to a meeting at Pangkor. Not content simply to solicit opinions and report back to London, Clarke, on his own initiative, on 20 January 1874 concluded with the chieftains what became known as the Pangkor Engagement. Several of its provisions were explicitly drawn from Indian practice. Article 6, for instance, provided that "the sultan shall receive and provide a suitable residence for a British officer to be called Resident . . . whose advice must be asked and acted upon on all occasions other than those touching Malay religion and custom." But article 10 called into question one of the chief tenets of the Indian princely system, which left the entire internal governance of his state, as well as control over religion and custom, in the hands of its ruler. That article read, "The collection and control of all revenues, and the general administration of the country, [shall] be regulated under the advice of these Residents."[43]

What moved Clarke to introduce this additional provision into the Engagement is not at once obvious. In part, no doubt, the insertion of

MAP 2. Malaya, c. 1900

article 10 reflected the growing late-Victorian disillusionment with the character and abilities of "native" peoples. As T. Braddell, the Straits attorney general had written, supporting Campbell's 1873 recommendation, the native chiefs "are indolent, self-indulgent, and averse to continuous exertion in any direction." Clarke himself wrote, in justification of his action, that "the Malays, like every other rude Eastern nation, require to be treated much more like children, and to be taught; and this especially in all matters of improvement."[44] The Malay ruler was, in this view, simply incapable of doing his job properly and could not be left unchecked in control of the levers of administration. British disillusionment with the post-1858 Indian princely system may also have played a part. Clearly, Clarke was reluctant to be drawn into the continuing round of threats, frustrations, and rebuffs that marked British efforts in India to mold the activities of princes now guaranteed possession of their thrones.

Still, Pangkor did not by itself resolve these difficulties. To the contrary, it only brought them visibly to the surface, for there was no easy way to resolve the ambiguity inherent in a system in which, on one hand, residents gave "advice" and that, on the other, authorized them to "regulate" the collection of revenue. Clarke himself spoke of the residents as "watching the collection of the revenue, and controlling its expenditure" and as inducing the sultan "to select proper men for the collection."[45] But how this was to take place was left designedly vague. Carnarvon, colonial secretary in the new Conservative government under Disraeli, when informed of the Pangkor arrangements, urged the Straits officials to move cautiously. Arguing that the history of Indian residents ought to "put us on our guard in the present instance," he pointed out that, while the presence of a resident was "an undoubted benefit" to a princely state, "we become through them much more closely connected than heretofore with things and persons and political combinations that may easily lead us further than we now intend to go." Determined to keep this "new phase" of colonial policy carefully in check, Carnarvon repeatedly insisted that residents, in keeping with the Indian precedent, should "in all ordinary cases, confine their action to advice tendered by them to native Rulers, under whose direction the government of the country should be carried on."[46]

Even though halting, this first step toward a "forward" policy in Malaya evoked substantial criticism. Most outspoken perhaps was Lord Stanley of Alderley. A widely traveled Arabist and Orientalist, friend of Sir Richard Burton, and, most unusually for the time, supporter of Indian nationalist aspirations, Stanley in the House of Lords presciently denounced the entire enterprise as one that "must inevitably lead to the invasion and conquest of the whole of the Malay peninsula." The local officials in the Straits, by contrast, unanimously backed Clarke's initiative. The colonial secretary, J. W. W. Birch, rapturously predicted that "the moment a British officer takes up his residence . . . we shall find an immediate influx of Chinese and even of Malays from other States; the revenues properly collected on fixed principles will naturally increase; justice will be administered and oppression prevented; order will be preserved, and security for life and property . . . will be ensured; while the country will soon be opened up by roads, and cultivation will everywhere increase."[47]

After Pangkor, Birch was appointed resident in Perak, while the adventurer T. C. S. Speedy, who had organized a private army for the subordinate chieftain the Mantri of Larut, took up the post of assistant resident in Larut. At the same time, the Straits government, anxious to establish the new system on a basis of accepted practice, requested from the foreign department of the Indian government "copies of any rules or regulations or printed code which may be in existence in India" that might serve as "guides" for those organizing the "new system" in Malaya. In reply, the foreign department said that its relations with India's princely states were "so various that it would be impossible to devise a set of rules which should be alike applicable to all." Instead, the department forwarded to Singapore a number of circular letters and instructions to residents that might, in its view, "indicate generally the spirit in which Political Officers are expected to conduct their intercourse with native princes and chiefs."[48]

Despite the provision of this well-intentioned advice, Birch and Speedy alike soon began to chafe at the restraints Indian-style indirect rule imposed upon them. Nor did they find the mere presence of a resident productive of the changes Birch had so enthusiastically predicted. Birch reported in April 1875 that the chiefs, although "by degree getting accustomed to it," were not yet "satisfied with the presence of a British officer," while the people of Perak, he resignedly announced, "are singularly averse to doing any work, even for hire, except cultivation of their own lands, or for their own purposes."[49] Hence, both men, on their own initiative, soon began to set up systems of administration under their own control. Whether this decision on their part was primarily a response to local chiefly inaction or was a calculated move to push forward British power in the absence of effective supervision from above, in either case the result was very quickly to undercut the "guidelines" for indirect rule so recently forwarded from Calcutta.

As news of these developments filtered back to Britain, most notably in Speedy's 1874 annual report for Larut, Lord Stanley led a chorus of critics both in Parliament and outside. Accepting for the moment the necessity for indirect rule in Malaya, Stanley chose to focus instead on Speedy's presumed "deviations" from Indian practice. Above all, Stanley told the House of Lords, Speedy in his report "invariably speaks as though he were the ruler of the country, instead of the adviser of the Ruler." Soliciting comments from a friend (unnamed) in the India Office, Stanley then proceeded to lecture the Colonial Office on how Speedy *ought* to have acted in Larut. Speedy ought not, for instance, he said, to have established courts on his own authority, and the presiding officer of any court should have been a native, sitting with a British assessor, with an appeal to the native ruler, not to the resident. In sum, as Stanley's "friend" put it, "under the present regime, the Mantri, in place of being judiciously trained to the wise exercise of his authority, is taught to regard himself as a puppet, equally destitute of power and responsibility."[50]

The Straits governor, now Sir William Jervois, disdaining to be taught lessons by Stanley or his friend, responded angrily that "Indian experience is not necessarily a qualification for forming a judgment on our officers and the chiefs of the Malay States." Contesting a central tenet of the Indian system, Jervois wrote that, "if native chiefs once felt certain that the Resident was there only to 'advise,' and that in the event of his advice being refused he would simply say, 'I wash my hands of this affair,' and then wait inactive till the next opportunity of offering his advice occurred, from that moment his position in the native State would be worse than useless." He urged that the residents be replaced with "Queen's commissioners" who would rule in the name of the sultan. Unhappily caught in the middle, Carnarvon contented himself with reminding the local officials that British residents were placed in the Malay states as "advisers not rulers."[51]

In November 1875 J. W. W. Birch, resident in Perak, was assassinated; this was followed within days by an uprising of disaffected Malays led by Sultan Abdullah. How far Birch's aggressively interventionist policy may have provoked the uprising matters less for our purposes than the British response. Faced with this challenge to their authority, the British poured troops into Perak and tracked down the perpetrators of Birch's murder. By the time the "Perak War" came to an end, an uncontested British supremacy had been established in Perak and in the adjacent states of Selangor and Sungei Ujong. In effect, the uprising and its subsequent suppression by force dramatically altered the balance of power in Malaya. To be sure, efforts were made to re-establish the status quo ante. A new Perak sultan was installed in place of Abdullah. The Pangkor Engagement, with its reservation of power over custom and religion to the sultans, was not repudiated, while Jervois's plan to formally annex Perak and other Malay states was turned aside. Sovereignty remained in the hands of the sultans, and in subsequent years the British elevated the ritual importance of the rulers, and their authority over the lesser chiefs.

Nevertheless, after the suppression of the Perak rising, it became impossible to rein in the officials in Malaya, now emboldened in their commitment to an interventionist strategy of governance. As Jervois pointedly told the colonial secretary, the residents in the Malay states had from the beginning taken to themselves "the control of public affairs," and so in practice exercised effective authority over the states to which they were accredited. To roll back this authority was out of the question. The power of the Malay sultan to act on his own, he insisted, was never more than "nominal." By himself he could neither carry out the advice of the resident nor control the petty chiefs and local usurpers who "set his authority at defiance with impunity." In the end, the beleaguered Carnarvon, unwilling to contemplate dismissing the Straits officials for insubordination, effectively abandoned the effort to restrain them. In a dispatch of 1 June 1876, while piously warning them not "to interfere more frequently or to a greater extent than is necessary in the minor details of government," he nevertheless authorized the officials in Malaya to take as "their special objects" the "maintenance of peace and law, the initiation of a sound source of taxation, with the consequent development of the general resources of the country, and the supervision of the collection of the revenue so as to ensure the receipt of funds necessary to carry out the principal engagements of the Government, and to pay for the costs of the British officers and whatever establishments may be found necessary to support them."[52] The 1858 settlement in India, in which defeat of the rebels led to the confirmation of the princes' authority over the administration of their states, was not to be repeated in Malaya. The Malay prince, so the British convinced themselves, was not like the Indian prince and could not be vested with power in the same manner.

Yet, despite the effective repudiation of indirect rule, India did not cease being a model for Malaya. Rather, Malaya's new British rulers now found organizing principles in the directly ruled districts of British India. Speedy and Birch had indeed already inaugurated this practice of "direct rule" in 1875. The court, for instance, which had drawn the wrath of Stanley's friend in the India Office was modeled on those in India, and enforced the Indian Penal Code. At the same time, on the administrative side, the British introduced Indian forms of local government into Malaya. Perak, for instance, was divided into four districts, each under the charge of a British official designated by the Indian term "collector and magistrate." His duties were identical to those of the Indian district collector; as F. A. Swettenham reported in 1879, he "collects the revenue of his district, defrays court expenses, and holds the surplus for the credit of the government." By 1886, Hugh Low, resident in Perak, recounted in his annual report that "business is now conducted almost precisely on the lines of a Crown Colony, and the returns and papers which lie before me in writing this report are such as would be sent in to the Colonial Secretary of one of the largest of Her Majesty's possessions."[53]

Of course, the Malayan administrative system possessed distinctive features of its own. State councils, in a way foreign to both princely and direct rule in India, incorporated the residents with the rulers and major chiefs. Substantive civil law, never codified, much of it dealing with religion and custom, was left in the hands of *qazis* appointed by the sultans. In 1895 the four states of Perak, Selangor, Pahang, and Negri Sembilan were brought together in the Federated Malay States, with a unified administration under a resident-general reporting to the Straits governor as high commissioner. In this way the ad hoc introduction of the principles of direct rule inaugurated after the Perak rebellion were formalized and consolidated. Surprisingly, even in this atmosphere, so different from that of princely India, Indian terminology still found a place. Swettenham, for instance, as resident-general inaugurated the new federation with a meeting that he called a durbar. Its substance, however, a four-day series of discussions with the princes and their British rulers all seated around a large table bore no resemblance to the ritual displays of sovereignty and homage that characterized Curzon's contemporaneous durbars.[54] Elsewhere in the Malay Peninsula, outside the federated states, from Kedah and Kelantan in the north to Johore in the south, the British presence was much more lightly felt. The rulers of these states were obliged to accept only British advisers, whose position was more comparable to that of a resident at an Indian princely court. Most exceptionally, the proud and outspokenly anglicized rulers of Johore managed to evade any subordination to the British at all until 1914.

As they spread their empire across Africa after 1890, the British had again to face the question of how to govern newly conquered territories. As before, Indian precedents helped shape the outcome. It is not possible here to assess the varied administrative structures the British established throughout Africa. One may identify three alternative strategies of governance: district administration on the pattern of British India; the Indian princely system with residents appointed as advisers to the rulers; and the transformed Indian model of Malaya, in which the resident ran the government in the name of the prince. The closest to the Malayan model was unquestionably the administration of Zanzibar, proclaimed a protectorate in 1890, where British officials were appointed to administrative posts while the sultan remained titular head of state.

The system of indirect rule established by Lugard, first in Uganda, then in Northern Nigeria, and finally throughout Nigeria and elsewhere, has been the subject of much commentary and analysis. Lugard was born in India and lived there as a child; after training at Sandhurst, he returned to serve in the Indian Army for a decade through the late 1870s and early 1880s. A personal romantic crisis provoked his resignation from the army and drove him in 1888 to seek adventure in Africa. As he set out from the 1890s to establish African colonial governments, there can be no doubt that Lugard was, as Margery Perham put it, "not unaware" of the working of India's administrative system in both its princely states and its directly ruled districts; and Indian example unquestionably helped inspire him as he set up his system of rule in Africa. He referred, for instance, in 1900 to Northern Nigeria as a "little India," and in his 1902 administrative report he spoke of Northern Nigeria, "though but a third in size, and many centuries behind the great Eastern dependency," as presenting "to my imagination many parallel conditions."[55]

Yet, apart from such features as the appointment of residents to princely courts — a defining feature of indirect rule anywhere — evidence that Lugard avowedly sought to apply Indian forms to African governance remains scanty. One might argue that as he moved across Africa, what Lugard brought with him from India was more the *idea* of indirect rule than any formal administrative arrangements. Certainly, the famed system of indirect rule Lugard set up in Northern Nigeria diverged considerably from any Indian model. Unlike its presumed Indian counterpart, the Nigerian system integrated into a single system the ruling emirs and the British colonial officials. As Lugard wrote in his influential *The Dual Mandate in British Tropical Africa,* "There are not two sets of rulers — British and native — working either separately or in cooperation, but a single Government in which the native chiefs have well defined duties and an acknowledged status equally with British officials."[56] The native ruler thus retained control over the collection of taxes and the administration of justice, but, unlike the prince in India, he was subject to strict and continuing supervision. Although Lugard did not go so far as his counterparts in Malaya in limiting the powers allotted native rulers, much of what he learned from what he called "the invaluable lessons of Indian administration" were lessons in what to avoid — above all, conceding to such rulers an unfettered control over the internal governance of their states.

Indian administrative forms may be said to have flourished more fully not in Lugard's system of indirect rule, but rather in the directly gov-

erned East African Protectorate after 1895. Here, Hardinge as commissioner carefully modeled the administrative structure on that of India. At
its heart, as in India, lay the division of the protectorate into districts, each
in charge of a "Collector." This official's responsibilities, and those of his
assistants, were to be "identical with those of the Collector and Assistant
Collectors in India or in the Bombay Presidency." The powers allotted to
the superior officers, the commissioner and sub-commissioner, were to
be equivalent to those of the Indian provincial governor (or lieutenant-
governor) and divisional commissioner. The introduction of such titles,
instead of more generic terms such as "district officer," Hardinge
explained, was undertaken with "the special purpose of its adaptability to
the various Indian acts."[57]

In its executive, as in its judicial, governance, Egypt stood apart.
Although, as Tignor makes clear, the Egyptian administrative system after
1882 was "guided" by Indian models, it could incorporate them only partially and incompletely. Despite the existence of many Indian-derived
plans and proposals, most notably Lord Dufferin's 1883 "Report on the
Reorganization of Egypt," Britain's inability — or unwillingness — to formally annex Egypt placed strict limits on what it could do as a ruling
authority. For the most part, Britain sought to control Egypt by placing
British officials in key ministries as "advisers" who wielded more power
than their nominal superiors. Even in 1882, already one thousand European officials were employed in the Egyptian government. Nevertheless,
as Tignor writes, the provincial administration remained "essentially
that created in the age of Mohammed Ali, while the social life of the
wealthy and sophisticated was dominated by French culture."[58]

The most visible Indian contributions to British rule in Egypt are to be
found not in the structure of its governing institutions, but in the provision of administrative personnel and, above all, in the construction of the
massive irrigation works that tamed the flow of the Nile. Lord Cromer,
as is well known, before taking up the post of consul-general in Egypt,
had served in India as private secretary to the viceroy Lord Northbrook
(1872–76) and as finance member of the viceroy's council from 1880 to
1883. The Indian Civil Service (ICS) officer Auckland Colvin went to
Egypt in 1878, where he served successively as head of the cadastral survey, commissioner of the debt, and controller-general; in 1883 he returned
to India as finance member of the viceroy's council. The British Indian
judge Sir John Scott served in Egypt as judicial adviser from 1890 to 1895.
Sir Colin Scott-Moncrieff, who had worked on the Ganges and Jamuna
canals and as chief engineer in Burma, joined the Egyptian public works

department in 1883, along with four subordinate engineers from India, including, as we have seen, William Willcocks. These appointments had lasting consequences, for they marked the first stage in the empire-wide diffusion of Indian practices of water management. "Irrigation," as Scott-Moncrieff wrote, "is an art which there is no occasion to practice in England," whereas northern India possesses a system of canals "far greater than in Egypt." For the reconstruction of the great Nile Barrage a few years later, as he wrote in an 1890 report on the project, "again I looked to India for helpers, and the services of four were lent to enable me to spend the Million [of a sterling loan to Egypt] to the best advantage."[59] The first Aswan Dam, with initial plans drawn up by Willcocks, followed.

Throughout a vast arc of the empire, then, India provided inspiration, precedents, and personnel for colonial administration. There was, one might argue, little alternative. By contrast with the English legal system, no one proposed introducing into the late-nineteenth-century empire English forms of local government. The Queensland law code might be considered suitable for Africa, but neither mayors and gentry-magistrates nor the kinds of elected local government bodies brought into being in Britain and Australia in these years, much less parliamentary elections, were appropriate, in the British view, for colonies that involved rule over "uncivilized" peoples. Ironically, the new Indian institutions that grew up after the 1880s — above all Lord Ripon's local self-government measures, which put in place partially elective municipal and district boards — had to be pointedly ignored. India was, to be sure, a rich and accessible source of administrative ideas, but it was always conceived of as being at a more advanced "stage" of "civilization" than Britain's other colonial territories. In Egypt alone did the British establish anything resembling legislative councils, and these had but little power. Much as Ripon's administrative reforms may have foreshadowed Africa's distant future, unlike district collectors and subordinated princes, they did not offer "models" for its present.

CHAPTER 2

Constructing Identities

From the earliest days of their rule over India, the British set out to order and define its peoples. In part this task reflected the imperative to make sense of and come to terms with the land over which they found themselves ruling. As many works written during the last decades under the influence of Michel Foucault have made abundantly clear, knowledge was an essential ingredient of power. Without knowing, authority could not be effectively exercised. The process may be said to have begun with Warren Hastings's construction of "Hindus" and of "Muslims" as distinct legal communities within India. During the Victorian era, however, and especially as the Raj consolidated its power after 1858, the study of India was made part of a larger scholarly enterprise in which the Victorians, as children of the Enlightenment, sought comprehensive ways of fitting the world around them into ordered hierarchies. Beginning with the photographic collection "The People of India," published in 1868, the British in India produced an array of volumes that purported to systematize the country's varied castes and ethnic groups. Not just intellectual exercises, these ethnographic categories, as they were embedded in censuses, gazetteers, and revenue records, shaped the administrative concerns of the colonial state. Further, the persistence of diverse ethnic identities at the heart of Indian society foreclosed any effective unity among India's peoples, or so the British colonial administrators believed. Divided by caste, religion, and ethnicity, India's peoples could not rise to any conception of unity. As H. H. Risley wrote in 1915, there existed in India "no national type and no nation or even nationality in the ordinary sense of these words."[1]

This chapter examines how this process of knowing and ordering India's peoples shaped British attitudes and assumptions about the societies the British encountered as they extended their empire into Southeast Asia and Africa in the later nineteenth century. I do not claim that the categories formed in India were transported wholesale overseas — there was of course no caste system in Malaya. Rather I argue that ways of thinking formed during the Indian colonial experience found expression, as the British struggled to come to terms with their new colonial subjects, in comparable, if different, forms of knowledge elsewhere. That is, the India of the Raj, with its richly elaborated hierarchies, existed always as a model, whether explicitly cited or not, for how the British ought appropriately to "make sense of" newly conquered colonial societies. India, with Ceylon, also made its presence felt more directly, through immigration, alike in Malaya and East Africa; and so forced the British to confront new problems in the ordering of multiracial societies. I endeavor here, with examples ranging from notions of "indolence" to land tenures to architecture, to show, primarily in relation to Malaya, how colonial knowledge incorporated Indian precedents and yet frequently challenged them.

The "Lazy" Native and the "Industrious" Immigrant

The British had entered the Malay world as far back as the early trading voyages of the East India Company, but their first attempts to come to terms with its peoples were a product of Stamford Raffles's conquests after 1810. Raffles's views of Malay abilities were not favorable. "From the comparatively rude and uncivilized character of the Malay nation, learned disquisition is not to be looked for," he wrote. Similar views were echoed by John Crawfurd, an associate of Raffles and author of the first extended British ethnography of the East Indies, the *History of the Indian Archipelago, Containing an Account of Manners, Arts, Languages, Religions, Institutions, and Commerce of Its Inhabitants,* published in 1820 in two volumes. With respect to their "intellectual capacity," Crawfurd wrote, "the Indian islander of the best capacity is unequal, in most respects, to an individual not above mediocrity in a civilized community." Such assertions involved, almost certainly, an implicit comparison with India, whose rich and ancient past British Orientalists were discovering during these very years. Yet there was also, for men like Crawfurd, much that was attractive about the Malay peoples. These characteristics too involved contrasts with India. The Javanese, for instance, possessed a "singular and unexpected candour" unlike the "almost universal disregard of truth which charac-terizes the inhabitants of Hindustan." In similar fashion the Malay pos-sessed a "kindness" and a "sympathy for distress"; hence, unlike the Indian, who "would see a man struggling for life in the water and afford him no assistance," the Malay would exert himself to come to the rescue.[2]

This making of the Malays into a "simple" people, though "good humoured and cheerful to a remarkable degree," persisted into the post-1874 colonial era. Most authoritative perhaps in its depiction of their char-acter was Frank Swettenham's *British Malaya,* first published in 1905 and reprinted into the 1940s. Swettenham (1850–1946) served almost his en-tire colonial career in the Straits and Malaya, rising to the posts of resident-general for the Malay states and governor of Singapore; in his lengthy retirement he made himself into a self-styled expert on colonial affairs. For Swettenham, as for other officials of the time, the "leading characteristic" of the Malay was "a disinclination to work." This caricature — the "myth of the lazy native," as it has been called — was grounded in the British con-ception of Malaya's tropical environment. A life of "inherent laziness" was, in Swettenham's view, a natural response to a warm climate that "inclines the body to ease and rest, the mind to dreamy contemplation rather than to strenuous and persistent toil," together with the fact that a bountiful nature had done "so much" for the Malay that occasional "fitful exertion" would produce enough rice and fish to supply his wants.

Yet, for Swettenham as for Crawfurd, the Malays remained still an attractive people. "Whilst the Malay has no stomach for really hard and continuous work, either of the brain or of the hands," Swettenham con-tinued, "if you can only give him an interest in the job he will perform prodigies; he will strive, and endure, and be cheerful and courageous with the best." "Take him on the war-path or any kind of chase," or even on an expedition through the jungle, Swettenham concluded, "and you will wish for no better servant, no more pleasant or cheery companion." Hugh Clifford, who served in remote Pahang in the 1890s, voiced similar sen-timents. "True children of the drowsy land in which they live," Malays were "lazy, indolent, and pleasure-loving" but at the same time "courte-ous of manner, soft of speech, and caressing by instinct."[3] This personal-ity obviously complemented the luxuriant wilderness in which the Malays lived — a land of sultry heat, teeming wildlife, and dense jungle. Land and people together, Malaya evoked a romantic vision of an arcadian time before the "boot of the ubiquitous white man" had trampled upon it.

Perfectly fitted to their lush tropical landscape, the Malays existed by contrast to those whom they were *not,* and should not be encouraged to emulate. The Malay, Swettenham pointedly observed, possessed "an absence of servility, which is unusual in the East." Further, he wrote, with the example of the educated Indian visibly before him, the Malay is not "a person who is always asserting himself, airing grievances, and clamouring for rights." The contrast with the Indian Bengali is instructive. Like the Malay, the Bengali, in the British view, was also given over to indolence and lethargy. Like the Malay, he was a product of a tropical climate. As Macaulay famously wrote of him, the Bengali passed his days in a "constant vapour bath," so that his "physical organization" was "feeble even to effeminacy." But the Bengali "babu," with his book learning and his mastery of English, appeared in the fearful shape of a caricature Englishman. By his mimicry of English manners and opinions, the Bengali represented that which had to be denied — a challenge to the legitimacy of the Raj. Progress surely had to come to Malaya, but the Malay was not to be reshaped in the image of the babu. Above all, it was essential, as Swettenham wrote in 1890, that the Malays not be taught English, for that would "only unfit them for the duties of life and make them discontented with anything like manual labor." There must be created in Malaya no "imitation, however remote, of the occasionally startling, sometimes grotesque, and often pathetic product of the British Indian schools." It was the task of the British to secure the Malay in the possession of his simple pleasures and to ensure that he remained as he was.[4]

Such a determination *not* to follow Indian precedents in education was widespread throughout the empire. Even in Egypt, with its sophisticated French-educated elite, men like Lord Cromer insisted that "India furnished rather an object lesson in what should be avoided." He determined not to create in Egypt another "superficially educated upper class," but instead to encourage elementary and technical education. "I want," he said, "to create as many carpenters, bricklayers, plasterers, etc., as I possibly can."[5] Whether in the Malay jungle or on the banks of the Nile, the local people were to be guided into paths far different from those Macaulay had outlined for India.

In place of an English educated elite, the British in Malaya sought to place the Malay sultans, since 1875 formed into loyal allies, at the center of the new political order. As they sought to understand the nature and position of the sultans, the British advanced theories devised more than a century before, during the conquest of India. There, in the late eighteenth and early nineteenth centuries, two visions of indigenous rulership had contested for supremacy. One, associated with the writings of Alexander Dow in the 1770s, argued that India's rulers were "Oriental despots" participating in an ancient tradition of unbounded personal authority. The second, elaborated by James Tod during the 1820s conquest of Rajputana, asserted that India's princely order resembled the feudal system of medieval Europe, with its hierarchy of rights and obligations based on military service.[6]

Though these two visions of Oriental rulership were fundamentally incompatible, both survived into the later Raj as descriptions of the "traditional" political order; and from India both found their way to Malaya. Hugh Clifford simultaneously elaborated both visions in an 1899 talk to the Royal Colonial Institute, as well as in a number of short stories. For Clifford the sultan was a man moved by "his whims," whose "lightest word brought death, swift and inevitable," and whose "passions were given to him to satisfy to the full, not to curb or restrain." Yet at the same time, Clifford insisted upon the feudal character of Malay society. To live in an independent Malaya, he asserted forthrightly, "is to live in the Europe of the thirteenth century," with the various sultanates divided into districts "held in fief" by chiefs bound to homage and military service. As with the Rajput states of India, so too in Malaya, the British believed, time had stood still for "some six centuries." Both societies possessed superior chieftains known as "rajas" set over peasant cultivators. In neither did there exist the springs of autonomous political development.[7]

Unlike the Muslim rulers of India, the Malay sultans, with the general populace, were not seen as men drawn to religion. Though Muslim in faith, as Clifford wrote, Malays "continue to be Malays first, and Muhammadans afterward." Custom, or *adat,* he insisted, is the "fetish of the Malay. Before it even the Hukum Shara [sharia], the Divine Law of the Prophet, is powerless."[8] Hence the British brought to their conquest of Malaya none of the suspicion and anxiety that accompanied the supersession of the Muslim rulers of India, or for that matter, the Dutch conquest of Indonesia. No Malay ruler was ever portrayed, like Tipu Sultan of Mysore, as a zealous fanatic driven by his Islamic faith. Nor were the people more generally, like the Muslims of northern India at the time of the 1857 revolt, ever regarded as potential participants in a "great Mahomedan conspiracy." As a result the British had no hesitation in allowing the sultans to retain authority over "Malay religion and custom," even as they took over day-to-day governance for themselves.

Despite their commitment to preserving a "traditional" Malay way of life, the British determined to develop the resources of the country, above all by encouraging mining and plantation agriculture. This endeavor necessarily involved encouraging immigration. The bulk of this was from China. Swettenham hailed the Chinese immigrants who flooded into the country from the 1870s onward for their pioneering work in the mining industry and in bringing capital into Malaya. They had, he said, introduced "tens of thousands of their countrymen when the one great need was labour to develop the hidden riches of an almost unknown and jungle-covered country."[9] But this migrant stream poured in from South Asia as well. Varied in character, it brought Sikhs from the Punjab, laborers from the Tamil country of South India, educated Ceylon Tamils, and British planters and officials from throughout South Asia seeking new opportunities in this new colonial territory. Aspects of this migration, especially that of Sikhs for the police, are discussed elsewhere in this volume, while the migration of plantation laborers from southern India — which brought some 200,000 Indians to Malaya by 1913 — has been the subject of a number of studies and will not be treated here. It is, however, worth noting briefly the exceptional character of migration from Ceylon (Sri Lanka) to Malaya.

Several circumstances together propelled migration from Ceylon. For the British themselves, many saw in the Straits opportunities denied them in the more settled colonial society of Ceylon. J. W. W. Birch, for instance, served in Ceylon for fifteen years before taking up the post of colonial secretary in the Straits in 1870. Others came over from the police or technical services, among them the engineer C. E. Spooner, who in 1891 left the Ceylon Public Works Department (PWD) to run the Selangor PWD, and ultimately the Malayan State Railways. In addition, many private Englishmen settled in Malaya as planters after the 1880s collapse of coffee production in Ceylon. In Malaya these men initially opened up coffee plantations but then, after 1900, shifted to rubber to take advantage of the booming market fed by the burgeoning automotive industry. Sydney W. Moorhouse, for instance, born in Ceylon in 1874, after six years planting tea, moved to Malaya in 1898; in 1905 he floated a rubber company that by 1916 had 16,000 acres under production for Dunlop.

Often family ties spurred these moves. Like many others, R. W. Harrison went to Ceylon from England as a youth in 1886 to join his planter brother, and some years later moved on to Malaya. Similarly, in 1905 Thomas R. Harvey at age twenty-two came out to Malaya to join his three elder brothers, tea planters in Ceylon who had recently shifted their enterprise to Malaya. Not only rubber planters but the rubber plant itself came to Malaya from Ceylon. Smuggled out of Brazil, the first British rubber seedlings were raised at Kew and then shipped to Ceylon in 1876, where they were grown in the Paradeniya Government Gardens. One of the first planters to come from Ceylon to Malaya, Thomas Heslop Hill, brought rubber seed with him in 1883 and thus laid the foundation for the export crop that was to bring immense prosperity to Malaya during the first decades of the twentieth century.[10]

Planters and officials alike brought to Malaya with them educated Ceylon Tamils. A minority community resident in the northern Jaffna Peninsula, Tamils took eagerly to English education in the decades following the early-nineteenth-century British conquest of the island. By midcentury they were represented in Ceylonese government service far in excess of their proportion of the island's population. By the 1880s, however, population pressure in the Jaffna area, combined with increasing competition from Sinhalese and Burghers for employment, encouraged ambitious Tamils to look for jobs off the island. At the same time, as British officials began to establish colonial-style governments in Malaya, they turned to Ceylon, where so many of them had themselves been previously employed, as a source of skilled labor.

As a result, Ceylon Tamils took up a range of employment opportunities in Malaya. Clerks, auditors, assistant surveyors, draftsmen, overseers — employed on plantations as well as in government offices — they found a remunerative role for themselves, as was so often the case with educated elites from South Asia, as intermediaries between Britain's colonial rulers and newly colonized peoples. Indeed, for some time, the effective operation of the government depended on them. In 1890, as W. E. Maxwell wrote from Selangor, only after "a Chief Clerk of some experience" was obtained from Ceylon was it possible to "enforce the due carrying out of the Indian Civil Procedure Code." For decades after the opening of the railways in 1885, all skilled jobs, from clerk to stationmaster, were held by Ceylon Tamils. By 1911 there were some 8,500 Ceylon Tamils in Malaya, and, some have argued, their remittances home sustained the prosperity of Jaffna.[11]

These various ethnic groups were not, of course, free from internal divisions of their own. These the British at times chose to recognize and at others to ignore. Among Indians, from the outset a distinction emerged between migrants from the south and those from the north. The former, the earliest and most numerous of Indian migrants, were initially designated "Klings," from their origin along the southeastern coast of India in an area corresponding to the ancient kingdom of Kalinga; they were then subsequently known as Tamils, from the preponderance of Tamil speakers among the South Indian migrants. All North Indians were lumped together as "Bengalis," presumably because they had passed through Bengal and taken ship in Calcutta on their way to Malaya. This was an odd, even paradoxical, usage, for not only were very few migrants from Bengal proper but, as we have seen, Bengalis were associated in the British mind with effeminacy. By contrast, North Indian residents of Malaya were commonly Punjabis and Hindustanis, and as members of so-called "martial races," they were often recruited, as we shall see later, for the police and security services. Nevertheless the label "Bengali" stuck. As the census commissioner noted in 1911, "the term 'Bengali' is used not only by Malays, but has become of such common use that many a local Punjabi will and does describe himself as a Bengali." This regional classification, with its implied racial distinction between Aryan and Dravidian, overrode other identities central to the colonial ordering of India, above all those of religion, such as "Hindu" and "Muslim." It ignored as well the existence of racially mixed communities, such as the Indo-Malay Jawi Peranankan.[12]

Malays were, by contrast, for the British simply "the people of the country," as Swettenham put it. But this definition hid more than it revealed. Above all, it took no account of residence. A racial classification, the term "Malay" excluded Chinese and Indians no matter how long they and their families had lived in Malaya. The Chinese, as Hugh Clifford acknowledged, had "toiled in the peninsula for centuries," but they nevertheless remained "alien."[13] Even though by the 1920s some 30 percent of the Chinese population had been born in the peninsula, the census takers refused to accept them as permanently settled. By contrast, the ethnic differences among migrants from the Netherlands Indies across the straits were blurred, as were the differences between them and the Malays of Malaya. For the purposes of colonial policy making the category "Malay" embraced those culturally cognate peoples who were of the same "ethnic stock" and who shared common language and customs, including the Muslim faith. Participation in the ordering world of *kampung* (village community) and *kerajaan* (kingly polity) alone made one "Malay."

Malay Society: Villager and Sultan

Even while working to encourage — by immigration and investment — the economic incorporation of Malaya into the world capitalist order, the British refused to abandon their vision of a Malay society composed of a people "unspoilt" by modern ways. To sustain the two visions side by side required an immense act of social engineering. Above all, Malays had to be kept separate from their Chinese and Indian neighbors; the economy had to be separated into subsistence and commercial sectors; and a political order had to be constructed that linked the Malays to their old rulers, while the immigrant communities were policed by the British and by community leaders such as "Kapitan China" in Kuala Lumpur. Although the classification and legislation that this endeavor required was not modeled on those of India, it shared similar concerns and objectives. Above all, the conviction that inherent characteristics shaped behavior was as compelling in the Malay peninsula as in India. Yet in Malaya, where caste did not exist and "tribes" (apart from scattered forest aborigines) were few, distinctions of race and ethnicity loomed over all others. Colonial Malayan society for the British was divided among "Chinese," "Indian," and "Malay" communities, each with its own presumably distinctive racial characteristics and occupations: the Chinese concentrated in mining and commerce, the Indians in plantation agriculture, and the Malays in subsistence cultivation. These ethnic differences took physical shape at the outset in the racially demarcated zones laid out by Raffles in Singapore. Spread along the harbor in a way reminiscent of the "black" and "white" towns that comprised eighteenth-century Madras, Raffles's Singapore placed the "European Town" in the center adjacent to the government offices. To one side, across the Singapore River, was the area set aside for the Chinese, while on the far opposite side was the "Bugis Campong" for Malays. The Indian sector of the city subsequently developed inland to the north of the Malay zone.

To secure the Malay in his village livelihood as a subsistence cultivator, the British sought to protect him from the disruptive influences of the colonial capitalist order. As they devised policies to achieve this objective, India offered models both to emulate and to repudiate. In both colonial territories, land legislation based on the principles of liberalism, by the award of individual title, opened up novel opportunities for indebtedness, sale, and transfer of holdings among the cultivating classes. In both too, but especially in the Indian Punjab and in Malay Selangor from the 1890s, the British, to preserve a settled agricultural community, embarked upon concerted efforts to restrain the operation of their own system of property rights.

In 1891 the Selangor Land Enactment created a special form of secure "customary" tenure for Muslim smallholders. In language strikingly reminiscent of the discussions then underway in the Punjab, one district officer wrote that it "was considered desirable that these people should be made permanent holders (as far as possible) of their holdings and that everything should be done to prevent their mortgaging their holdings and then in default of payment being ejected and their places taken by Chinese, Chetties [south Indian bankers], and others." The "inhabitants of Selangor" ought not, he insisted, be reduced to "a class of vagrants in their own country." With the growth after 1900 of widespread rubber cultivation, peasant landholdings took on a new value and spurred British efforts to preserve the Malays in possession of their land. In 1911 Selangor landholders could secure a reduction in land tax by accepting a prohibition on their right of transfer to others than members of the "Malayan race." The following year, to encourage subsistence cropping, the owners of such "ancestral lands" were prohibited from growing rubber for the market. Finally, in 1913 the major provisions of the Selangor scheme were incorporated into the Malay Reservations Enactment, which covered all of the Federated Malay States. Under this act no land owned by a Malay cultivator within a reserved area could be sold or transferred to a non-Malay.[14]

Meanwhile in India in the Punjab, a similar process of legislative restriction on land transfer was underway. The sale of land for debt in India had long troubled the British and had led to various acts meant to protect the peasantry from eviction. But only in the Punjab did this anxiety take the shape of a full-scale curtailment of an individual's private property rights. By the Punjab Land Alienation Act of 1900, the British prohibited the transfer of agricultural land in the province to anyone other than a member of a registered "agricultural tribe." No longer were commercial or urban castes, largely Hindu, to be allowed to displace the Punjab's Sikh and Muslim agriculturalists. The capitalist property market was henceforth subordinated, as in Malaya, to the ideal of a stable agrarian order kept in place by its "traditional" elites. To be sure, in the Punjab the British had no objection to production for the market. Further, the province's strategic location adjoining the North-West Frontier, together with its status as the main recruiting ground for the Indian Army and even for colonial police forces, made its stability essential to the security of the Raj in a way that was not the case in Malaya. Nevertheless, the structural rigidities introduced into both societies by these restrictive patterns of landholding generated similar styles of political activity and sustained the dominance of rural elites well into the era of independence. In India outside the Punjab, where land transfer remained less rigorously restricted, the country's land tenures provided for Malayan administrators, not a model to follow, but a cautionary tale of that which was to be avoided. As with the insistent concern to prevent the creation in Malaya of a babu class, so too with land legislation, the British prided themselves, in the words of one colonial official, that there was not in Malaya "any tendency as in parts of India to the dispossession of permanent proprietors in favor of moneylenders or European estate owners."[15]

As they endeavored to fit themselves into the new colonial order, the Malay rulers — in large part because they had been stripped of so much of their authority — determined to take full advantage of those powers that remained to them in the sphere of "custom and religion." Although they had always embodied ritual elements of Islamic kingship in the represen-

tation of their authority, they now moved energetically to deploy ortho-
dox Islamic symbolism. As they sought to regulate and control religious
life in their states and to preempt and contain their critics, they not surprisingly became caught up in the larger currents of Islamic reform that
coursed through southern Asia in the later nineteenth century. Indeed, as
one official remarked in 1906, the sultans were in the process of becoming "less of a Malay and more of a Mussulman." The new Islamic sensi-
bility was in no way limited to Malaya, nor was it directly connected with
colonialism. Still, the growing networks of trade and travel across the
Indian Ocean facilitated the growth of a more outward-looking sharia-
based Islam. Singapore, in particular, became a center of Islamic education
and publication. The British had no love for what they called "Wahabi-
ism," which they pictured as a conspiracy driven by "fanaticism," and they
opposed it forcefully in India. In Malaya, by contrast, it advanced British
interests to represent the sultans as men devoted to Islam. Insofar as the
sultans portrayed Islam through the idiom of rajaship, they presented
themselves as the leaders of a community at once Malay and Muslim. In
so doing, the Malay people could be made "Muslim," yet the faith could
be kept out of the hands of threatening "Wahabi" preachers.[16]

Muslims, Malays, Mosques: A "Saracenic" Architecture

But how was this ordering conjuncture of Malay, Muslim, and sultan to
be made compelling to its intended audience of both ruler and ruled,
Malay and Briton? This was accomplished most visibly through the cre-
ation of a new public architecture. This architecture took two forms. In the
major Malayan cities — above all in Kuala Lumpur, capital after 1895 of the
Federated Malay States (FMS), and to a lesser extent in Singapore — the
British erected civic structures, from government offices to railway stations,
for the use of the new colonial state. At the same time, in the capitals of the
Malay sultans the British built palaces and even, as they had never done in
India, where rulers were left scrupulously alone to put up religious structures as they wished, state mosques. With these buildings, erected in what
is called the Indo-Saracenic style, the British made vividly manifest their
vision of Malaya, of its rulers, and of themselves at its center.

In India during the late nineteenth century, the British endeavored to
create an architecture that would at once enable them to lay claim to mastery of India's past and announce their own connection to that past.
Imagining the Mughals as foreign conquerors like themselves, the British

sought to follow the example, as the architect William Emerson, a fore-most designer of Saracenic structures, put it, of those whom they had sup-planted and who, they supposed, had "seized upon the art indigenous to the country they had conquered, adapting it to suit their own needs and ideas." In so doing, as they erected structures for their own use, the British appropriated architectural elements associated with the Mughal Empire, as well an eclectic array of stylistic forms drawn from various medieval Muslim dynasties. These forms — above all the arch and the dome — they conceived of as "Saracenic" or as "Mahometan," and hence appropriate for representing themselves as a truly "Indian" power. This architecture was never a mere antiquarian exercise. To be sure, as an architecture of façades, the Indo-Saracenic looked to the past. But these buildings were erected to meet the requirements of the modern colonial state, and they housed law courts, colleges, banks, and railway stations.[17]

The British took with them to Malaya the same set of assumptions about how to represent the British Empire in stone. In Malaya a Saracenic public architecture, the British expected, could make the new colonial regime appear to be an integral part of an enduringly Muslim land and, as well, accommodate the new colonial state's requirements for office space and the like. Yet, despite Malaya's Muslim character, the British could not help but realize that this land was profoundly different from India. As they surveyed the landscape, the British, as we have seen, saw only a jungle-clad wilderness. Monumental architecture of the sort they were accustomed to in India was conspicuous by its absence. For the most part Malaya's rulers erected unpretentious wooden residences and other structures. As the trav-eler Isabella Bird wrote with some surprise, "It is strange that a people con-verted from Arabia, and, partly, civilized both from Arabia and from Persia, should never have constructed anything permanent. If they [the Malays] were swept away tomorrow, not a trace of them except their metal work would be found." Hence, the British saw their task, as one official pro-claimed on the occasion of the inauguration of the Kuala Lumpur secre-tariat, as that of developing a city from a "virgin forest where man scarce ever trod, and whose only inhabitants were the beasts of the forest."[18]

Lacking indigenous examples of Islamic-styled work to serve as mod-els, the British pressed into service for their own building in Malaya a wildly eclectic array of elements presumed to be "Mahometan." The first and most notable such structure was the Selangor Secretariat (1894–97), even now the most prominent landmark in the center of Kuala Lumpur. Designed by the state engineer C. E. Spooner, who had served in the Ceylon PWD for fifteen years, the secretariat adopted, as the local news-

FIGURE 1. Secretariat, Kuala Lumpur, Malaysia.
Photograph by Thomas Metcalf.

paper the *Selangor Journal* put it, an "Arabesque" style of architecture "judiciously mixed with Indian detail." The design, they admitted, was "quite new in this country" but of a "pleasing and varied" character. The newspaper singled out as of especially "beautiful proportions" the building's 130-foot-high clock tower, decorated with corner minarets and a copper-colored dome. J. P. Rodger, the resident, similarly described the structure, meant to accommodate all the departments of the new government, as incorporating a "Moorish style of architecture." The choice of the Moorish style was not uncontested. The PWD architect R. A. J. Bidwell had initially drawn up an elevation in "Classic Renaissance"; but,

FIGURE 2. Kuala Lumpur railway station. Photograph by
Thomas Metcalf.

Spooner told the crowd at the opening ceremony for the new secretariat,
"I then decided on the Mahometan style."[19]

Other civic buildings were erected in Kuala Lumpur during the boom
years after the turn of the century. Most notable perhaps were the high
court (1909) and the railway station (1911). Most of these buildings were
designed by the FMS government architect from 1900 to 1914, A. B.
Hubback. They joined forms drawn from northern India, among them
the platform-based cupola or *chattri* with horseshoe arches and bands of
color typical of North Africa and Spain, together with elongated spirelets
somewhat reminiscent of Ottoman Turkey. Of the railway station one

traveler wrote that, with its "Moorish" design, "painted snow-white, and with turret towers like minarets at each end in pairs," the station was "unique in style and architecture." Indeed, he continued, "it is difficult to realize the real purpose of the building, and one may be forgiven for writing it down as a mosque."[20]

Singapore, though the metropolitan center for the Malay Peninsula, stood largely apart from this architectural style. Peopled by Chinese and Indian immigrants, the island colony of Singapore looked outward to the Straits of Malacca and the trade that flowed through them. Singapore's architects sought inspiration from colonial India, but in a different architectural tradition — that of European classicism. The colony's first architect, G. D. Coleman, modeled Singapore's first government building (1827), a villa-type structure with balanced columns, porticos, and pilasters, on the neo-Palladian architecture of Calcutta. Subsequent civic buildings, among them the Empress Place Building (1867) and Government House (1869), in their classical styles followed Coleman's lead. Nor was the choice of this style only a matter of fashion or aesthetics. Classical architecture, with its "eternal principles of ordered beauty," proclaimed Britain's enduring imperial authority and hence appropriately represented Singapore's position as a nodal point in a worldwide empire. Only one major Singapore building, R. A. J. Bidwell's Oriental Telephone and Telegraph offices (1904), adopted a Saracenic style (figure 3). In similar fashion, Hong Kong, though adjacent to China, did not incorporate Chinese architectural elements in its civic building, but rather, through the patronage of classical forms, announced itself as an imperial city.

Even in India, where the British meticulously compiled volumes of "architectural elements" drawn from the massive structures about them, they did not in their own Saracenic-styled buildings adhere strictly to any pre-existing models. The Indo-Saracenic was always an architecture of eclecticism. In the "virgin forest" that was Malaya, the British had space to create, far more than was possible in India, an architecture defined purely by Orientalist fantasy. All Muslim forms, that is, could equally well represent and so constitute what was, for the British, the central fact about Malaya and the Malays: that being Muslim was an essential component of being Malay and that that Muslim identity could most appropriately take architectural shape through those forms that the British, largely on the basis of their extensive experience in India, had determined were properly Islamic. Whether these forms in fact originated in India or even in Muslim Spain, they still defined Malaya as a Muslim society ordered by the British as its legitimate rulers. That the whole was a colonial en-

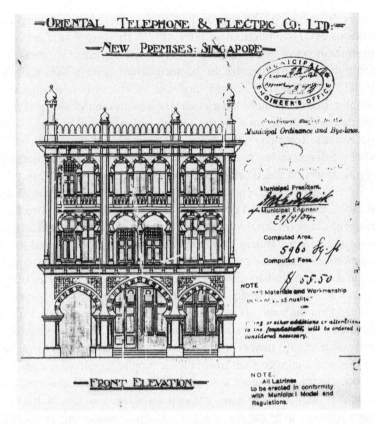

FIGURE 3. Oriental Telephone and Telegraph Company, Singapore (front elevation). Courtesy of the National Archives, Singapore.

terprise was made visibly manifest in the looming clock tower of the Selangor secretariat. Wholly idiosyncratic in its design, the clock tower, like similar structures in India, announced the British determination to enforce upon their colonial subjects a novel regularity and punctuality in place of their presumed indolence.[21]

In striking contrast to India, where they sought to distance themselves from all involvement with religion to avoid unsettling the country's diverse populations, in Malaya the British designed and built mosques. As their building in the colonial capital of Kuala Lumpur sought to make the British-run government appear part of an Islamic Malaya, so too were the mosques and palaces they erected at the capitals of the Malay sultans meant to make the sultans, along with their subjects, participants in this vision. In so doing, the British dramatically altered the accepted conventions of Malay religious architecture. In the precolonial era Malay mosques incorporated a wide variety of design elements. The mosque at Kampung Laut, for instance, in the northeastern state of Kelantan, built in the mid-eighteenth century, and one of the earliest mosques still extant in Malaya, is built of dark rich wood, with interlocking pieces and a wide overhanging roof. In the southwest, in the old colonial city of Malacca, the Terengkera mosque, of the same period, is constructed in a wholly different style, characterized by squared sloping roofs adjoining a pagoda tower modeled on Sumatran or even Chinese precedents.

By the early nineteenth century, as Singapore and Penang, with Malacca, grew into cosmopolitan urban centers integrated into larger maritime networks, local Muslims devised ever more eclectic styles of religious architecture. Indian Tamil merchants, for example, erected shrines (*dargahs*) in Singapore and Penang devoted to a holy man whose grave site in the South Indian town of Nagore was regarded as a place of spiritual power and pilgrimage. The Malayan counterparts, though necessarily lacking the tomb, were modeled on that of Nagore. Erected at both Penang and Singapore, these shrines incorporated, along with the layout and multilevel twin towers of the original, fluted pilasters with Corinthian capitals and a cornice with iron bracket supports, reflecting a growing European influence (figure 4); and at Penang, a dome. Undoubtedly the most distinctive of the early colonial mosques was the 1846 Hajjah Fatima mosque in Singapore. Built by a Malay woman married to a Bugis merchant, with a British architect as designer, this mosque possesses a striking single minaret. With its classical elements, this tower was likely modeled on the spire of the nearby Anglican church. Clearly, even as late as the mid-nineteenth century, domes, arches, arabesques, and the like were not required to make even a mosque "Muslim."[22]

All this was to change by the end of the century as the British set out to encourage mosque construction. Convinced that only certain architectural elements could properly represent Islam, the British were determined that the sultans utilize these forms in their building. Inasmuch, however, as these exotic architectural elements had never formed a part of indigenous building traditions, the sultans by themselves had no way of incorporating them into their structures. Hence, of necessity, British architects took charge of the designs, and government funds were used to pay much of the construction costs. The first such mosque was that of Kuala Lumpur. Situated at the confluence of the city's two rivers and designed by the local architect A. B. Hubback, the mosque remained the

FIGURE 4. Nagore Durga, Telok Ayer Road, Singapore. Courtesy of the National Museum of Singapore, National Heritage Board.

city's principal (*jami*) mosque throughout the colonial period (figure 5). Praised by the resident as "one of the finest examples of this class of building in Malaya," the building, opened by the Selangor sultan in 1909, included an open courtyard, a small prayer hall topped by three domes, and two eighty-foot-high minarets, all in a northern Indian Islamic style. In addition, it incorporated in its façade alternating horizontal bands of color, and scalloped arches, not drawn from any Indian model.[23]

As they moved from state to state through Malaya and even into Singapore itself, Hubback and his fellow architects allowed their Orientalist fancies free rein. Typical of the transformation brought about by British direction was that of Singapore's Sultan mosque. The original structure of 1825, built for the sultan who had ceded Singapore to the British, adopted the traditional Southeast Asian form of a double-tiered roof in the shape of a truncated pyramid. One hundred years later, in 1924, the British firm of Swan and Maclaren reconstructed the mosque in Saracenic style, with a verandah, elaborate moldings in arabesque designs, four tall slender minarets at the corners, and above the main prayer hall, a gold-

FIGURE 5. Jami Mosque, Kuala Lumpur. Photograph by
Thomas Metcalf.

colored dome springing from a base of glass bottles.[24] In Perak state,
whose wealth in tin made possible an elaborate architecture, colonial
Islamic exoticism found unquestionably its most exuberant expression.
The Ubadiah mosque in Kuala Kangsar (1913), set upon a hilltop, with a
huge golden dome and towering minarets, conjures up nothing less than
a Victorian illustrator's fantasy from the *Arabian Nights*. Designed, once
again, by Hubback, this mosque combines such diverse elements as
horseshoe arches reminiscent of Andalusia and Morocco, Indian *chattris*
atop its minarets, glowing red glass around the base of the main dome,
and a covered carriage entry, or portico, with its own golden dome.

FIGURE 6. Ubadiah Mosque, Kuala Kangsar, Malaysia.
Photograph by Thomas Metcalf.

Not all Malay sultans were willing to conform to the British expectation of how they ought to represent themselves. Defying the Saracenic model of architecture, as well as the whole notion of traditional rulership, the sultans of Johore, especially the English-educated Abu Bakar (ruled 1862–95), sought to portray themselves as modern rulers. Ruling a state located directly across from Singapore at the southern tip of the peninsula, Abu Bakar determined, by manipulating the elements of British liberalism, to save Johore from imperial intervention. He enacted for Johore a constitution that presented the state and its government as independent from the person of the sultan. In so doing, he managed to stave off the state's accepting a British resident until 1914. Abu Bakar's political liberalism found its architectural complement, not surprisingly, in a palace and mosque designed in a European neoclassical idiom. Completed after Abu Bakar's death in 1895, the mosque, on a spacious hilltop site in Johore Bahru, boasts a marble colonnade and Italian Renaissance detailing.[25]

The Johore ruler's defiant rejection of the place marked out for him in the colonial order parallels the resistance of a number of Indian princes. The maharajas of Gwalior and Kapurthala, among others, sought to define themselves as modern by repudiating the colonial Saracenic in favor of European styles, especially the neoclassical and baroque, as they built palaces and other structures. Such resistance makes abundantly clear that those most committed to the ideals embodied in Saracenic styles were the British themselves. Indeed, the British, one may say, were the primary audience for what they had constructed. Yet, for the most part, defiance was not a practicable strategy for either Indian or Malay princes. In each case, whatever power they possessed derived wholly from the support given them by the British. As the British insisted that they act as "traditional" rulers, the princes had of necessity to adopt those institutional as well as architectural forms that would make them appear, in British eyes, "traditional" and, in Malaya, Muslim.[26]

As a style for building, the Indo-Saracenic, with its imagined Islamic past turned to the purposes of British colonialism, took shape outside India most fully only in Malaya. The historicist assumptions that undergirded this style, however, found expression not only in the construction of colonial buildings but also in historic preservation. In India this involved an effort, overseen by the Archeological Survey of India, to preserve and protect the monuments of earlier rulers. Such structures were imagined as belonging properly to a fixed moment in time. Set in garden plots, these buildings were meant to evoke romantic visions of grandeur and of fallen majesty in a narrative of Indian history whose endpoint was the coming of the British. Of these historic monuments, the most compelling (apart from those of the ancient Buddhist era, seen as classically inspired) were those of Saracenic design, spanning the period from the Ghorid builders of the Qutb Minar (1193) to the Mughal dynasty of the late sixteenth and seventeenth centuries. Of the isolated fifteenth-century Mandu, for instance, the architectural historian James Fergusson wrote, the "simple grandeur and expression of power" of the city's "Pathan"-styled structures showed how its builders had "grasped the true elements of architectural design."[27]

The British brought these assumptions with them to Egypt when they took responsibility for its governance. The great monuments of Egyptian antiquity, cherished since Napoleon's time, of course stood apart. But, as Paula Sanders has argued, as the British set out to "preserve" Egypt's Islamic monuments, they already knew what an architecture worthy of preservation ought to look like. The Indian "Saracenic" and the Egyptian "Mamluk," as they saw it, were comparable, and hence equally deserving of preservation. Curzon, for instance, in 1905 determined to get from Egypt a "beautiful hanging lamp of Saracenic design" to hang in the tomb chamber of the Taj Mahal, because, as he wrote to Cromer, the "style of the Taj you know to be what we call Indo-Saracenic, which is really Arabic, with flowering substituted for geometric patterns." The "Arab," furthermore, was the "pure form" from which the Saracenic architecture, first Islamic and then colonial, had been derived. The preservation of such buildings was therefore essential not only in India but in Egypt as well. The celebration of the Saracenic came of course at a cost. As "Hindu" architecture in India was deprecated as the product of a "corrupt and idol-atrous" society, so too was Ottoman building in Egypt disdained. The Ottomans, though rulers of Egypt for several hundred years, were "Turks," ruling over a society "in decline." Seen through the lens of the Indian Saracenic, their buildings, subject to much alteration and decay, were not worthy of historic preservation.[28] Saracenic design, by contrast, at once knit the empire together and proclaimed British mastery over the societies, from Egypt to India to Malaya, that it comprised.

Swettenham described the relationship between the India of the Raj and Malaya as one in which "that Great Dependency of the British Crown" offered "a hundred cases of kindly help" to the "struggling little Malay States."[29] Matters of course were not so simple, for the "help" was frequently unwanted or ignored. India stood forth, too, especially in such matters as education, as a model to be avoided. Nevertheless, in funda-mental ways, ranging from Macaulay's legal codes and the ideals of tra-ditional rulership, to demarcations of racial and ethnic difference, to the architectural styles deemed suitable for colonial building, the "Great Dependency" of the Indian Raj defined what empire was all about and laid down its institutional framework. A "struggling" Malaya or Kenya could never wholly be free of its gravitational attraction.

CHAPTER 3

Projecting Power

The Indian Army Overseas

On the first of November 1875, J. W. W. Birch, recently appointed as British resident in the Malay state of Perak, was assassinated, and the state erupted in rebellion against its new British overlords. From the outset, it was assumed as a matter of course that the Indian Army would be given the task of suppressing this rebellion. As the Indian secretary telegraphed the viceroy from London on November 8, "Serious disturbances reported in Perak. Sir W. Jervois [Straits governor] states that he may require troops. In that case he has been directed to apply to you. Please immediately comply with any such requisition in the manner you think best." The following day the Straits colonial secretary wrote requesting the dispatch from India of five hundred men and a ship of war to Penang. On the 16th the military secretary in Calcutta told the brigadier commanding the contingent that "it is highly desirable that no time should be lost, and that as troops and ships are ready, they should start." Some six hundred British soldiers of the 3rd Buffs embarked for Malaya on November 20; they were followed six days later by four hundred men of the 1st Gurkhas. So rapid was this mobilization that when the first of these troops disembarked at Penang, Birch had been dead less than a month. By February the uprising had been suppressed, and the troops returned to India.[1] Once again, the Indian Army had marched to the rescue of an imperiled British Empire.

The use of the Indian Army to extend and secure Britain's empire throughout the vast region "east of Suez" was no new phenomenon in 1875. The East India Company, from the days of its first conquests, had

68

deployed Indian troops eastward in Manila, Sumatra, and Malacca and to the west of India in Mauritius, the Persian Gulf, and Aden. Company troops participated as well in both opium wars with China, not to mention their continuing engagement in regions closer to India, including the 1855 Persian war and the successive campaigns in Burma. With the abolition of the East India Company in 1858 and the subsequent reorganization of the Indian Army, deployment overseas became a regular feature of Indian military life. Connected to this deployment of Indian troops was the construction of an arc of power emanating from the government's mountaintop aerie at Simla and extending throughout this Indian Ocean arena. India remained always, to be sure, a subordinate partner in the larger British Empire, but from Africa to eastern Asia, its army made possible that empire's very existence. At the same time, sheltered by this military umbrella, India's Foreign Office claimed responsibility for the movement of troops and making of imperial policy throughout much of Asia. The power that was projected across these vast spaces was unquestionably directed to British imperial interests, but, as often as not, it marked out as well what R. J. Blyth has called "the empire of the raj."[2]

Despite the large number of publications on the Indian Army and on the colonial campaigns of the British army, no one has undertaken a comprehensive study of the Indian Army's deployment overseas in the late nineteenth and early twentieth centuries. This chapter does not endeavor to remedy that shortcoming. Rather, by examining several selected overseas campaigns between the 1870s and the First World War, it illuminates the ways in which the Indian Army secured and sustained the British colonial empire. Success in these expeditions was not guaranteed. Indeed, even apart from the catastrophic defeats sustained at the siege of Kut in the First World War (1916) and the fall of Singapore in the second (1942), officers and men of the Indian Army regularly fell in skirmishes with Britain's colonial opponents. Nevertheless, by its very size and discipline, the Indian Army provided an unmatched imperial ready reserve. No other, or subsequent, imperial power has ever had access to a comparable force.

That the Indian Army could, and should, be used in Britain's colonial expeditions was a commonplace of Victorian thinking. At an 1869 parliamentary hearing on the Abyssinian war of 1867–68 — in which a British Indian force from Bombay under the command of Sir Robert Napier, commander-in-chief of the Bombay Army, overthrew the regime of King Theodore — the then Indian secretary, Sir Stafford Northcote, was asked whether consideration had ever been given to deploying a force from

England. There "was a general feeling," he replied, "that if an expedition was undertaken at all it had better be from India." Indeed, he continued, "it was taken almost for granted that if an expedition were undertaken it would be most convenient to use Indian troops, and that if the Indian troops were used the expedition must be from India." A year before, in 1868, a select committee on the army had already come out in favor of the deployment of Indian, rather than British or locally raised, forces in colonial territories around the Indian Ocean.[3]

There were obvious advantages for the British in using Indian troops to conquer their empire for them. Indian troops were cheaper in pay and equipment than British. Their deaths in battle was less likely to trouble the British conscience than the loss of British troops. In addition, Indians were deemed better able than Britons to survive in tropical climates. In such places as Ceylon and the Straits Settlements, where the climate was "unsuitable to the European constitution," the 1868 army committee recommended more frequent use of Indian troops. Political and strategic considerations also played a role. Designedly obscuring the "divide and rule" mentality that underlay such a decision, the committee asserted that "the evidence they have received points rather to the employment in our Eastern possessions of our native Indian troops, to be from time to time relieved in the same manner as British troops, than to the maintenance of local corps raised for service in the particular colony."[4] Use of Indian rather than British troops carried with it the further substantial advantage that the Indian Army's deployment was not subject to a Parliamentary vote beforehand, so that the government possessed a freer hand in sending contingents on campaigns abroad on short notice, as to Perak in 1875, or when popular support at home was uncertain.

There were, of course, limits to the reliance on Indian troops for imperial security. One earlier objection to overseas deployment — the reluctance of high-caste soldiers to travel across the sea — disappeared with the enforcement of the 1856 General Enlistment Act, requiring Indian soldiers to agree to serve wherever they were sent. Even so, however, the Nepali Gurkhas, because they were recruited in a foreign land, were not covered by the provisions of the act, so that, as we shall see, their caste objections to overseas deployment had to be taken into account. In any case, Indian troops could not be sent too far from India, for such deployment, with the attendant necessity of regular relief, would be uneconomical. The anxieties that underlay "divide and rule" also discouraged the British from leaving any colony to the "exclusive protection" of Indian troops. There must always, they insisted, be at least a small contingent of British troops. After all, the loyalty of Indian troops, as mercenaries, could never be taken wholly for granted. This was of course the bitter lesson of 1857. Overseas, the Singapore mutiny of 1915, not to mention Subhas Chandra Bose's formation of the Indian National Army to fight against the British from among the Indian prisoners of war taken after the fall of Singapore in 1942, further demonstrated the truth of this assertion.

There was always, too, the vexed matter of who should pay when India's army was deployed overseas. Were these expeditions undertaken to enhance the security of India, and hence appropriately charged to India's finances? Or were they purely imperial in nature, so that the resulting costs ought to be charged to the imperial British exchequer? As the recurring expenses of the Indian Army were met by the Indian, not the British, taxpayer, the temptation to offload onto India's finances so much of the cost of these expeditions as possible was ever present. The Royal Commission on the Administration of the Expenditure of India (1900) defined geographic zones in which, in its view, India had a "direct and substantial" or a "modified" interest, primarily the regions along the rim of the Indian Ocean, and hence could be expected to contribute to the costs of troop deployment — in contrast to those areas where India had no interest, such as Europe, Japan, or West Africa, and should be exempt from payment. But how the costs should be allocated for particular expeditions or particular types of expenditures, in the absence of an authoritative arbiter, could not easily be resolved and often led to bitter disputes between the Indian and London governments. From their side, educated Indians, most notably Dadabhai Naoroji in his dissent from the conclusions of the royal commission, insisted that all wars carried on in "distant parts" beyond the Indian frontier advanced only "Imperial" interests, not Indian; and hence "no expenditure should be placed upon India, either ordinary or extraordinary" for such expeditions.[5]

"Martial Races" and the Indian Military

As the Indian Army underwent reorganization in the years after 1858, it embodied in its structure the theory of "martial races" as they were seen to exist in India. The army's deployment overseas was in many ways simply an extension of martial races ideology. Colonial subjects elsewhere, say in Malaya, did not possess the inherent martial ability that permitted recruitment into a colonial army, and hence required policing by more martial Indians. In other regions the eruption of "savage" violence, as in the Somaliland of the "Mad Mullah," or transfrontier Afghanistan, required for its suppression the force that India's "martial races," disciplined into the Indian Army, could alone provide. Over time, as well, as the British conquered such regions as eastern Africa, they began to look for indigenous martial races in the expectation that, disciplined in such units as the King's African Rifles, they might complement and even in time displace Indians as guardians of the colonial state.

Much has been written about the Indian martial races ideology as it emerged from the traumatic upheaval of 1857. The initial recruitment of so-called martial races, however, had little to do with race theory of any sort. Rather it was a pragmatic response to the mutinous behavior of the Bengal Army. Those who rallied to the British cause, for whatever reasons of their own, such as Punjabi Sikhs and Nepali Gurkhas, won favorable commendation at the time and subsequently secured a preferential entry into the reorganized Indian Army. With the growth of race theory in subsequent decades, the British came to believe that inbred and enduring differences in martial skill existed among the peoples of the "East." As G. F. MacMunn put it in his definitive study of India's armies, whereas in Europe "every able-bodied man, given food and arms, is a fighting man of some sort," hence capable of serving his country in time of war, in the "East" only "certain clans and classes can bear arms; the others have not the physical courage necessary for the warrior."[6]

This theory drew sustenance from a range of elements in the cultural baggage of Victorian England. As Aryan racial theory saw fair-skinned peoples from Central Asia conquering northern India in ancient times, it was assumed that the descendants of these Aryan invaders possessed superior military capabilities. One favored "martial" race, the Dogras, were presumed, MacMunn wrote, to retain the "old Aryan Hindu stock." More generally, the British favored in their recruitment policies those who could be deemed racially pure in their patterns of descent, for they believed that racial mixing would inevitably lead to degeneracy and hence to military weakness. "Great pride of race usually accompanies those qualities which we look for," as one officer wrote. It is important always to remember that these racial categories had very little substance in reality. Indeed, as we will see, often men were first recruited into the army and only then shaped to fit the requirements of martial race ideology. Neither "Gurkha" nor "Sikh," much less "Aryan," were ever stable categories.

Theories of climatic determinism complemented those of racial descent. Their "hardy, active, and alert life" in a land of brutal winters and often rugged mountains had, the British believed, inured India's northern peoples, including even the Jat Sikhs of the Punjab plains, to hardship and thus fitted them for military life. These northern peoples also embodied a style of personal interaction the British found attractive. Unlike the caste-bound plains Hindu, the Sikh and the Muslim of the northwest were free of prejudice; as MacMunn wrote of the Pathans, "to the best type of Englishman their open irresponsible manner and delight in all exercise and sport, with their constant high spirits, appeal greatly." Neither the urban resident nor the educated Indian were suitably "martial." City dwellers, so the British conceived, had been corrupted and softened by urban life and were threatening in their potential for disorder, while the educated middle classes, especially the Bengali, who mocked the British by mimicry, were disparaged for their "effeminacy." The ideal recruit was always the sturdy yeoman, personified above all by the Jat Sikh of the Punjab, who with his Punjabi Muslim neighbors had become by the later nineteenth century the predominant group in the Indian Army. By 1914 Punjabis and men from the North-West Frontier, together with Nepali Gurkhas (of whom more presently), made up nearly three-quarters of India's infantry forces.

Such beliefs — of climate and descent forming a martial race — were not wholly without parallels at home. In the British imagination, Scotland had much in common with the Punjab, with the result that the "sturdy" Highlander, much like the Sikh, was invested with a distinctive martial ability. Both Highlander and Sikh had valiantly fought against the English subjugation of their homeland, and this stout resistance secured for each, the one in the late eighteenth century, the other in the late nineteenth, a preferential place in the army. Each group too was set off by a distinctive dress — of flowing kilt and feathered bonnet, of full beard and turban — that served as a visible reminder of their martial prowess. The British often imagined the Sikh and the Scottish Highlander loyally marching side by side to the support of the British Empire. From the relief of the Lucknow residency in the 1857 revolt on through the frontier engagements of the 1880s and 1890s, Sikh and Highlander were frequently seen as "brethren-in-arms" engaged in a "generous rivalry" as together they stormed the enemy's entrenchments.[7]

As part of the larger construction of colonial knowledge by which the British sought to convince themselves that they could master, and so more effectively rule, Indian society, each of the various martial races was conceived of as possessing its own distinctive set of characteristics. By the early twentieth century these had become codified in a set of recruiting handbooks, which elaborated in intricate detail the customs and character of each desired clan or caste. Such ethnographic accounts endeavored to ensure that "the men enlisted should be the very best of their type." It is needless to rehearse here these characterizations, in which Indians were depicted not as individuals but as "specimens" or representatives of groups. The varied qualities ascribed to the prospective soldier included, among others, for the Jat, "a slow wit and dogged courage," for the Dogra, "enthusiastic courage and an almost boyish simplicity of character," and for the Gurkha, the supreme accolade of the "bravest among the brave." In every case the British imagined themselves as providing the ordering intelligence that made the "childlike" native into a disciplined and effective force. So compelling were these characterizations that they not only shaped Indian recruiting strategy but may even have helped inspire the soldiers to act up to the expectations held out to them. Further, as we will see in a subsequent chapter, these stereotypes informed colonial recruitment of Indian police. Those whom, as members of martial races, the Indian authorities depicted as the ideal soldier the colonial governments, not surprisingly, sought to employ in their forces as well.

One martial race stood apart in important ways from the others. Tough, sturdy, a product of the demanding climate of the Nepal hills, "imbued with the warlike qualities of their ancestors," the Gurkhas were a classic martial race.[8] Like Sikhs and Highlanders, the Gurkhas had initially won praise for their resistance to the British, in their case during the course of the 1814–16 Nepal War. This unstinting admiration of the Gurkhas' courage soon took the form of their induction into the Indian Army. By 1833 the British resident in Katmandu, Brian Hodgson, had labeled the Gurkha tribes as "martial classes." Doubters were convinced by the steadfast determination and steadiness under fire of the Gurkha units at the siege of Delhi in 1857. By the 1870s there were five Gurkha regiments, each with a single battalion. Yet, unlike Sikhs, they were short in stature, physically unimpressive, and wore no distinctive uniform; as citizens of the independent state of Nepal they were not British subjects; and, most important for our purposes, by contrast with other army units, their deployment outside India was limited. Apart from the Perak expedition of 1875 and the 1900 China expeditionary force, Gurkhas participated in none of the extensive overseas campaigns of the Indian Army before 1914; and as individuals they were never made available for recruitment by colonial police forces. Why this extended exclusion of the "bravest among the brave" from participating in the larger imperial enterprise?

As Nepal was never brought within the British Empire, successful recruitment depended on the collaboration of the Nepal authorities. Always hostile to foreigners, the Nepal government adamantly refused to allow British recruiters to set foot in the country, and until 1885 they refused to sanction any open recruitment. Hence recruiting was undertaken sub rosa by parties of soldiers on furlough, who, as the Gurkha recruiting handbook recounts, were "obliged to smuggle their recruits across the border as best they could." With the coming to power of the more accommodating Prime Minister Bir Shamsher, recruiting was regularized, with depots opened at Gorakhpur and Darjeeling near the Nepal border, and regiments were authorized to send recruiting parties into the interior. British officers themselves were still denied access. Nevertheless, in 1886, in a first step, second battalions were added to the existing regiments. By 1908 the establishment of Gurkha troops in the Indian Army comprised ten regiments of two battalions each, for a total of some fourteen to fifteen thousand men under arms.[9]

In the early years, the British wavered as to whether Gurkhas ought to be deployed in overseas campaigns. On one hand, as the commander-in-chief of the Indian Army, W. R. Mansfield, wrote in 1870, "we have localized our Goorkha Regiments, because of the expediency of keeping Goorkhas in countries and climates similar to those in which they are bred." It was, nevertheless, he acknowledged, "a great inconvenience" to exclude Gurkha forces from taking a "share in the general movement of the Army." Hence the decision was taken to include them in the 1875 Perak expedition, where their distinctive fighting skills made Gurkhas "preferable to Pioneers for employment on special field service" in a jungle-clad land.[10] This unit was, of course, composed of Gurkhas surreptitiously spirited out of Nepal. With the regularization of recruiting after 1885, the British had to pay greater attention to the concerns of the Nepal authorities and the wishes of the Gurkhas themselves. Gurkha troops could no longer be so easily dispatched wherever the Indian military wished.

Central to British reluctance to dispatch Gurkha regiments overseas was fear of compromising the soldiers' caste status during the course of such travel. It is not clear how widely this anxiety was shared among the Gurkhas as individuals, nor how far such concerns played a role in the British decision to confine Gurkha troops to service within South Asia during the 1880s and 1890s. The late-nineteenth-century growth of this sentiment, whether among the Gurkhas themselves or among their British officers, may well have been an instance of the "invention of tradition" so common during those years. In any case, at the time of the Boxer expedition of 1900, when a unit of the Gurkha Rifles joined the large force sent to Peking, the Gurkha soldiers found themselves, on their return home, stripped of their caste privileges. This was a substantial hindrance to Gurkha enlistment in the Indian Army. Given its limited resources as a mountain kingdom, Nepal was by 1900 heavily reliant on military service as a means of employment for its citizens. As the prime minister pleaded on their behalf with the priests, "We have no means of supporting these men [who join the Indian Army]." Hence he secured from the priestly establishment a commitment that, when Gurkhas returned from active duty overseas, a Hindu priest would perform the expiatory rite of *pani patya* for the men. In this way they could clear themselves of the sin of their sea voyage and be re-admitted to caste. By the time of the 1914–18 war, pandits were even being dispatched to the Indian Army depots at Dehra Dun and elsewhere so that soldiers could go through the *pani patya* ritual immediately upon their return to India and so go home to Nepal with their caste position intact.[11]

Acceptance of the *pani patya* ritual made possible the massive expansion of the Indian Army's Gurkha troops — from twenty battalions to forty — during the First World War, and their deployment from Gallipoli to France and beyond. But this dispensation applied only to soldiers who went overseas on active military duty, not those who went for other reasons or in times of peace. Hence those Gurkhas who participated in ceremonial events, such George V's coronation, found themselves denied the *pani patya* ritual on their return. In similar fashion, although the Nepal *darbar* made no objection to Gurkhas serving in Mesopotamia during the First World War, once the peace treaty had been signed they refused to send further troops. This placed the British in an awkward position during the 1920 rebellion, when, as the Indian foreign secretary wrote to the resident in Katmandu, "the military authorities find it essential, in view of the serious fighting now taking place in Mesopotamia, to reinforce these battalions." In the end, Nepal agreed to send further troops; in return the Indian government provided an assurance that such service would "in no way create a precedent for similar treatment in the future."[12] Over the long years that followed, the Gurkhas built an enduring reputation as tough fighters for the British Empire, especially during the Second World War. These exploits, celebrated in a massive literature, testify to the power of the martial races ideal to shape military recruiting and even, perhaps, to inspire behavior in combat.

As the British extended their empire across the globe in the later decades of the nineteenth century, they not unnaturally endeavored to turn the "experience and expertise" they had gained in India to identifying "martial races" in their new colonies, and so to recruit local military forces of comparable prowess. As in the case of India, a steadfast resistance to the imposition of colonial rule helped convince the British that a given "race" might appropriately be labeled martial. But rarely did the transformation from enemy to ally occur so smoothly elsewhere as with the Sikhs and Gurkhas. Often, lacking the trial by fire to which Sikhs and Gurkhas had been subjected in 1857, the British continued to mistrust those whom they had defeated. Sometimes too, conquered peoples, among them the Malays and the Chinese, were regarded as insufficiently martial because they did not fit the British vision of a proper martial race. Their opposition, as a result, was viewed not as the manly combat of opposed armies but as treacherous and stealthy, and so unworthy, as in the assassination of Birch or the Boxer rebellion itself. The Hong Kong Regiment, raised in 1892, was composed wholly of Indians, not Chinese.

The case of Malaya is instructive. From 1902 onwards, the military authorities there pressed for the creation of a Malay battalion, along with volunteer companies in each Malay state. As the inspector-general of overseas forces argued in 1913, "A loyal and patriotic Malay nation, trained to arms, might well prove in future a fitting guardian for the western portal to the Pacific, a doughty defender of one of the richest and fairest portions of the British Empire." But this plea, like those before it, fell on deaf ears. Malays were, after all, in the British view, "soft" and "indolent," not a "martial" race. The governor, Arthur Young, insisted that they would resist discipline, and that the formation of volunteer corps would interfere with rice planting and harvesting. Young put forward instead a suggestion, never taken seriously, that Malays should be formed into a naval force.[13] Only after the First World War, punctuated as it was by the 1915 mutiny of the Singapore Indian garrison, did the Malayan authorities begin seriously to consider forming Malays into a military force.

Still, inspired by the experience of the Raj, where many had served previously, and anxious to secure a force of their own, the British in East Africa from the 1890s set out to identify martial races that might be fashioned into soldiers comparable to those of the Indian Army. The criteria for inclusion in this category, and by extension in what became known as the King's African Rifles (KAR), were much the same as in India. A stout resistance generated an initial British respect, as was the case with the Nandi of Kenya, who were widely recruited for the KAR. But fighting spirit did not by itself produce recruits. The Maasai, for instance, impressed the British from the outset for their martial abilities, but, as Timothy Parsons recounts, they "showed absolutely no interest in the

army." As the Maasai pastoral economy remained intact despite disloca-
tion from their Rift Valley homeland, "no amount of persuasion, short of
conscription, could convince them to enlist." An experimental Maasai
Company of the King's African Rifles was disbanded in 1907 on the
ground that the Maasai warriors would not accept military discipline.[14]

As in India, the East African recruiters preferred agriculturalists and
pastoralists to urban dwellers and the educated. Further, in East Africa,
with the alienation of the White Highlands to settlers, the colonial economy began to undermine traditional pastoral lifestyles and so drove
many Kenyans to search for paid employment. Many saw military service as preferable to life as laborers or as squatters on white farms. Pastoral
peoples, such as the Kamba and Samburu, Parsons argues, "became martial races when population growth, unfavorable climatic conditions, and
colonial economic policies began to limit their ability to maintain large
herds." Martial races did not exist apart from the colonial economic policies — and the cultural politics — that created them.[15]

Campaigning Overseas: The Indian Army in Africa

The Indian Army found employment overseas in two related kinds of
imperial enterprises: the initial conquest of new territories, and the subsequent suppression of rebellions when reliable local forces did not exist
or were insufficient for the task. The extended stationing of units of the
Indian Army in colonial territories overseas, however, met with the
adamant opposition of the Indian government. Individual soldiers, as
demonstrated in the following chapter, often signed up for extended periods of duty with contingents recruited for service in particular colonies.
But the government of India refused to allow units of the army to
remain on colonial service once the immediate objective of their overseas
deployment had been secured. All units were meant to be held in readi-
ness in India for service on the frontier or wherever required. Then too,
although Parliamentary consent was not required for the initial deployment of Indian troops, a lengthy stay abroad required confronting an
always contentious House of Commons. This insistence upon short-term
deployment was not without its inconveniences. A British regiment due
for relief, for instance, was brought from Hong Kong to help quell the
1875 Perak uprising. After its suppression the local authorities had planned
to retain the Gurkhas in Malaya to fill up the gap once the British soldiers
had left for home. The War Office, however, vetoed this proposal. "In

view," it wrote, "of the serious objections which exist to the employment of Indian troops in the Malay peninsula without the consent of Parliament, he [the secretary of state for war] has decided to postpone the relief of the 10th Regiment so as to enable the troops lately sent from India to return to that country."[16]

Similar objections arose in connection with an 1890 plan by the War Office to post a battalion of Indian infantry at Hong Kong, where these men would join a battalion of British troops to form a total garrison of one thousand. Although the War Office possessed the ultimate responsibility for troop deployment in the colonial territories of the British Empire, the Indian government refused to permit any regiment of its army to undertake such a tour of duty. Altogether apart from questions of promotion and relief, they argued, while the Indian recruit "is bound by his obligation and oath on enlistment to serve beyond the seas and beyond Indian territories, it appears open to question whether this obligation equitably extends to garrison service in a British colony in a time of peace." In the end, the China Regiment (as it was called) was raised by soliciting volunteers from various Punjab regiments. The posting of Indian troops abroad nevertheless remained attractive, for, as one officer put it, "the service was popular and the Indian budget profited." By the years just prior to the Great War, the Indian government was supplying occasional battalions for service in nearby colonies, among them Mauritius, Ceylon, and Singapore, as well as for Hong Kong and North China.[17]

Although a detailed discussion of the overseas campaigns undertaken by the Indian Army during the half century from the 1860s to the First World War is beyond the scope of this work, it might be useful to look at some of the occasions when Indian troops saw service in Africa. During the scramble of the late nineteenth century, when that continent saw the greatest expansion of the British Empire since the conquest of India itself, the British, stretched thin across immense distances, frequently called on their Indian forces for assistance. Units of the Indian Army participated in several of the assaults that brought down African rulers and in the suppression of uprisings in Uganda and Somaliland. India, one might argue, conquered Africa for Britain.

As we have seen, the 1867–68 Abyssinian campaign that brought down King Theodore was a wholly Indian enterprise, carried out by Indian troops under the command of officers of the Indian Army. Indian troops also participated in the British-led 1882 campaign, culminating in the battle of Tel-el-Kebir, that overthrew the regime of Urabi in Egypt and so inaugurated some seventy years of British control over that strategically

FIGURE 7. Balooch Regiment, Abyssinia, 1868. Photograph by the Royal Engineers. Courtesy of the Council, National Army Museum, London. Negative no. 18089.

important land. The Indian contingent on that occasion comprised three infantry battalions, three regiments of cavalry, and a reserve force of two battalions of infantry stationed at Aden, for a total strength, apart from British officers, of over five thousand men. In the decisive encounter at Tel-el-Kebir under Sir Garnet Wolseley, the Indians played a key role in the final assault and then pursued the remnant enemy force into Cairo. Two weeks later, after the reinstallation of the khedive as the nominal ruler of Egypt, the Indian force embarked at Suez for Bombay.[18]

Three years after Tel-el-Kebir, in 1885, an Indian force some three thousand strong was landed at Suakin on the Sudan coast. This campaign marked the first stage of the extended war against the Mahdi, whose "dervish" army repeatedly defied British and British-led forces sent against it, most notably in the siege of Khartoum that led to the death of Charles "Chinese" Gordon. The Suakin campaign, in the aftermath of Gordon's death, was an attempt to secure the eastern flank of the Sudan along the Red Sea. In this conflict, with the Mahdi's lieutenant Osman Digna and his "dervish" forces, the Indian Brigade participated in a series of indecisive encounters until they were finally withdrawn in May 1885, after some three months' active service.[19] For the next thirteen years, until the 1898 Battle of Omdurman, the Sudan was left to the control of the Mahdi. In that final assault Kitchener's army, marching up the Nile from Cairo, included British, Egyptian, and Sudanese but not Indian troops.

With the defeat in the Sudan and the intensification of the scramble for Africa, the British turned their attention in the late 1880s to East Africa. Initially, the Imperial British East Africa Company, put in charge of the territories constituting what is now Kenya and Uganda, endeavored to extend British authority into the African interior by the ad hoc recruitment of local soldiers, primarily Sudanese, Swahilis from the coast, and Egyptians from the khedive's defeated army. From 1890 the company also, over the intense opposition of the Indian government, began recruiting soldiers from India for its local contingents. This recruitment from India, extended and developed further after the British government took over East Africa from the bankrupt company in 1895, is taken up in the next chapter. Here, my concern is to ascertain when and for what purposes regular units of the Indian Army were sent to East Africa.

Sudanese formed the backbone of the chartered company's small force. Initially some seventy soldiers drawn from the Egyptian army, these men were recruited by Major Frederick Lugard in 1890, when he was sent as the company's agent to assert a British presence in the kingdom of Buganda. This force was soon augmented by the inclusion of soldiers stranded in the southern Sudan after the fall of Khartoum, as well as those left behind by Emin Pasha after his departure from the Equatorial province with H. M. Stanley in 1888. When the British government declared a protectorate over the Buganda kingdom in 1894, these men were formed into the Uganda Rifles. By 1897 the Uganda Rifles comprised some 250 Sudanese and an equal number of Swahilis, together with some 190 Somalis; an Indian contingent of 300 was stationed on the coast at Mombasa.

For the British the Sudanese possessed many of the attractive characteristics of a martial race. Tall, a Nilotic people, allegedly of ancient "Nubian" heritage, bred in the harsh environment of the desert, they had fought well against the Egyptian armies sent into the Sudan. "As fighting men pure and simple," wrote one British officer, "they possibly have not their equal in the world." The Sudanese, nevertheless, proved to be less than staunch supporters of the new regime in Uganda. In 1897 three companies of Sudanese troops in the Uganda Rifles mutinied, alleging inadequate pay and excessive campaigning.[20] The result was a crisis of colonial order that the protectorate's fledgling government could not contain by itself. Hence they turned, as colonial authorities elsewhere had so often done, to India and to the Indian Army. The requisition for troops reached the government of India on November 20; two weeks later the 27th Bombay Light Infantry, with some 750 officers and men, embarked for Mombasa.

The uprising enforced upon the local authorities a lesson their Indian counterparts had learned forty years before, in 1857. As the acting commissioner, F. J. Jackson, wrote to the foreign secretary as the revolt was unfolding, Indian troops might prove costly, but "it is scarcely wise to rely solely on Sudanese, who already realize, and presume on the fact, that it is through them that we are masters of the Protectorate."[21] The presence of the Bombay Infantry — reinforced in February 1898 by the 4th Bombay Rifles — did not, however, at once put an end to the uprising. To the contrary, the Indian force, landing in an unfamiliar territory, found itself confronted by unforeseen problems of transport and supply. The Uganda Railway, then under construction, had progressed only 150 miles beyond its coastal terminus at Mombasa; while East Africa, infested with the tsetse fly, could not support the mules and horses the Indian Army customarily used for transport. Hence movement of the force to the rebel-controlled area of Uganda, some six hundred miles into the interior, posed exceptional difficulties.

Some indication of what the Indian troops faced can be found in the report submitted by the commissariat officer Lt. E. G. Vaughan.[22] Writing from the Kikuyu district of central Kenya to headquarters in Poona in July 1898, the frustrated Vaughan reported that he had arrived in Mombasa some three months earlier with no orders and no information about conditions in East Africa. Unable to secure supplies from an Indian firm — Cowasjee Dinshaw and Bros. — in Zanzibar, Vaughan sought tenders from Mombasa firms only to discover that there were "no reliable Firms of any experience in contracts for supplies" in that city and that, in any case, as far as he could ascertain, apart from maize and sugar cane, "the country does not as yet produce anything in sufficiently large quantities for Indian troops." Undaunted, Vaughan set off upcountry by the new rail line. A comedy of errors ensued. "I myself left Kilindini by goods-train in the guards van," Vaughan reported; "was delayed at Voi one day by the engine going off the line; had to transfer my baggage and camp by the rails; again delayed four days at Ndi; and eventually only reached the rail-head . . . by changing to a coal-truck and doing the last part of the journey on the engine itself."

Beyond the railhead, reliable transport could be secured only by employing porters to carry head loads, and these were engaged "only with great difficulty." The imported draft animals were all useless. As Vaughan wrote in despair, "Rinderpest has killed all the bullocks; camels brought up from the coast cannot stand the colder climate about Kikuyu and the Ravine [Rift Valley]; and the toetze fly poisons the mules." Donkeys were the "least affected" transport animals, but they were not readily procurable. As a result, on his arrival, Vaughan found some eight hundred loads destined for the 27th, abandoned at Kikuyu. "Only the fifty men at the Ravine were receiving commissariat rations, the others on in front were living on what the country could give them — black flour and plantains chiefly — and consequently going sick from the inferior food." Eventually Vaughan located a contractor from Mombasa "whose bullocks had died and carts broken down" and with his assistance sent up to the front over seven weeks, by donkey and head porter, some fourteen hundred loads. Even then, Vaughan reported, he was "hampered by my having no interpreter or clerk, no godown [storeroom] or office establishment of any sort, no cash assignment, and from the fact that the natives of these parts only appreciate beads, cloth, and brass wire as currency."

Some of the losses incurred in such expeditions were more symbolic than consequential. Two years before, in 1896, when a detachment of the 24th Bombay Infantry was sent to suppress a rising on the East African coast, the officers of the regiment claimed compensation for the loss of their chargers, eleven of which, out of thirteen animals taken to Africa, died of tsetse. These chargers, mostly purchased from Pathans on the frontier, so the claim alleged, "were brought over by all officers as they formed part of their equipment, and no information was received as to the unsuitability of the country for horses."[23]

Once the supply problems were overcome, the Indian force in Uganda set out to pursue the Sudanese mutineers; after a series of hard-fought encounters across the protectorate during the summer and autumn of 1898, the operation finally succeeded in December. Meanwhile, a detachment of the Indian force had been redeployed in the eastern Jubaland region of Kenya to put down cross-border cattle raiding by the Ogaden Somalis. This operation did not begin in promising fashion. In June 1898 a detachment of forty men of the 4th Bombay Rifles, marching through thick bush with their swords sheathed, and so unable to respond promptly, were ambushed by Somalis with the loss of one Indian officer and twenty-six men. Though the Somalis of the Ogaden were to rise again in 1900, on this occasion by October they were forced to sue for peace.

The 4th sailed to Bombay in December, while by April, following the suppression of the Sudanese mutiny, the 27th Bombay Infantry had returned to Karachi.[24] Though the local authorities had "eagerly" awaited the arrival of the Indian force, they were happy to see it depart. As Col. W. A. Broome, the officer commanding in Uganda, wrote at the end of the campaign, he preferred even Sudanese troops to Indian, for the former could at least "feed themselves from local produce" and so relieve the "strain" on commissariat and transport.[25] Ultimately, as we shall see in the next chapter, Uganda was garrisoned by Indians recruited specifically for African service, together with local recruits of various communities who formed the King's African Rifles.

Clearly, overseas deployment of the Indian Army, especially when carried out with little notice and to unfamiliar regions, was not always or inevitably a simple matter. Although Indian casualties were usually low — only twenty soldiers of the 27th were killed in Uganda — and the mission in East Africa was successfully accomplished, pacification of the imperial borderlands was never mere child's play. Queen Victoria's "little wars" were not little for the participants, on either side. Occasional setbacks, however, did not slow the pace of deployment of Indian troops, for the British had no other force available that could secure their expanding empire so effectively and economically. Furthermore, the Indian Army could be made to serve purposes beyond that of actual fighting. Above all, its presence made visible the power of the British Empire. In July 1896, following a campaign on the East African coast, the troops of the 24th Bombay Infantry were paraded on the open square in front of the palace of the sultan of Zanzibar. "In the presence of the sultan, some of his principal adherents, and a large crowd of Arabs, natives, and Indians," the consul Basil Cave reported, "they were put through such exercises as the somewhat limited space permitted." The sultan, Cave exulted, "was considerably impressed by this example of our military strength in India." "I cannot but think," he concluded, that "the visit will have had a good moral effect both on him and on his subjects."[26] When the sultan died a month later, the recollection of this parade, combined with a brief bombardment by gunboats in the harbor, no doubt helped discourage resistance when the British enforced the accession of their candidate as sultan over the claimant who had occupied the palace.

At the conclusion of these African expeditions, the question inevitably arose of who was to pay for them. As East Africa fell into an ambiguous middle zone between clearly defined Indian and imperial interests, the imperial and the Indian governments each attempted to secure payment from the other. At the outset the Treasury endeavored to justify charging the continuing costs of the borrowed regiments against India by pointing to the "close commercial ties of Zanzibar and East Africa to India," together with the alleged "need of protection" for the Indian laborers working on the railway then under construction. The imperial exchequer would, the Treasury insisted, pay the extraordinary costs incurred in transporting the troops to and from Africa and while they were employed in Africa, but no more. The government of India in return argued that there was "no justification" for charging to Indian revenues any portion of the costs of the force so long as it was out of India. After all, it pointed out, "it is a very great advantage to the administration of the British East African Protectorate to obtain the services of a regiment fully equipped and disciplined, without having had to bear the charges incurred in bringing this regiment to a state of efficiency, or becoming liable for any portion of the ordinary pension charges." Citing the precedent of earlier expeditions, the imperial government insisted that the charges be apportioned and that India bear all "ordinary" charges.[27]

The Uganda campaign was immediately followed first by the South African War (1899–1902) and then by a long-drawn-out and inconclusive struggle with the so-called Mad Mullah of Somaliland, against whom expeditions were launched from 1901 to 1904. The Indian Army's contribution to the Boer War little resembled those conflicts in which it had previously participated. Although some 5,500 soldiers were sent from India to South Africa at the outbreak of the war and thousands more soon followed, the fighting force consisted wholly of troops from British regiments, together with some civilian volunteer corps. A mere twenty of those in the front lines were Indian rank and file, and these were all attached to hospital units. Still, the Indian contribution to the war was not negligible. Several thousand noncombatants were sent to South Africa, where they served the British Army in a variety of capacities, as orderlies, transport personnel, cooks, water carriers, and the like. These Indians complemented the ambulance corps raised by South African Indians under Mohandas Gandhi. India's native cavalry regiments, in a strange irony, contributed their horses, some five thousand remounts in total, but not the cavalrymen who normally rode them into battle![28] This skewed deployment, of course, was the product of a conscious decision that the Boer War was to be a "white man's" war. Despised and discriminated against by the settler community, Indians were no more to be sent into combat against the superior whites than were South Africa's own blacks. At no time during the war or the subsequent reconstruction did the

British wish openly to challenge a racial ideology in which, after all, they themselves to some degree participated.

The British had no such hesitation in sending Indian troops against the "fanatical" Muslims of Somaliland. By 1904 some four regiments of infantry, complemented by smaller contingents of artillery and sappers and miners, had seen service in Somaliland.[29] In 1899 the "Mullah," Haji Muhammad Abdullah, who had recruited followers among the local Somali tribesmen, first came to notice when he began raiding into the British-controlled protectorate along the Horn of Africa. The War Office wasted no time in deciding that "repressive measures" against this "fanatical Mullah" were "inevitable" and that the "troops to be employed should be drawn from India." They ordered the dispatch of a native cavalry regiment, which in their view could presumably best track and capture the Mullah —"clearly the main object to be kept in view" — supported by four companies of infantry together with two machine guns. The adjutant general in Simla quietly pointed out a problem with this scheme. How, he asked, was it proposed to man the guns when native troops — a legacy of the anxieties of 1857 — were not "trained in working machine guns"?[30] Before any troops could be sent, however, the Mullah's followers dispersed and the plan was abandoned.

A year later, at the end of 1900, further raids convinced the British authorities finally to launch a punitive expedition. On this occasion, to avoid the expense of sending men from India, the troops employed were a local Somali levy of fifteen hundred men. India contributed only some fifty Punjabi Muslim soldiers, who were engaged as drill instructors. These half-trained Somalis managed to drive the Mullah out of British territory, only to see him return in early 1902. The Somalis were now joined for a second campaign by troops of the King's African Rifles dispatched from Central and East Africa, and in November by regular troops from India. These included Punjab Mounted Infantry, Sikhs of the Punjab Frontier Force, a regiment of Pioneers, sappers and miners, and two hundred men of the Bikaner Camel Corps, a private force maintained by that state's maharaja. This unwieldy force, some forty-five hundred men in all, including amongst its members Britons, Boers, Indians, East Africans, Sudanese, and Somalis, chased the elusive Mullah all around the desert reaches of Somaliland. Camels and sheep were taken as he abandoned encampments to escape his pursuers, but there was no sign of the Mullah himself. Effective pursuit was not made easier by the lack of "really trustworthy information" and of water and transport. But the Mullah was not wholly quiescent. In April 1903, appearing from thick bush, his

FIGURE 8. "Out into the Sandy Deserts of Somaliland: An Indian Camel Corps in Pursuit of the Mullah," 1903. Wash drawing by Arthur Garrett. Courtesy of the Council, National Army Museum, London. No. 1961–10–42.

forces overwhelmed an isolated column of Sikhs and Africans. The column's British officers and Indian soldiers, a total of some two hundred men, were all killed in a desperate fight. Only eleven Africans survived unscathed.

Following this disaster, in July, the Somaliland Field Force was reorganized under new command and reinforced with further troops from India. The Indian portion of the force now consisted of 3,650 men. Thus strengthened, the British kept the Mullah on the run and defeated him whenever he chose to stand and fight. His forces nevertheless continued to exact casualties from the imperial force and forced it to remain continuously on the move in difficult terrain. The Mullah himself was as elusive as ever; ultimately, his forces scattered, he sought shelter among the desert tribes of the remote interior. This expensive and futile campaign thus finally came to an end in the summer of 1904, some four years after it had begun. Following the subsequent withdrawal of the regular Indian troops, Somaliland was garrisoned by a specially recruited Indian contingent of the King's African Rifles.

The Somali campaign overlapped to a substantial extent with the largest deployment in half a century of Indian troops overseas — the expedition to suppress the Boxer uprising in China (1900–02). At its height this massive deployment saw some 15,000 Indian troops in action in China, in company with forces drawn from throughout the empire and from other Western countries and Japan. There is no need here to recount the well-known events of the Boxer uprising and its suppression. One can, however, get something of a glimpse of the opportunities and the tensions generated by overseas service, at least at the officer level, from the diary entries of Amar Singh, a Rajput nobleman who went to China with the Jodhpur Lancers, a body of troops raised by that state's maharaja. For the most part, India's princes eagerly sought occasions to display their loyalty to the empire that sustained them in power. Frustrated by the rejection of their offers of troops for the Boer War, several leaped at the opportunity to participate in the suppression of the Boxers. Amar Singh exulted at the "joyful news" that he was to be sent to China. Arriving after the main fighting, he participated in only one battle with the rebels. On that occasion, after spearing three men and dodging bullets on the battlefield, he wrote, invoking Rajput traditions of bravery under fire, "I can safely say without exaggeration or boasting or self-praise that my temper and nerve seemed to me to be quite calm."[31]

Amar Singh nevertheless intensely disliked the demeaning way he and other Indian officers were treated by the British. Again and again, his diary entries recount instances of snubs and disrespect. These angered him the more because, as a soldier in the force of a princely state, he regarded himself as a member of an autonomous contingent allied in a position of "subordinate cooperation" with the British military. But such comfortable fictions could not withstand the reality of British racial sentiment. As Amar Singh wrote bitterly in July 1901 on his return to India, "The Indians are looked upon as inferiors in the scale of humanity. . . . No Indian can rise above the rank of a rissaldar or a subadar major, and however young or junior a British officer may be he always looks down upon the other as an ignorant fellow. . . . Even if someone offered me a direct rissaldarship [appointment as the Indian equivalent of lieutenant] in the British Indian Army I would straight away reject [it]. I would not like to be treated like a coolie."[32]

Amar Singh has little to say about the ordinary Indian soldiers he encountered in China except to praise their behavior. "The Indian Army here made a good show," he wrote, "and as far as I can see was never behind any other foreigners." Carefully picked and of "good physique," the Indians were "taller and stouter" than many of the Europeans, and better horsemen. Unfortunately, we do not possess any published accounts by Indian rank-and-file soldiers of their experiences in the Boxer campaign or indeed in any of the other overseas expeditions undertaken by the Indian Army prior to the First World War.³³ Nevertheless, it would seem that overseas service was attractive. Certainly, as we will see in the next chapter, Indian soldiers never hesitated to sign up for duty with the contingents recruited for local service in the African colonies. The British too, aware of the importance of contented Indian troops for their colonial wars, endeavored to accommodate their special requirements, even shipping Indian foodstuffs under difficult circumstances to Africa and (as we have seen) arranging for priests to perform expiatory rituals for returning Gurkhas.³⁴ Only with the rise in casualties during the 1914–18 war, and the simultaneous growth of Indian nationalist sentiment, did overseas service begin to lose its luster. Even then, however, as David Omissi has made clear in his selection of letters home from Indian soldiers in France, loyalty to the soldier's unit and his officers and even to the king-emperor, together with internalized caste ideals of bravery and honor, sustained soldiers in the cold and wet of the trenches so far from home.³⁵

The Mesopotamian Campaign: From Conquest to Colonialism in Iraq

During the First World War, Indian troops saw action on the Western Front in France and participated in the campaigns in Gallipoli and German East Africa. India's largest contribution to the war effort, however, took place in Mesopotamia as the British endeavored to wrest from the Turks, once they had joined the German cause, the Basra and Baghdad provinces of their empire. Of the total number of 1.3 million Indians sent overseas to fight for the British Empire, some 600,000 — or close to half the total — saw service in Mesopotamia. These 600,000, split almost evenly between combatants and noncombatants, saw action from November 1914 until the end of the war and beyond. Further, until the spring of 1916, the Mesopotamian campaign was organized and led from India. Throughout the conflict, India supplied not only the officers and men of its army but also civil officials, administrative staff, and corps of laborers, together with almost all the transport, stores, and supplies that enabled the army to function. This enormous outpouring of men and material from India transformed much of Mesopotamia, above all the province of Basra, into a de facto Indian colony. Hence, although the story of the Mesopotamian campaign is well known and will not be rehearsed in detail here, the conquest of Iraq sheds a powerful light on

India's enduring role as an imperial center in the larger region of the Indian Ocean.

Begun as a defensive operation to secure Persia and its oil resources, the Indian Army's Mesopotamian Force "D" rapidly expanded its objectives to encompass the conquest of the city of Basra, secured by the end of November 1914, and then the ousting of the Turks from the whole of the lower Tigris River region. Stunningly successful in its initial encounters, the Indian Army, under the command of Gen. Charles Townshend, found itself drawn ever farther into the interior as the Turks retreated toward Baghdad. Outrunning its supply lines, the overconfident Indian force was finally stopped at Ctesiphon, some twenty-five miles from Baghdad, in November 1915. There, after sustaining heavy losses, the force turned back with the aim of finding a secure place to regroup and make a stand. Townshend selected for this purpose the village of Kut el-Amara, protected by embankments along the river, only to find himself promptly besieged by the Turks. Three rescue expeditions failed to break though the entrenched Turkish lines. After a siege of some 146 days, Townshend surrendered on April 29, 1916. Apart from the humiliation of surrender, the human cost of this fiasco was immense. During the campaign, Townshend's force suffered some 10,000 casualties, while the relieving forces lost more than 20,000 troops in their botched attempts at rescue. As one officer wrote, the "flower of the Indian army was buried on the banks of the Tigris from Shu'aiba to Ctesiphon."[36]

Following this debacle, the War Office took charge of the operations in Mesopotamia and placed Maj.-Gen. Stanley Maude in command. Maude resumed the advance on Baghdad and eventually took the city in March 1917. India nevertheless remained the base of supply and troops for the campaign. Indeed, endeavoring to make amends for its ineffectual organization of the initial campaign, the Indian government after 1916 redoubled its efforts to provide needed supplies, including laborers for the unloading of ships and the construction of docks, roads, and embankments as well as the provision of menial services for the military. Often coercively recruited and treated harshly as "coolies," these porters, sweepers, washermen, mule and camel drivers, and others, many of them tribals from remote areas such as Chota Nagpur, received little pay for exhausting work and frequently found their one- or two-year terms extended as long as the war continued. In addition to those recruited from the countryside, over the years from 1916 to 1919 a total of some 17,000 men held in Indian prisons were induced by promise of remission of their sentences to serve in Mesopotamia in the special Jail Labour Corps.[37]

The difficulty of securing willing labor — whether in Mesopotamia or India — was frequently substantial. Most telling perhaps is the case of the Shaiba bund. This embankment project originated in 1915 from the military's desire to protect its camps at Basra against flooding and to develop the district's irrigation potential. Initially the British sought labor from the local sheikhs, but these desert dwellers saw no gain for themselves from the project and so refused to participate. Efforts to secure labor through local contractors fared no better. The "demands of the Force in Basrah were enormous and very high prices were being paid there, so there is little wonder that coolies preferred well paid work in congenial surroundings to heavy work in the desert." So the army turned to India, where it found that the laborers first recruited for the project "suddenly had an attack of nerves and refused to embark," instead fleeing to their homes. Only when the coolies were placed in camps under military guard was it possible to secure the three thousand laborers needed for the project. Nevertheless, by the last years of the war, the extraordinary demand for labor in Mesopotamia enabled even jail coolies to insist on strict enforcement of their contracts, sometimes even their renegotiation at higher rates of pay. Many too saw in such service a way to gain artisanal skills they could take back with them to India.[38]

One of the most striking yet least known contributions of India to the Mesopotamian campaign was the provision of naval craft. Until roads and railways could be put in place, the only transport network in Mesopotamia was that provided by its rivers. Too shallow for ordinary gunboats and British coastal vessels, these rivers could be navigated only by local craft. As the supply lines lengthened and the demand for river craft increased with the intensification of the war effort, the British authorities turned to India. By the end of the war some one thousand boats of varying sorts and sizes had been shipped from India to Iraq. As the war correspondent Edmund Candler wrote, "To supplement the self-respecting paddle steamers of the Tigris, the most heterogeneous collection of scrap-iron and remnants of river traffic were gathered in, taxing the resources of India's inland navigation from Bhamo [Burma] to Sind." This demand for transport vessels in turn stimulated the moribund Indian shipbuilding industry and so set the stage for the postwar revival of the industry, culminating in the founding of the Scindia Steam Navigation Company in 1919. In Mesopotamia, India had, as it were, found a space between the modern steamship and the old-fashioned dhow in which it could at once advance the objectives of the British Empire and contribute in a small way to its own industrial growth.[39]

Supply of river craft was complemented by such related activities as the rebuilding of the Basra harbor. Sir George Buchanan, brought to Mesopotamia from Burma in 1915, began the construction of new wharves utilizing Indian labor and Indian teak, with the aim of reorganizing Basra "along the lines of an Indian commercial port"; he then proceeded upriver with schemes for river conservancy, irrigation, and flood control. "So far as irrigation is concerned," he wrote, evoking Scott-Moncrieff and William Willcocks, "I need hardly point out that India, who supplied the original engineers for Egypt, possesses the most extensive irrigation works in the world and the engineers with the widest experience." Nor was India's contribution limited to raw materials. It included iron work and other finished metals, including rails, pontoons, bridgework, together with telephone and telegraph lines. In effect, India was no longer simply a "traditional" agrarian society deservedly colonized, but a leader in state-led technological development. The "expert advice, modern irrigation, and up-to-date agricultural machinery" provided by India, as Edwin Montagu, the secretary of state for India, proudly told the House of Commons in August 1918, "were gradually changing the appearance of the country [Mesopotamia] and eradicating the blight of Turkish rule."[40] This sense that India was, in some degree, now visibly modern could not but help strengthen its claim to the measure of self-rule, with eventual dominion status, that Montagu had enunciated in Parliament a year before. This evident technological prowess gave weight as well to India's claim to a share in the governance of the still "backward" lands along the Tigris.

From the first days of the war, some British Indian officials had anticipated the possibility of annexing Mesopotamia, or at least the Basra *vilayet* (province), to the Indian Raj. Most outspoken perhaps was Sir Arnold T. Wilson (1884–1940). An officer of the 32nd Sikh Pioneers who had joined the Political Department in 1909 and served in Persia, Wilson saw in the outbreak of war with Turkey an unrivaled opportunity to expand the Indian Empire. As he wrote within a week of the fall of Basra, in a letter forwarded to Sir Edward Grey at the Foreign Office, "I should like to see it announced that Mesopotamia was to be annexed to India as a colony for India and Indians, that the Government of India would administer it, and gradually bring under cultivation its vast unpopulated desert plains, peopling them with martial races from the Punjab." A "few hundred thousand Indian colonists," he argued, in addition to developing the resources of Mesopotamia, would be an "immense accession of strength to us politically and strategically" in keeping the Turks or other hostile powers at bay. Further, Wilson argued, by giving India control of the Shia holy sites, annexation would reassure India's Muslims that their sacrifices in the war would be rewarded by a "place in the sun" in the Islamic world; while throwing Mesopotamia open for settlement would, he hoped, by providing an alternative arena for "expansion," still the Indian demand for entry into white settler–dominated colonies.[41]

The viceroy, Lord Hardinge, only a few days later wrote the secretary of state in the same vein, proposing "permanent occupation" of Basra. Returning from a tour of the Gulf in February 1915, he reiterated once again his commitment to Indian rule over Mesopotamia. The "interests concerned, strategic, commercial, political and religious alike," he insisted, "are mainly Indian." Indeed, "commercially the connection of the province [Basra] with India is closer than that existing in the case of Burma, and Basrah is as near Delhi as Rangoon." Like Arnold, Hardinge argued that Mesopotamia should "prove attractive to a good class of Indian colonist," who would find there a field "more attractive than emigration to British colonies." "The irrigation and Indian colonization of the Basrah *vilayet*," he concluded, "open up a vista of endless opportunity and wealth in the not far distant future." In similar fashion, the now retired Sir William Willcocks, who had been employed in Mesopotamia by the Ottomans before the war, imagined the Tigris-Euphrates delta "reclaimed and settled by millions of natives of India, who will make it again the Garden of the East."[42]

Critics wasted no time in pointing to what they saw as the shortcomings of the scheme. Although no one saw fit to question the fundamental legitimacy of the British appropriation of Mesopotamia, men such as A. H. Grant, the foreign secretary in Delhi, wondered "how the Arabs with prescriptive rights there" would welcome the alienation of their land to Indians; and he wondered as well, in view of the rise of radical nationalism in the Punjab, whether "it would be to our political advantage to have a vast Moslem colony astride our interests in the Gulf." Grant nevertheless supported the assumption of "complete administration over [Mesopotamia] . . . like an Indian province," albeit with "the understanding that the Arabs were to be admitted to such share in it as they were competent to undertake and with the eventual object of reducing our control over ordinary internal administration to a minimum as soon as the Arabs were fit to relieve us of it."[43]

Opposition at home in England was far more intense. Given the contradictory objectives of British government policy in the larger Middle East region and the desire not to antagonize European allies while the war was in progress, the London authorities were anxious not to appear to be

94   PROJECTING POWER

embarking on a premature expansion of the British Empire. Again and
again, Hardinge and his government were urged to make no announce-
ments of sovereignty or permanent occupation. Further, with the 1916
creation of the Arab Bureau in Cairo, the Arabists associated with that
office began to put forward their own claims to control the conquered territories of the Middle East, including Mesopotamia. In their view, there
existed a natural affinity between Mesopotamia and its neighbors to the
west. As Mark Sykes, who was to play a crucial role in the final settlement,
put it, "Indian and Arab civilization and mentality are poles asunder."
Contesting the claims of those who saw India bringing "civilization" to
the region, he insisted that "there can be no doubt that the native stan-
dards of Egypt and Syria are far higher than those of India, and owing to
language and racial affinity it is from these regions that the civilization of
Irak [sic] would naturally be drawn."[44]

As this debate over high strategy lurched forward, with one proposal
after another put forward only to be shot down as Delhi, Cairo, and London jockeyed for control, the authorities on the ground in Mesopotamia,
all of them Indian officials, proceeded to establish an Indian-style colonial administration. The central figure in this enterprise was Sir Percy Cox
(1864–1937), chief political officer with the Indian expeditionary force,
assisted by Arnold Wilson as deputy chief political officer from 1915. Cox
had begun his career, after receiving a commission in the Indian Army in
1885, with a series of political appointments as agent or resident under the
government of India in the princely states of Kolhapur and Baroda and
overseas in Somaliland and Muscat; for the ten years prior to the war he
had been political resident in the Gulf and consul-general in Persia. Cox
served as chief political officer in Mesopotamia until 1918 and returned as
high commissioner from 1920 to 1923. Between 1918 and 1920 Wilson held
charge as civil commissioner.

On November 23, 1914, a "ceremonial march" through the streets by
the troops, the hoisting of the Union Jack "on a prominent building," and
the reading of a proclamation in Arabic announced the British conquest
of the city of Basra. One month later, the commanding general moved to
set up a proper civil administration in place of military government. The
establishment of civil courts, wrote General A. Barrett, was a "pressing
need," as was the setting up of the entire array of governmental functions
from police and customs to land settlement and survey. Although a few
minor officials were available, he reported to the authorities in India, "all
the leading Turkish officials have fled," and he urged that "selected civil
officials be sent over as early as possible." Within a day H. R. C. Dobbs

of the Political Department had been ordered to proceed to Basra from his post on the Indian frontier in Baluchistan with instructions to take charge of government and *waqf* (religious endowment) property and the collection of land revenue.[45]

The raising of a police force was not so easily accomplished. While acknowledging that in time a force could be raised locally, Barrett recommended that "about one hundred good police" be "drafted in as a temporary measure from Northern India." Punjabis, he said, half to be Sikhs and half Muslims, would be "suitable"; and he preferred "men with some knowledge of Arabic." The Punjab government replied, with perhaps droll understatement, that "men with a knowledge of Arabic would probably be unobtainable." Cox insisted that, though "a useful accessory," knowledge of Arabic was "not essential." What was essential was that the men be of "good fighting stamp." Further, he said, "Indians from the Punjab would be more effective and a much less complicated body to deal with than numbers of strange men from Egypt requiring to maintain their families there." Ultimately, after extended correspondence, the Bombay government found in Aden (still part of that presidency despite its location in southwestern Arabia) some fifty Arabic-speaking constables whom it could spare.[46] By June 1915 these men were on the streets of Basra. Already, in these early encounters, the tension between a vision of Mesopotamia as a colony of India and as a part of the larger Arabic-speaking Middle East was palpable.

But, both Cox and the military insisted, fifty men were not enough. Men were needed both to patrol Basra city and at the same time to form the nucleus of, and help train, the local force of some six hundred being gradually enlisted. Indeed, with the likelihood of an advance on Baghdad, Cox envisaged the need for a "nucleus of two hundred men from India." If Muslim Punjabis were not available, he would accept men from the United Provinces or even elsewhere. Considerations of expense, together with a reluctance to confront a home government still undecided as to the territory's fate, encouraged the Indian authorities to refuse further police. In the end, as "the best solution of the difficulty," Cox opted for the recruitment of Kurds.[47] This decision, though perhaps not an open avowal of "divide and rule," nevertheless effectively sustained that principle of imperial policing while avoiding the appearance of prematurely transforming Basra "into an Indian district."

Recruitment of police from India was at once followed by that of civil officials and subordinate staff. Some were senior technical personnel, such as Sir George Buchanan, chairman of the Rangoon Port Trust, and F. E.

Gwyther, formerly chief engineer of the Punjab; others, Cox's four
deputies among them, were Indian Army officers assigned to civil duties
in Mesopotamia; yet others, transferred from midlevel postings in the
Indian government, took up similar duties in the newly conquered territory. Among those appointed in 1916 alone were customs officers from
Bengal, assistant surgeons, four civilian dentists, executive and assistant
engineers of the Public Works Department, and an inspector-general of
police and several assistant superintendents, along with other Europeans
of lesser status such as office superintendents and cipher clerks.[48]

Among the subordinate non-European staff, some few were Arabic
speakers drawn from the existing consulates in the region, at Bushire,
Sistan, or Basra. But the bulk of those employed by the new government
were Indians brought over from India. Cox, for instance, secured for the
post of treasury officer at Amara an extra assistant commissioner from
Gujrat (Punjab), Malik Bakhsh Khan, a member of the landed Tiwana
family, who brought with him an entire treasury staff of accountants and
clerks. When Lt.-Col. S. G. Knox, a lawyer and member of the Indian
political department, was directed to set up a judicial establishment at
Basra, he at once "proceeded to Bombay and there enlisted" the necessary
clerical staff. Among these were C. A. Braganza and J. B. Kotewal, clerks
in the court of small causes at Bombay, and E. R. Mehta, fourth clerk in
the jail department office at Thana. The last appointment occasioned some
surprise. As one official in Delhi noted in the file next to this appointment,
"Originally a temporary hand in the Bombay Jail department on Rs. 25 a
month, this official has passed through the stages of 90, 100, and 120 till
at last we find him as assistant record keeper on Rs. 125." Such promotions
by leaps and bounds were not uncommon, as Indians, despite the frequent
hardships of service so far from home, sought to take advantage of the desperate need for staff in the newly conquered territory.[49]

With this extensive employment of staff from India went the effective
Indianization of Basra's administrative structure. Two projects in particular pushed forward this process. One was a detailed revenue survey proposed by H. R. C. Dobbs as revenue commissioner; the other was the
bringing into force of the Iraq Occupied Territories Code through the
efforts of Lt.-Col. Knox as senior judicial officer. Dobbs, during his two-
year stay in Mesopotamia (1915–16), collected information on local
tenures and promulgated regulations for the settlement of disputes
among the desert tribes based on his Baluchistan experience in compiling
tribal codes. Nevertheless the initiation of large-scale survey and assess-
ment operations was postponed until the end of the war for fear of antag-

onizing the local populace.[50] The administration of justice, however, could not be left for the future, with the result that Knox, from the very outset, set about introducing into Mesopotamia Indian laws and judicial personnel.

As Knox's legal reforms were brought into force, the British endeavored, somewhat disingenuously, to avoid giving the appearance of change even as they were fundamentally altering the working of the courts on the ground. Gertrude Bell, in a 1916 report on the working of the judiciary, asserted that the occupying authorities in Iraq had accepted the "general spirit of the Hague Convention, which required that the law of the country previous to the occupation so far as possible be administered"; and, she pointed out, the Iraq Occupied Territories Code adhered to this requirement by stating that "subject to stated exceptions Turkish civil law shall be applicable." Yet, as Knox himself openly acknowledged, the "exceptions" included "the bulk of cases coming before the courts, which are thus justiciable under such specific Indian laws as have been applied under the code." Knox insisted that these acts, including the Indian Penal Code and Indian Succession Act, had been "worked successfully with suitable modifications." These "modifications" largely involved technical changes, in favor of the Turkish Civil Code, in the laws of inheritance, transfer of property, and the collection of debt.[51] In his annual report for 1917 Knox went on to argue for a regularization of the judicial structure by the appointment of a separate legal secretary to handle legislative functions and an independent judge advocate-general. Only a trained legal secretary fluent in Arabic, he wrote, could oversee "the publication of our laws in a form intelligible to those affected by them."[52]

As reports of Knox's activities filtered back to Delhi, his zeal for legal reform prompted a degree of alarm. By November 1915, even sympathetic officials had begun to worry "whether the administration of the occupied Turkish territory is not tending to assume rather too rapidly the complex character of a British Indian district." Reviewing Knox's 1915 report, one not altogether pleased official commented, "The Report and the Code seem to indicate that our legal administration of the Occupied Territories of Iraq has been remarkably thorough and efficient: indeed the main criticism one is tempted to make is that it has been almost too thorough and too efficient." As Knox elaborated his legal arrangements, the same criticism — that the judicial work was being "overdone" — was repeated in subsequent years.[53]

Maude's conquest of Baghdad brought matters to a head. The question of whether Iraq was to be, in any sense, an Indian colony had now to be faced. In the ensuing discussions, the government of India sought desperately to maintain a footing for itself in the region. At the very least, the viceroy Lord Chelmsford insisted, India "must control Basra," along with the Gulf, and Iraq must remain open for Indian migration. "It must be recognized," he told the Indian secretary in London, "that India has shed her blood in the conquest of these territories in which she already has large commercial, political, and religious interests, and that any restrictions on free Indian immigration into Iraq for trade or other purposes would cause bitter and legitimate resentment." Such views received a cool reception in Whitehall. Arthur Hirtzel at the India Office, for one, reflecting the views of men like Sykes, bluntly denied that India could play any useful role as a colonizing power. "The Arabs may endure the white man — that remains to be seen — but it is surely doubtful if they will endure the Indian; if the Government of India administer Irak, the Indian public will certainly look upon the country as their preserve."[54]

Slowly, but with a determined persistence, the British government forced its Indian counterpart to abandon any claims to predominance in Mesopotamia. The first setback took place in the newly conquered Baghdad *vilayet*. As the Indian secretary, expressing the War Cabinet's views, instructed the viceroy in March 1917, with a disingenuousness equivalent to Bell's description of Knox's code, Baghdad was to be "an Arab state with a local ruler, under a British protectorate in everything but name." In keeping with this "Arab façade," Baghdad was to be administered "as far as possible as an Arab province by indigenous agency and in accordance with existing laws and institutions." Above all, there was to be no reliance on the Iraq code, and no employment of Indian staff. The "local judicial system would be maintained as regards both law and personnel, with only the substitution of Arab for Turk."[55]

Hence, as the Baghdad *vilayet* was brought under British control, its administration bore little resemblance to Knox's Basra. To be sure, Indian officers gained a number of senior posts, including the new position of civil commissioner at Baghdad, held by Cox's one-time deputy Col. A. T. Wilson; and Indian civil servants still predominated in the revenue department that H. C. Dobbs had set up. But for the rest, Arabic-speaking staff were recruited from the Egyptian, Sudan, and Levant services. By 1918, with the exception of H. F. Forbes of the Indian Civil Service, who sat on the Baghdad court, the British officers in the Iraq judicial department consisted of E. Bonham-Carter, Major E. M. Drower, and B. H. Bell, all of the Sudan Civil Service, together with Major H. A. Bros of the Cyprus Civil Service and a barrister from New Zealand. Beneath these few British officers, Bonham-Carter crowed in his 1918 report, "the whole of the clerical staff and the majority of the judges are Arabs, and the courts are following the law and customs with which the people are familiar."[56]

Inevitably, Knox's code, with the Indian laws it incorporated, fell victim to these changed circumstances. As early as 1917, at the time of the fall of Baghdad, Cox had pressed for the creation of a uniform code embracing both the Basra and Baghdad *vilayets*. The postwar abolition of a separate administration for Basra, with the subsequent creation of the state of Iraq from the union of the three Turkish *vilayets* of Basra, Baghdad, and Mosul, provided the occasion to bring Basra "into line with the Baghdad system and practice." To affirm the new order, Knox was denied promotion to the senior position of judicial secretary at Baghdad to which he was otherwise entitled.

More than mere administrative convenience was at stake. Despite agreement that the Indian codes were "much in advance" of the Turkish codes, the British in Iraq now prided themselves that they had built the "foundations of the fabric of justice" on the "firm rock of the native law and customs of the people." All the people of Iraq, not just the residents of Baghdad, were entitled to these "benefits."[57] Like the larger façade of the mandatory government itself, this "firm rock" was also a façade, in which British "supervision" complemented the employment of "Arab hands." Furthermore, the law administered in these courts was hardly indigenous to Arab Mesopotamia. As the British openly acknowledged, the Ottoman Penal Code as adopted in Iraq was based largely on the French Napoleonic code as amended for use in Egypt, while the criminal procedure regulations were "based on the Sudan Criminal Procedure Code prepared under instructions from Lord Kitchener" following that country's 1898 conquest. This did not bother the new British legislators, for, as Bonham-Carter argued, "local conditions in Egypt and in this country have so many resemblances that provisions which have been found to work well in that country are likely to be suitable here." On the civil side, the Ottoman code of 1869, based as it was on the sharia, had to be put in force, Bonham-Carter commented, because it was "regarded with much respect in Mesopotamia, but it is not a satisfactory code by which to regulate modern transactions."[58]

In Iraq, as in the contemporaneous controversies over the Indian codes in Kenya, India could not be seen to be an imperial center. But the situation in Iraq was especially sensitive. In the era of the League of Nations, the British claim to exercise authority as mandatory power had to rest upon the repudiation of "strange and foreign" institutions, however "advanced" they might be, in favor of those "familiar" to the local people. Any visible appearance of direct colonial rule would be unseemly, even embarrassing. India's role in Iraq had to be brought to an end, and Britain's kept suitably veiled.

The withering away of direct Indian influence on the governance of Iraq was complemented by the discouragement of Indian immigration. This objective had been enunciated as part of London's larger strategy for Iraq's future as far back as 1917. Both the Indian government and the local British authorities in Iraq, however, each for their own purposes, sought to delay the introduction of an exclusionary policy. From its side, the Indian government, as we have seen, sought to assuage mounting nationalist sentiment in India by presenting a British Mesopotamia as a land where Indians could prosper as settlers and where Indian Muslims could be assured that the region's holy places would be secure. By the end of the war, with the rise of Gandhian nationalism, such conciliation had become ever more urgent. But this expectation was misconceived if not wholly delusionary, for the Indian people had no enthusiasm for Britain's imperial conquests in the Middle East, and no desire to settle in a Mesopotamia awarded to them in place of the free movement throughout the empire they craved. Much of this was evident to the authorities in Delhi. As early as 1916 the viceroy had noted the Indian people's "indifference to the Arabs" and had deprecated proclamations of annexation on the ground that any such act would "jar on Indian Muslims as the first tangible proof of the disintegration of the Ottoman Empire."[59] The powerful Khilafat movement in India after 1919 — dedicated to preventing the imposition of harsh peace terms on Turkey — only further underlined the futility of rallying Indian support for Britain's Middle East policy by offering Indians a privileged place in the conquered lands. Increasingly too by the 1920s, Indians in Iraq found themselves vulnerable to attack by an aroused Arab populace.

Iraq's British rulers, on their side, wanted Indians, but only as soldiers and as laborers who could contribute to the development of its resources. Given continuous rumblings of rebellion in the immediate postwar years, culminating in a full-scale uprising in the summer of 1920, continued deployment of the Indian Army was essential to the security of the British position in Iraq. So late as October 1919, a full year after the end of the war, some eighteen Indian infantry battalions, eight batteries of mountain artillery, and six companies of sappers and miners — a total of some 44,000 troops — remained posted in the country. During the 1920 uprising, a desperate government summoned to its aid further Indian troops, including a Gurkha contingent reluctantly made available by the Nepal authorities; these Indian troops, as Wilson later acknowledged, "endured the hardest and worst brunt of the fighting in Mesopotamia."[60]

From the wartime mobilization of the Jail Labour Corps on into the 1920s, Indian labor remained indispensable for the ambitious public works programs the British had initiated in Mesopotamia. Sir Percy Cox, high commissioner in Baghdad, reported in December 1920 that his government employed some 25,000 Indian laborers on military works, a further 10,000 on irrigation projects, and 20,000 on the railways. Of these men, some 15,000 were recorded as skilled artisans, with the remainder unskilled. That recruiting labor in peacetime for work in Iraq contravened the restrictions on indentured labor embodied in the Indian Emigration Acts did not bother Cox. Ignoring Delhi's feeble protests, he simply pretended that these laborers, even though constructing railways or irrigation canals, were all employed by the military on military works and that therefore they did not fall within the usual regulations. The mandatory government further depended on thousands of skilled Indian and Anglo-Indian technical staff in the railways, telegraphs, and other offices. An additional 3,000 Indians were employed in Iraq by private firms as clerks, fitters, mechanics, chauffeurs, and general laborers.[61]

The Indian Army, then, made possible the expansion of the British Empire across territories as widely scattered as Malaya, East Africa, and Mesopotamia. But apart from soldiers and laborers, Indians were rarely sought as immigrants in these newly conquered lands. In Mesopotamia, despite the expansive vision of such men as William Willcocks, no Indians were settled on the land, and after 1920 all seeking entry were subject to scrutiny at the port of Basra to make sure they were not "undesirables," among whom were included peddlers, small shopkeepers, and "political agitators."[62] For a brief six years, from 1915 to 1920, Mesopotamia could be imagined as a colony of an Indian imperial center — a place where Indians of all classes might find opportunities not so readily available at home and where Indian laws, institutions, and technical expertise might flourish. In 1921, as India's contract laborers began to return home, control over Iraq was formally transferred from the India Office to the Colonial Office. Iraq was to be British and Arab, not Indian.

CHAPTER 4

Recruiting Sikhs for
Colonial Police and Military

During August of 1873 Captain T. C. S. Speedy, sometime lieutenant in
the 10th Punjab Regiment, recruited some two hundred Sikhs and
Pathans in the Punjab on behalf of the Mantri of Larut, a petty chieftain
in Perak (Malaya), who planned to use them to subdue the growing
power of the Chinese clans in the state. The next year, with the advance
of British authority into Malaya after the Pangkor Engagement, Speedy
was appointed assistant resident at Larut, and his force was taken into
government service as the Perak Armed Police. Subsequently reorganized
as the Perak Sikhs and then, after the creation of the Malay federation in
1896, as the Malay States Guides, this force remained the premiere body
of armed police in Malaya until 1919, when it was finally disbanded. In
Hong Kong as well, the late 1860s and early 1870s saw the recruitment of
Sikhs for the colonial police. Together with Punjabi Muslims, these
Sikhs constituted the predominant element in the colony's police until the
mid-twentieth century. In 1922 there were 435 Indians in the Hong Kong
police; in 1939, 774.[1] The same tale of recruitment and policing can be told
of the Chinese Treaty Ports, of the Straits Settlements, and, with the
British conquest after 1890 of East and Central Africa, of Nyasaland,
Kenya, Uganda, and Somaliland. By the end of the nineteenth century,
across a great arc ranging from Zomba to Tientsin, Indian, predominantly
Sikh, contingents patrolled and policed the British Empire. The Indian
Army, as we have seen, often conquered these territories for Britain. But
day in and day out over the decades that followed, Indian policemen

made visible the reality that India was not simply a colonial territory but itself a center of Britain's imperial authority.

This chapter asks why and how Indians were recruited for service in colonial police forces; why Punjabis, above all Sikhs, were singled out for such recruitment; and how this transport not only of men but also of the shaping ideas and institutions of the late-Victorian Raj to colonial territories around the Indian Ocean produced a distinctive policing strategy connecting India with the colonies from the 1870s to the First World War.

Singapore and Malaya

We can conveniently begin with Tristram Charles Sawyer Speedy (1836–1910). Born in Meerut, son of James Speedy, a lieutenant in the 3rd Regiment of Foot, Tristram Speedy was commissioned into the Indian Army in 1854. By 1860, posted first in Meerut then in Peshawar, Speedy had risen to the position of adjutant in the 10th Punjab Regiment. In that year, restless, he gave up his commission and commenced a life of wandering adventure. This took him first to the court of King Theodore of Abyssinia, where he also served for a time as British vice-consul in Eritrea; then to New Zealand, where he enlisted in the local militia fighting the Maori; and ultimately back to Abyssinia in 1868, when Lord Napier summoned him to act as interpreter and adviser for the campaign that was to culminate in the siege of the fortress of Magdala and the death of King Theodore. After the Magdala campaign, Speedy took charge of Theodore's orphaned infant son Alamayu, whom he brought with him to England and subsequently to India, where Speedy secured the post of district superintendent of police in Sitapur (Oudh). After two years in India Speedy moved on to the Straits, where in 1872 he took up the position of superintendent of police in Penang. After little more than a year, in July 1873, he resigned this post, at less than a month's notice, to take up service with the Mantri of Larut. A month later he was on his way to Lahore.[2]

Speedy's recruiting strategy was simple enough. Returning to an area with which he was familiar from his army days, he signed up, within a few weeks, some two hundred men, some residents of Wazirabad and Gujranwala, others Pathans and men from the hill tribes. As the district superintendent of police in Lahore later wrote of Speedy's activities, "He would not enlist residents of towns or cities, but villagers only. Each man received one rupee on enlistment as bounty, and was to receive three annas a day until the date of leaving Calcutta, their [sic] pay would then

FIGURE 9. "T. C. S. Speedy in Abyssinian Dress," 1868, from a woodcut published in the *Illustrated London News*. Courtesy of the National Archives, Singapore.

be Rupees 20, 25, and 30 respectively; they were informed that they were going across the water; that the Government were going to abandon the Andamans as a penal settlement; and that some other 'tappoo' or island had been selected; and that they were being enlisted for service there. . . . The men were dispatched from Lahore in small parties daily, and their expenses paid to Calcutta." (Whether deception was employed on this occasion is an open question. Clearly the financial incentives were substantial, and the senior police authorities doubted that Speedy had in fact implied that the Andamans were to be abandoned. Still, as he was recruiting on behalf of the unknown ruler of an unfamiliar state, Speedy may have found some judicious bending of the truth helpful.)

Speedy had not bothered even to inform the government of India of his recruiting mission, much less obtain its permission. Hence, when his recruits were discovered milling about on the docks at Calcutta, the government, suspicious of this seemingly surreptitious venture on behalf of a foreign power, delayed Speedy's departure and sought explanations for his behavior from both the Punjab and Straits authorities. The Punjab inspector-general of police somewhat disingenuously replied that "as there are no orders on the subject of enlistments, and it being no uncommon occurrence, the maharajah of Cashmere constantly having agents enlisting men, and in regard to crossing the sea, agents from both China and the Andamans have lately been in Lahore, no notice was taken by the police."[3] Singapore, on its side, said that the Larut *mantri* was a ruler with whom it had friendly relations and that it had no desire to interfere with his effort to regain control of his country from the Chinese. Speedy too insisted that the *mantri* had turned to India for police "as he had neither faith nor trust in the inhabitants of his own province, as the Malays instead of keeping order often sided with one faction or the other, and thereby only enhanced disorder."[4] Consequently, on 25 September, Speedy embarked for Penang with the one hundred of his recruits who remained.

From Speedy's enterprise a number of consequences followed. A furious government of India discovered to its surprise that, as the Bengal secretary wrote, "so long as the government cannot prove *belligerent* intention against a friendly power any one, be he who he may, may come and raise soldiers in India without leave or license. . . . A coolie to till the land may not be taken without very special precautions, but a soldier may be taken without any precautions whatever."[5] As a result, by Act IV of 1874 the Indian government reserved to itself the power to prohibit or to regulate, subject to any conditions it might impose, the "obtaining or attempting to obtain within India recruits for the service of any foreign state in any capacity." Although, as we shall see, this act did not conclusively settle the question of how recruitment for colonial police forces was to be carried on, it did put an end to the activities of such rogue adventurers as Speedy.

In Malaya, Speedy's troopers received an enthusiastic welcome, and not only from the Mantri of Larut. After the Pangkor Engagement and even more after the 1875 Perak War, the British were anxious to secure the presence in Malaya of a force sufficient to control the Chinese tin miners and secret societies and, more generally, to sustain the authority of the Malay sultans in whose name the nominal sovereignty of the country still resided. Since units of the regular Indian Army could not be stationed permanently overseas, Speedy's militia pointed the way to a solution. As the colonial secretary in Singapore wrote to Calcutta in November 1874, "Great difficulty has been found in procuring in the Straits men properly qualified to serve as guards for the Residents and as military police, but a number of Siekhs serving for some time in Perak . . . have given so much satisfaction . . . that Sir Andrew Clarke [the governor] considers it would be very beneficial for the service if a well selected body of men of that class could be procured from India."[6] The resulting request for one hundred men met with the sanction of the Indian government. These recruits, however, scattered across the country in small groups, and lacking, after Speedy's transfer to civil employment, an officer who could communicate with them in their own language, remained ill-disciplined and so of little use. After the Perak War, Governor Sir William Jervois renewed, now more urgently, his predecessor's request for an Indian police force and determined as well to organize the force more efficiently.

Dissatisfied with the remnants of Speedy's recruits, whom he derided as "of low caste and bad character," Jervois proposed "to keep only the best of them to form the nucleus of the Resident's Guard" and to procure the remainder of the new force in India from among "Sikhs of good character who have been discharged from Punjab regiments." This force of about two hundred men he proposed to employ as sentries at residencies, jails, and public offices. It is unclear how far either Speedy or Jervois, as they sought recruits for their new force, adhered to an avowed theory of Indian martial races. Speedy no doubt preferred Punjabis not only because he had served in that province but also because, ever since John Lawrence had turned to them in the dark days of 1857, Punjabis were perceived as loyal and trustworthy. Speedy's preference for villagers also anticipated a continuing theme in the recruitment for the Indian Army. In any case, Speedy clearly had no scruples in taking on board almost anyone who would join his force.

Once the decision had been taken to employ Sikhs in Malaya, there remained the question of discipline. Above all, Jervois insisted, the force had to be "under the superintendence of an officer who can speak Hindustani and who can understand their habits and prejudices," and who could also speak Malay. The choice fell upon Lt. Paul Swinburne, an officer of the 80th Regiment of Foot who had served in both India and Malaya.[7] A cousin of the poet Algernon Charles Swinburne, Lt. Swinburne took charge of the Perak Armed Police in December 1876 and set out to discipline it on an Indian military model. In this endeavor he received the hearty support of the Indian government, which for some years had been concerned about the way such men were treated by the local authorities in the colonies.

Above all, the Indian government was anxious to avoid a reoccurrence of the events of 1863, when some one thousand Punjabis "of the superior military classes" had been recruited to form what they were led to believe was a Pioneer Corps of sappers and miners attached to the Ceylon Public Works Department. When they arrived in Ceylon, the Indians found themselves called on to do the work of laborers, breaking stones on the roads; insisting they had been recruited as soldiers, the men refused to work, and in the end all had to be sent back to their homes. The government's concern of course was not wholly disinterested, for "the unfortunate result of this experiment," it wrote, "may exercise an injurious result on the temper and behaviour of a valuable class of men whenever they may be required by government for service beyond the sea."

The Hong Kong government, by contrast, when it sought Indian recruits in 1867, had supplied detailed terms of service, with rules, regulations, and grades based on those in force for the Punjab police. The term of engagement was set at five years with a free return passage to Calcutta at its termination and the opportunity of re-enlistment. All of this was meant, as the Indian government acknowledged, to reassure the men that the force was in fact raised for police duties. Further, the Hong Kong government had hired an officer of the Punjab police, a district superintendent from Multan, one Mr. Creagh, to enlist the men required and then to accompany them to Hong Kong, where he took up the permanent position of superintendent of the Indian contingent.[8] Although Swinburne was not a Punjab officer and he recruited the bulk of his men on the spot in Malaya, the Hong Kong regulations shaped the structure of the Perak force, which in 1878 numbered some 247 Sikhs.

Despite the imposition of discipline under an Indian-trained officer, the Perak Sikhs, like their counterparts in Hong Kong, did not fit easily into colonial society. They were not meant to. The disaffected Emily Innes, whose husband, in Perak service, had been exiled to the obscure post of Durian Sabatang, described the police there, Sikhs and Pathans, as "too sacred to be made of use in any way that was not strictly military. These lordly beings therefore confined themselves to marching up and down below the house, gun in hand, as sentries, and begging for brandy whenever they saw me, under pretext of drinking my health."

Somewhat more sympathetically, the traveler Isabella Bird, from the comfort of the Perak residency, described the Indian police she met as "splendid looking men with long moustaches and whiskers," wearing "large blue turbans, scarlet coats, and white trousers," and as "to all intents and purposes soldiers, drilled and disciplined as such." Their joy, she wrote, "would be in shooting and looting, but they have not any scent for crime." They are "devoted to the accumulation of money, and very many of them being betrothed to little girls in India, save nearly all their pay in order to buy land and settle there. When off duty they wear turbans and robes nearly as white as snow, and look both classical and colossal. They get on admirably with the Malays, but look down on the Chinese, who are much afraid of them. . . . I have been awoke each night [at the Residency] by the clank which attends the change of guard, and as the moonlight flashes on the bayonets, I realize that I am in Perak."[9] A near-total linguistic isolation reinforced this social distance. The overwhelming majority of the Indian police — in Malaya as in Hong Kong, Punjabi speakers with little incentive to learn Malay or Chinese — could communicate with no one apart from their comrades and commandant.

These social barriers did not much trouble the British. The solving of crime was the task of the Malay police, some 220 strong on land and water in 1878; while rural policing fell to the lot of the village headman (penghulu). Similarly, in Hong Kong the 177 Indians on the force in 1874 were complemented by some 110 Europeans and 204 Chinese constables. The Indians were there in large measure simply to overawe and intimidate the local population, in part by their sheer physical size. Isabella Bird told of seeing "a single Sikh driving four or five Chinamen in front of him, having knotted their pigtails together for reins." Many resident Europeans, especially among the nonofficial community, considered the Perak Sikhs as a "useless extravagance," while their arrogance excited widespread comment. Even a senior official like Hugh Clifford could write of the Sikh that "he is possessed of as absolute a conviction of his own superiority to the men of any other race — Europeans alone excepted — as is the White Man himself. He is quite frank about this opinion, and he is accustomed to act upon it at all times. To other Asiatics he is as arrogant and overbearing as can well be conceived, and he displays none of the tact which helps to make a European less hated for his airs of superiority than he might be."[10] Despite, perhaps because of, this behavior, the usefulness of the Sikh policeman remained unimpaired.

As time went on, the arena open to Sikh employment in Malaya widened and their numbers increased. In Perak itself Swinburne was replaced as commandant of the Sikh police in 1879 by Capt., later Lt. Col., R. S. F. Walker (1850–1917), an officer who had served in India with the

British Army and had participated in the suppression of the Perak rising. Walker set out to strengthen and reorganize the force. In 1883 he recruited a troop of cavalry, consisting of fifteen sowars drawn from Fane's Horse, to patrol the roads at night. The following year he reconstituted the force, rather grandly, as 1st Battalion, Perak Sikhs (at no time was there ever a 2nd battalion) and at the same time increased the size of the force to 701 Sikhs, together with 175 Malays and the 15 troopers.[11]

In 1884 a Sikh contingent of forty men was formed for Perak's southern neighbor, the state of Selangor. When initially established in 1875, with a superintendent, H. C. Syers (1853–97), who secured the post even though he was only a twenty-two-year-old private in the 10th Regiment of Foot, the Selangor police had consisted primarily of Malays whom Syers recruited from Malacca. For years Syers resisted the employment of Sikhs or other Indians. Similarly, unlike his neighbors in Perak, Syers did not concentrate his force as a strategic reserve at the residencies, but rather dispersed most of it throughout the interior to check crime. In part this strategy no doubt reflected the fact that, unlike most of his police contemporaries, Syers had never served in India or in the Indian Army. Hence he did not possess his peers' unwavering confidence that Sikhs alone could be disciplined into an effective force. Nevertheless the pressure to employ Sikhs was unrelenting. As early as 1879 F. A. Swettenham as resident was arguing that "it would be more advisable . . . to employ as in Perak a proportion of Sikhs." Behind this preference lay also a belief on Swettenham's part that to place police on civil duty in villages would undercut the village headmen by setting up a rival source of authority. In the end a compromise was reached in which Syers agreed to accept Indians as "semi-military guards" for the residency and other public buildings, while retaining his force of some three hundred Malays.[12] By 1894 the Sikh contingent in Selangor comprised some 210 men.

In 1889 a Sikh contingent of one hundred men followed the extension of British authority across the Malay peninsula into the eastern state of Pahang. On this occasion both the incoming resident, J. P. Rodger, and the Pahang sultan opposed the introduction of these men into the state. The sultan, Rodger wrote, "strongly objects to the importation of Sikhs into Pahang saying that they are rough and ignorant of Malay customs," while Rodger concurred that Sikhs were "out of place in a purely Malay state" such as Pahang. None of this altered the governor's conviction that a Sikh guard was required in Pahang as elsewhere. Putting the best face on the decision, Rodger concluded that "the main, if not the only, objection to the Sikhs is that so few of them can speak Malay, but the Pahang force is called upon to perform a comparatively small amount of purely police work."[13]

Two years later, in 1891, the Pahang Malays rose in rebellion. Mobilized jointly, the Selangor and Perak Sikhs took the lead under Syers in containing the uprising. One encounter, however, ended in disaster when in June 1894 portions of both the Selangor and Perak forces, surprised in the jungle, commenced firing wildly and in the confusion shot and killed a British officer. The resulting inquiry, by Maj.-Gen. H. T. Jones-Vaughan, called into question both the recruitment strategy and the organization of the Indian forces in Malaya, and so helped bring about their complete reconstitution in 1896. Concurrent with the inauguration of the Federated Malay States, the Perak and Selangor Sikh police were consolidated into a new Malay States Guides under Col. Walker, while Syers became commissioner of police for the federation. Syers's force was composed mostly of Malays, together with a few Sikhs brought over from the disbanded Perak force. (Syers retained his new post for only one year, for in July 1897 he was killed by a wild beast he had wounded while hunting in the jungle.) Walker's "smart little troop" of mounted cavalry, now twenty-three in number, alone survived the upheaval. Although, as the Perak resident acknowledged, "with the development of roads, telegraphs, and railways, the necessity for the 'Troop' as a practical working body has nearly disappeared," and although the road patrols were now entrusted to Malays on bicycles, nevertheless, as the sultan was "much attached" to them, these troopers were retained as his ceremonial bodyguard.[14]

In the Straits Settlements too, after a long and agonizing debate, a Sikh contingent of 165 men joined the force in 1881. Through the 1870s the Straits police consisted of almost equal numbers of local Malays and Klings (South Indians). As the police inspector-general reported in 1876 with satisfaction, "the present force is one recruited without expense from the population of the Straits Settlements, and the wages paid do not exceed the ordinary rates of household servants and coolies. They all speak Malay, the common language of the inhabitants of these settlements." Nevertheless, as the evidence given before the 1879 police commission made clear, there existed much dissatisfaction with Malay and Kling alike. What was required to secure an effective force, the commissioners argued, their views shaped by the conventions of colonial racial ideology, was a way to join "the truthfulness and sobriety" of the Malay with the "greater intelligence and activity" of the Kling. The Chinese, distrusted because of their ties to the secret societies, were perceived as "too dangerous" to employ in any number, and so were excluded from the force altogether except as detectives. Hence, guardedly, the 1879 commission recommended introducing a "certain number" of Sikhs. Within a year of their arrival, the inspector-general, impressed by the Sikhs' "very remarkable aptitude for acquiring a knowledge of military exercises," was already, despite their possession of an "overbearing" disposition, clamoring for an enlargement of the Sikh contingent.[15] By the late 1890s over three hundred Sikhs were employed in a Straits police force some two thousand strong.

Throughout these years, who was to be recruited and where remained contentious issues. From the earliest postmutiny years, there existed always a consensus that Sikhs were to be preferred as soldiers and policemen. Only in the early 1880s, as Indian Army recruiting shifted to the Punjab and Nepal, did the theory of martial races, as we have seen, become fully elaborated.[16] By contrast to India, however, where army officers claimed intimate knowledge of the "essential character" of the various groups described in recruiting handbooks, in the colonies a term like "Sikh," set apart from its Indian context, often existed as little more than a floating signifier indicating martial ability. In much of Southeast Asia a Sikh was anyone having the appropriate physique who wore a turban and called himself a Sikh. As the British commissioner of police in Siam noted in 1905, "'Sikh' is, in this part of the world, a grand name for all kinds of Indians. I have seen Madrasi Pariahs and Gonda Barwars masquerading as Sikhs."

In similar fashion, Jones-Vaughan commented of the Selangor Sikh Police, half of which was not Sikh at all but "Pathan," that its Pathan company was "composed chiefly of so-called Pathans, who were really no more Pathans than I am, coming from the southern Peshawar district." In fact, these men, like most "Pathans" in the Sikh Police forces, were Punjabi Muslims.[17] Perhaps the most extreme instance of this uncertainty was found in far-off Africa, where in 1892 H. H. Johnston, requesting the service of a contingent of Sikhs to aid in the conquest of Nyasaland, acknowledged that "I am afraid I derive most of my ideas of the Indian Army from the works of Rudyard Kipling"![18] To compound confusion further, Sikhs, and North Indians more generally, as we have seen, were popularly known in Malaya as "Bengalis" because they embarked at Calcutta — and thus were the carefully constructed ethnic stereotypes of British India turned upside down.

In Perak, the Straits, and Hong Kong, a police force was initially constituted by officers and men brought from India. Subsequent recruitment, however, for the most part came from among those who offered themselves for enlistment at headquarters. In 1885, 251 men sought to join the Perak Sikhs at their Taiping headquarters; three years later, some 365 trooped up to the enlistment desk. On average, of these men usually about one-third were taken on, and the remainder sent away. Most had found their way to Malaya on their own, drawn by the prospect of employment. Some few — 37 of 72 recruits in 1884, and 12 of 129 in 1888 — had seen service in the Indian Army, while others were actively recruited by the members of the Perak force, who were, as Swettenham wrote, encouraged "when on leave in India, to bring with them on their return to duty men selected by them, many of them being their own friends and relatives."

On occasion, recruiting in India was officially sponsored. In July 1887, for instance, subahdar Chanda Singh was sent on a tour of the Punjab, from which he returned with fifty recruits averaging, he proudly reported, five foot, ten and a half inches in height and thirty-four and three-fourths inches in chest measurement. (Height and chest size were always seen as signifiers of appropriate fitness.) Colonel Walker, an enthusiast for recruitment in India, believing that it would thus be possible to "secure a much finer body of men," himself undertook a recruiting tour of the Punjab in 1884, and the district army recruiting officer in Amritsar was subsequently empowered to enlist men for service with the Perak Sikhs. Nevertheless, the Perak authorities, with their neighbors in Singapore, preferred to do their recruiting at home, where recruits could be secured much more cheaply and as easily as in India. Those who were rejected rarely returned to India, but rather took up employment as "carters, gharrymen, syces, and watchmen" in Malaya or struck out in search of greener pastures in Borneo, Sumatra, or China.[19] Labuan and British North Borneo alone provided employment for over two hundred Sikhs, Punjabis, and Afghans by 1898, while Sikh migration to China, and from there to Russia and even Canada, was, as we shall see, to provoke a crisis in the first years of the twentieth century.

The colonial authorities wrestled too, like their counterparts in India from the time of the 1858 Peel Commission onward, with the vexed question of whether different "classes" should serve together in mixed units or be kept apart. The ultimate dividing lines of race were never crossed. Malay and Chinese units were always kept rigorously separate from those manned by Indians. But, particularly given the small numbers and the often rather vague notions of Indian ethnicity held by many in Southeast Asia, it was uncommon, despite the increasingly class-based organization of the Indian Army, to organize local troops on such a basis.

In Selangor, as we have seen, the so-called Sikh contingent was divided into one company of "Sikhs" and another of "Pathans." After the 1894 disaster, General Jones-Vaughan argued strongly for the elimination of the "Pathan element" altogether. The Pathan, he said, "at best and when obtained from the best districts is unreliable in time of need, gives a great deal of trouble especially as regards the women of this country (as he is a Mohammedan), [and] requires a strong hand and constant supervision." Echoing most contemporary colonial opinion, he insisted that "military considerations are greatly in favor of a homogeneous force which would be free from jealousies and would be animated by a common bond of brotherhood in the field." As constituted after 1896, the Malay States Guides, under Walker's leadership, comprised some 540 Sikhs, together with a vestigial group of 80 Pathans and Punjabi Muslims. Always, the objective was to make colonial police forces as much "Sikh" as possible.[20]

Central and East Africa

The apparent success of Sikh police in Southeast Asia inspired the British, as they moved into East and Central Africa after 1890, to request Sikh police and military units of their own. No sooner had the Imperial British East Africa Company, the British government's chosen agent to administer the territories it had reserved for itself north of German Tanganyika, been set up than its officials began clamoring for Indian police. In similar fashion, in Central Africa, even before the formal establishment of the British protectorate over the territory later known as Nyasaland, the administrator H. H. Johnston requested permission to recruit a military force in India. For Johnston and the company alike, the reputation of the Sikh as the premier colonial soldier was so great that from the outset they insisted that Sikhs, and Sikhs alone, must be supplied to them.

The Indian government, anxious to preserve the recruiting grounds of the Punjab for its own use, was not pleased to see this new demand for Sikhs spring up on the far western side of the Indian Ocean. It had already, some years before, refused the request of the "white raja" James Brooke of Sarawak to recruit Sikhs for service in his dominions, and it initially sought to prevent any recruitment for Africa. When that proved unsuccessful, it then endeavored to deny African recruiters access to the Punjab, or at the very least, to its Sikh population. The first, unauthorized recruitment took place under Col. J. Pollock, a retired officer of the

Madras Sappers, who took with him to Mombasa from Bangalore in 1889 some one hundred pensioned artisans to supervise construction work for the Imperial British East Africa Company. He then requested formal permission to engage two hundred Sikhs for police work. Of the one hundred men whom he had initially engaged, he wrote reassuringly to the Indian government, "not a man has been sick with malarial disease . . . they are very content, and, as there are many Indian shopkeepers in Mombasa, they do not lack the company of their own countrymen and women."[21] In 1890, following urgent appeals to the Foreign Office by the company's president, Sir William Mackinnon, the Indian government authorized the company to recruit, not Sikhs, but two hundred residents of the predominantly Hindu Haryana districts of the eastern Punjab. These men, volunteers recruited for a three-year tour of duty, sailed from Bombay in June 1890 under the command of Alexander S. Rogers (1862–1930), a young assistant district superintendent of police at Lahore.

By the time the three years had expired, in July 1893, the Imperial British East Africa Company was staggering toward bankruptcy. Uganda and the bulk of the interior had already been abandoned, and the Indian troopers were concentrated in the coastal districts of Lamu and Witu. The return of the Indians to their homes thus opened the way to anarchy throughout the company's territories. To preserve something from the chaos, Witu and Lamu were made a British protectorate and placed under the government of the sultan of Zanzibar, with Rogers appointed as administrator. But, with a mere fifty Nubian (Sudanese Arab) police, along with untrained local Swahilis (Muslims of the coast), Rogers had no hope of maintaining order. As Rennell Rodd, the consul general in Zanzibar, wrote, pleading desperately for more Indians, "The utter debacle of the Company has rendered the situation all along the coast extremely critical. . . . I am at my wits end where to find men; the Arab irregulars cannot be relied upon as recent events at Kismayu have shown; the Swahili troops are unseasoned . . . and not very courageous." Rogers concurred. "A force of one hundred sepoys," he wrote, "is more valuable than three or four times their number of Swahilis." Rodd requested permission to recruit in India one hundred Punjabis, who would be drilled in Africa by Rogers to form a military police force. He was prepared to offer free rations and clothing, and pay at rates ranging upwards of fifteen rupees a month, to prospective recruits.[22]

Despite the backing of the Foreign Office, the Indian government did not receive this request with enthusiasm. To the contrary, it used this occasion to reiterate its objections to such recruitment. As one official in the Military Department put it, echoing widespread opinion, "what is objected to is the frittering away of Indian soldiers, actual or potential — and Punjabis especially — in these regions," while another argued forthrightly that "the proper field" for the recruitment of troops for Africa was in Africa itself. The viceroy, rather as though swatting away a swarm of flies, deplored the colonial "tendency to indent upon us for small bodies of troops to serve in all sorts of remote places." Rogers's willingness to recruit and train soldiers of his own, far from easing the burden on the Indian Army, in the army's view only made matters worse. As the adjutant general shrewdly observed, "to allow a recruiting party offering more than Rs. 7 a month [the standard Indian Army pay scale] to compete in the open market with our own parties does infinite harm, not so much on account of the actual number of men withdrawn from India, as by reason of the effect on the minds of possible recruits who absolutely refuse to enlist on Rs. 7 a month when once they know their brothers have gone off with a party offering Rs. 20." Hence, in October 1893, with the concurrence of the Indian secretary in London, the government of India rejected Rogers's request for troops.[23]

Meanwhile, to the south, Harry Johnston was engaged in establishing his own protectorate, that of Nyasaland (now Malawi). Isolated in the heart of Africa, confronted with hostile Arab slavers, and dependent on the Portuguese in Mozambique for trade and transit rights, Johnston lost no time in requesting an Indian force to bulwark his regime. In April 1891, two months before the protectorate was established, Johnston's request for fifty, soon raised to seventy, Sikhs or Punjabi Muslims was already before the Indian authorities. Capt. C. M. Maguire of the 2nd Hyderabad Lancers was entrusted with the task of securing the men and, once in Africa, commanding the force. Unlike the ongoing recruiting operations in Southeast Asia or those for the Imperial British East Africa (IBEA) Company in East Africa, Maguire sought his troopers directly from the Indian Army rather than through open recruiting in the Punjab countryside. This decision was prompted in large part by the fact that, as Johnston told Maguire, "the duties of the men will be chiefly fighting." Those recruited, in other words, had to be available for immediate deployment in campaigns of conquest and pacification. For such purposes, only "trained and disciplined men" would do.[24] Time did not permit the luxury of an extended period on the parade ground.

Johnston was anxious also to avoid any appearance of rivalry, such as that implied in Rogers's recruitment scheme, with an Indian military determined to protect its recruiting grounds from those offering higher pay. For himself, Johnston would "willingly" have recruited his own "raw" Sikhs, for he could then have gotten more men more cheaply and engaged them for longer periods of service. But he thought it preferable to ask for that which "it would be easier for the Indian government to grant." Further, the Indian authorities, though still worried that overseas recruitment might "materially weaken our military resources," had also come to the conclusion that such service might be advantageous for the individual soldier. "From the point of view of the army," as one military official wrote, "it appears expedient that such highly paid employment, especially when calculated to foster an adventurous spirit among the men, should be placed within their reach as it is within the reach of their British officers." On this ground and, further, because Johnston represented a British protectorate, not a chartered company or the sultan of Zanzibar, the request for men was approved.[25]

The vexed question remained of whether Johnston should be permitted to recruit Sikhs. The India Office insistently urged on this and other occasions that colonial recruiting should be directed toward other classes, most notably South Indians and Hindustanis from the Gangetic plain. Yet in the end, no such proposal could succeed, for the Indian military was trapped by its commitment to the idea of martial races. The army, that is to say, had to permit recruitment of Sikhs and Punjabis, for, as one official wrote, "assuredly no other natives of India will be fit for the work." Hindustanis, or men from southern India, were "predestined to failure in a service of the kind proposed. It was found in the case of the Burma Military Police that the Hindustani with his pots and pans, his prejudices, and his prostration as soon as removed from his own country, his own diet, and his native 'ab-o-hawa' [climate], proved himself not only a lamentable failure but a grave difficulty to the administration. And if he failed in Burma, how much more, and more disastrously, would he fail in Africa? The same objections, but intensified, would exist to taking men from Bombay, Madras, or the Hyderabad Contingent." Even within the larger Sikh community, the British believed, different clan groups possessed distinctive characteristics. Maguire preferred Mazbi, or lower-class, Sikhs on the grounds that they, he was informed, were "less particular as to the food given them than Jat Sikhs"; and he was further urged to take only "*true* Mazhabis, not Lohanas or Ramdasis."[26] In June 1891 Maguire set sail for Africa with forty-nine Sikhs chosen from two pioneer battalions, and a further twenty-two cavalrymen selected from his own former unit, the Hyderabad Lancers.

No sooner had they arrived in Nyasaland than Maguire's troopers went into action on and around Lake Nyasa. These initial encounters were not wholly successful. On one occasion, attacking a shore fort from the lake, Maguire himself was shot and drowned while trying to climb back aboard the steamer, while three Sikhs were killed and ten wounded. The cavalrymen too, unused to such combat, were ineffective, and they were ultimately sent back to India after their horses had all died of tsetse infection. Still, Johnston remained convinced that Sikh forces were essential for the pacification of Central Africa. As he wrote the Indian commander-in-chief in July 1892, requesting a further one hundred soldiers, "Great Britain can only maintain her supremacy in these countries of Central Africa by the employment of Indian troops." When, he continued, "our skirmishing force of Zanzibaris was repulsed by the enemy or temporarily disappeared, the Indians always saved the day." If we cannot, he said, "for the next few years, be allowed to maintain a force of one to two hundred Indian soldiers, we had better retire from Nyasaland altogether and allow the slave trade to go on unopposed."[27]

Two years later, Johnston laid out in detail for the Foreign Office the reasons for his conviction that without Sikhs the Nyasaland protectorate would be exposed to "serious risks of military disaster." Zanzibaris, he said, were of "little use as fighting men especially when directed against Arabs and [Nyasa] Yaos, who were practically their brothers"; Sudanese were "undoubtedly brave, but prone to drunkenness and excessive immorality and treat friendly and hostile natives with equal harshness and cruelty"; while Makua from Mozambique were "thoroughly brave and easily disciplined," but their recruitment was restricted by the Portuguese authorities. Inspired by the stories of Kipling, Johnston was tempted to ask for Gurkha troops, for their "daring and bravery" made them, he imagined, "just the men for some of our hazardous operations in the hill country in the Shire highlands." But he was deterred by what he had heard of their "difficult and expensive diet," including a large allowance of meat that he could not easily supply. Sikhs, by contrast, he wrote, echoing martial races ideology, were seemingly without faults. "Not being Muhammadans, they are quite out of sympathy with the Arab slave traders. Not being Hindus of high caste, they give no trouble about their food or any inconvenient religious ceremonies. They are brave, strong, vigorous, and well suited to the rough life and exhausting climate. . . . [In addition] their behavior to the natives is admirable, and their popularity in this respect is one of the most potent tendencies toward the spread of friendly relations between the Administration and the more recalcitrant of the native tribes." Nor was it, in Johnston's view, at all surprising that India

should be called upon to garrison eastern Africa. Something of an imperial center in its own right, India had, he wrote, by degrees "become the
dominant factor in the lands bordering the Indian Ocean within the tropics, and towards India all Eastern Africa turns as the mainspring of commerce and the source of power." What India lost by the provision of
troops it gained by opportunities for profitable trade and outlets for its
manufactures.[28]

Confronted with this array of arguments, the Indian government
sanctioned the further enrollment of Sikh contingents for Central Africa.
One hundred men under Lt. C. A. Edwards of the 35th Sikhs sailed in
February 1893. A further one hundred, to relieve Maguire's now depleted
force, whose two year tour was approaching its end, followed a few
months later under the command of Lt. W. H. Manning of the 1st Sikhs.
How, one must ask, were these men selected? What induced soldiers of
the Indian Army to sign up for service in remote Nyasaland? One might
follow Lt. Edwards as he described his recruiting tour. He began by having the conditions of service translated into Urdu and Gurmukhi, with
copies sent to the commanding officers of the regiments, six in number,
from which he was authorized to accept recruits. From each regiment he
was permitted to take no more than twenty men. The various commanding officers were requested to read aloud the conditions of service
at roll call. Edwards then visited each regiment in turn, and had all those
who wished to go, generally about 80 to 150 men per regiment, fall in
before him. From among this number, Edwards selected some 30 or 35
"likely looking" soldiers and dismissed the remainder. He then examined
the service records of these 30 and rejected those who were "of bad or
indifferent character" or were "bad shots." The rest then proceeded to the
regimental hospital. "After the medical officer had thoroughly inspected
the men and signed a certificate that the men were physically fit for service in British Central Africa, I inspected again the men who were passed
as fit, and finally selected the 20 men I required." After the final inspection the conditions of service were "most thoroughly and carefully
explained to the men." Once he had secured the one hundred he was
authorized to engage, he had them all dispatched to Agra, where they
were outfitted and sent off together by train to Bombay and thence to
Africa.[29]

Edwards's 1893 batch, all Sikhs, came from five regiments, each of
which supplied the full twenty men. He acknowledged that "very few
havildars, buglers, and signalers volunteered so I hadn't a good number
to select from," but as a whole, he insisted, the contingent comprised

"good men" who were all "very happy and are looking eagerly forward to active service in Central Africa." The inducement to sign up for African service operated most strongly at the lowest level, that of the ordinary sepoy, and was weaker at the level of the noncommissioned officer (NCO) and skilled artisan. An 1895 recruitment drive for East Africa, for instance, produced only one subahdar and four jamadar applicants for six available NCO positions. Recruiting in 1898 for Central Africa, Lt. C. Godfrey found himself unable to procure soldier artificers from Pioneer regiments and, after taking all who volunteered, was still short of buglers and drummers. Ironically, forewarned by Edwards's report that NCOs were in short supply, Godfrey accepted all who presented themselves in the early stages of his tour, in Burma and Bombay, only to find, when he did reach the Punjab, fifteen volunteers for the one NCO position he still had open. He grumbled, "If I had known this before I could have made a better selection of non-commissioned officers than I have done, as I should have obtained men from Punjab regiments thoroughly experienced in active service and naturally more valuable men to have had."[30]

Of critical importance in securing volunteers was the pay differential compared with that of the Indian Army. By contrast with the army's seven rupees a month, with rations to be paid for out of this sum, the African colonies offered ordinary sepoys eighteen rupees, with free rations, and a one hundred–rupee gratuity payable at the end of the term of service. NCOs received pay on a scale ranging from twenty-five rupees for naiks up to one hundred rupees for subahdars, with correspondingly higher bonuses ranging up to one thousand rupees. The Indian commander-in-chief estimated that "a prudent Sikh who serves three years in British Central Africa may contrive to save out of his pay about 35 pounds — a sum in India sufficient to start a man as a landholder and cultivator." Service in the Indian Army itself could of course, and did, produce the same result — but over a much longer period of active duty. The reluctance of the higher ranks to enlist for overseas service, as well as the rarity of re-enlistment — only five of the 175 men Godfrey engaged had previously served in Africa — might be taken as evidence that, once a soldier had put aside money enough to give himself and his family a start on the land, he preferred to remain closer to his home and, if an NCO, to take advantage of the greater opportunities for promotion offered within the Indian Army.[31]

As time went by, the colonial authorities found it ever easier to secure the men they wanted. Johnston himself accompanied his recruiters on one Indian tour in 1895 and came back, self-satisfied, to report that "the men selected are the very cream of the Sikh regiments: a finer fitter body of soldiers never left India before for foreign service. The eagerness with which they volunteered for service was most gratifying, and (apart from the Sikh love of adventure) is attributable to two causes: the award of the Central Africa medal to their comrades serving in previous campaigns; and the encouraging reports sent home by Sikh soldiers of previous contingents." In marked contrast with Edwards's experience two years before, Johnston reported that "in some cases the number of volunteers in a regiment of 900 men would be as many as 500, out of which we had to select only twenty."[32] Such successful recruiting, as we shall see presently, kept alive the Indian government's fear that the recruiting grounds of the Punjab were becoming depleted. It also often antagonized the commanding officers of the targeted regiments, who disliked losing their best men to African forces and so sometimes endeavored to obstruct recruiters' activities.

Once in Nyasaland the Sikhs joined a mixed force whose different elements were assigned different tasks. During the initial period of pacification, the Sikhs performed the role of shock troops, leading attacks against various hostile chieftains. By 1895, as the country became more settled, the Sikhs undertook garrison duty at a half-dozen forts scattered across the protectorate. Their role was frequently that of "stiffening" African troops. The 185 Sikhs in Nyasaland in 1898, for instance, comprised one company in the British Central Africa Rifles. The other six companies, totaling eight hundred men, were formed from the local Atonga, Yao, and Marimba peoples. The Sikhs, Johnston's successor Alfred Sharpe reported, were "distributed to the various companies so that each garrison of a fort is able to move out a complete force of Sikh and native troops to any point. About one hundred Sikhs are stationed in Zomba [the colonial capital] ready to march out at a few hours' notice."

Further, the Sikh was "as useful in times of peace as in war. . . . [He] makes himself useful in road making, in the construction of bridges, in the organization of telegraphs, and in all work where an active intelligence is needed." Perhaps the Sikhs' greatest contribution, in Sharpe's view, was the example they set of effective military discipline. Their presence, he wrote in 1897, has "enabled us to get together a native force which I have no hesitation in saying will in the course of a few years meet all the requirements of the Protectorate." Native soldiers, so Sharpe reported, "in drill, marching, good behavior, and also fighting qualities . . . compare very favorably with the fighting races of India." They could not yet, however, he continued, be trusted to exercise command functions. Hence, it was necessary to employ trained Indian soldiers "to supply the senior NCOs for the native companies, to act as drill instructors, to keep the accounts of stores and rations issued to the men, and also to take charge of all escorts, guards, detachments, posts, and forts in the absence of British officers."[33]

In 1895, following the bankruptcy of the Imperial British East Africa Company, the imperial government took over the governance of East Africa. Under these new conditions, the Indian government could no longer so easily refuse to supply troops for service in the region. Before the year was out, a contingent of 300 Punjabi Muslims drawn from some nineteen regiments had been formed on the same terms and conditions as the Central African force and shipped off to Mombasa. This contingent joined some 250 Sudanese and 575 Swahili, Arab, Somali, and other locally recruited troops; together, as the East Africa Rifles, they formed the garrison of the new protectorate.[34]

In 1897 a mutiny among the Sudanese troops posted to Uganda, discussed above, enforced upon the British authorities once again the value of Indian troopers. Hence in 1898, once the mutiny had been put down and the regular Indian Army units withdrawn, a contingent of some four hundred Indian troops, half Sikh and half Punjabi Muslim, was raised for service exclusively in Uganda. There, together with seven hundred locally recruited Swahilis and seven hundred "loyal" Sudanese, they formed the Uganda Rifles. On the model of the Central and East African contingents before them, the Uganda force was raised for a three-year tour of duty, with base pay of eighteen rupees for ordinary sepoys. As the commander Lt. Col. J. R. L. Macdonald reported to Salisbury at the Foreign Office, "Without these [Indians] the Soudanese cannot again be considered a reliable force, as there have been grave symptoms of disaffection even among those who have not joined the mutiny; but, with an independent force of Indians in the country, the Soudanese would probably prove a useful manageable body of soldiers."[35]

Together these three Indian contingents comprised by 1900 a total of some 940 men who helped enforce British rule across hundreds of miles of territory stretching from Zomba to Mombasa to Kampala. Apart from a brief period in Somaliland, no attempt was made to raise special contingents for other African regions. Nevertheless, Indians formed small but critical components of the forces deployed elsewhere across Britain's African empire. In Rhodesia, confronted twice in a decade by massive native uprisings, the British South Africa Company, following a proposal by Alfred Sharpe, in 1898 abandoned the attempt, in the region north of the Zambezi (later Northern Rhodesia, now Zambia), to use white mounted policemen and instead recruited a force of 40 Sikhs placed over a contingent of 350 Africans. Whites were "unsuitable" on grounds of expense and susceptibility to fever, while a wholly African force ran the "risk" of a repetition of the "evil results" of the previous employment of native police.[36] In far-off West Africa too, the ongoing campaigns of Sir Frederick Lugard's West African Frontier Force during 1899 and 1900 opened up a window of opportunity for members of the Indian military, both British and Indian. Lugard, indeed, with his extensive Indian military background, wasted no time in turning to India for the trained men he needed.

Apart from his own brother, Capt. E. J. Lugard, whom Lugard brought over from the Indian Army to serve as political resident in Northern Nigeria, the most eminent British Indian officer in Lugard's force was Sir James Willcocks (1857–1926). A Sandhurst graduate and officer in a British regiment, the 100th Foot, posted to India, Willcocks, brother of the irrigation engineer William Willcocks, served in frontier campaigns during the 1890s from Baluchistan in the west to Manipur in the east. Joining Lugard, he took up command of the West African Frontier Force in 1899, where he gained a knighthood (KCMG) in 1900 for the relief of Kumasi. In 1906 he returned to India as a major-general, where he commanded the Northern Army and then, in 1914, the Indian Army Corps in France. Willcocks's career, better perhaps than most, illustrates the importance of India as a reservoir of experienced military personnel for service anywhere in the British Empire.[37]

But Lugard required for his force not just British officers from India but Indians as well. Among these were sappers, senior NCOs, Sikhs from the Central African contingent, and, as he began to set up a government after 1900, Indian artisans, clerks, transport officers, and the like. First to be called to West Africa were a group of twenty Madras sappers, required initially for the construction of houses and barracks. Lugard argued that the climate of West Africa was not "very dissimilar" to that of South India, while Madrasis, he claimed, "have a very remarkable facility in acquiring languages, and would probably become adepts in Hausa in a marvelously short time." More to the point, however, Lugard continued, "for the same total outlay a far larger number of them than of Europeans can be obtained," while Africans by contrast required "constant supervision" if the "maximum of work" was to be got out of them. The Madrasis, on a three-year engagement, sailed for Africa from India in the summer of 1898.[38] For fighting troops Lugard turned to the Sikhs of the Central

African Regiment. Serving under Willcocks's command, 73 Sikhs and 267 African troops from Nyasaland reinforced the West African Field Force in the relief of Kumasi, and subsequently at Obassa, where the Indian-trained Willcocks, trusting the military qualities of the Sikhs, placed them in the center of the line, in the face of withering fire, during the assault on the Ashanti stockade.[39]

To "stiffen" his African forces, Lugard sought some twenty-three Indian NCOs of the rank of jamadar. As he wrote to Joseph Chamberlain at the Colonial Office, British NCOs were far too expensive to employ widely, while African NCOs were so few in number as to be unobtainable, and where they did exist, in the Coast Battalions, they were "not the men to keep in discipline the fighting Hausas and Yorubas which form a large part of the West African Frontier Force." He proposed instead appointing a Sikh or Punjabi Muslim officer to each company of 150 native African infantry. British Indian native officers, he insisted, were "first class fighting men," acclimatized to the tropics and having "the requisite bravery to lead in the field." Mindful of the dictates of imperial security, he argued further that "as aliens whose interests are identified with the Europeans they [the Indians] would form a check which local native officers even if they were obtainable would not." Willcocks envisaged these prospective officers as young men "full of vigour, good English scholars in some cases, who would have all to gain by good service and who would gladly come." Neither Chamberlain nor the Indian government, however, regarded this proposal with any great enthusiasm. Above all, the Colonial Office insisted that as Hausa and Yoruba became "sufficiently trained" to undertake the duties of NCO, the number of Indians would have to be "gradually diminished" until, preferably no later than mid-1902, none would remain. Given these constraints, the scheme appears not to have been implemented.[40]

In his first annual report for Northern Nigeria, in 1900, Lugard argued his case for recruitment in India of "so-called skilled labour, viz., clerks, artisans, engineers, and pilots, etc." In all these spheres, he said, "British Indians of a much more efficient type than the class available here, and doing half as much again in a day's work, can be engaged in India at less than half the rates paid here." In 1905 ten clerks were brought from India "for distribution among the various departments in the senior most grades." That same year the assistant transport officer, a Mr. Carrigan, returned from India with some twenty-eight transport attendants, including veterinarians, blacksmiths, and shoeing smiths. These men, Lugard reported, "have already proved invaluable in teaching the natives how to use and repair carts, break in oxen to draught work, and tend animals," along with making available crafts hitherto unknown in West Africa, such as shoeing, packsaddle making, and wheel making. Carrigan also brought with him samples of Indian country carts, an "ekka" and a "tonga," "with a view to their local construction if they prove adapted to the country."[41]

As in the East Africa Protectorate during the same years, the result was to create a colonial government staffed by Indians at the middle levels. The Indian presence, however, was much less enduring in the West. The clerks had to compete with educated Africans from Sierra Leone and the coast. Complaining of harsh treatment at the hands of their British superiors, they all left within two years. Although Lugard praised the work of the Indian artisans and sought replacements from the Indian Supply and Transport Corps for those whose initial terms had expired, difficulties of transport and repatriation, in which some Indians were left stranded in England for months, brought the scheme to an end in 1909.[42] Clearly, West Africa was too far from India and possessed in its own educated elites and trading communities many of the skills that Indians elsewhere brought to the colonial enterprise. It was simply not possible to deploy an Indian military force effectively at such a distance from the subcontinent, much less to generate in the West the extensive Indian immigration that marked East Africa. Nevertheless, as soldiers and as artisans, Indians did make a visible contribution to the founding of Britain's West African empire. Furthermore, the almost reflexive turning to India and to Indians by such men as Lugard and Willcocks testifies to the power of the *idea* of India as a center of crafts, skills, and peoples who could be drawn upon to make empire more efficient and economical.

Controversy and Crisis

Throughout the 1890s and into the new century, the Indian government continued to grapple with the twin problems of military pay and the presumed depletion of its Punjabi recruiting grounds. At the same time, Sikhs remained in great demand as armed police from Africa to Asia. Yet by 1920 colonial Indian contingents had ceased to exist outside Hong Kong and the Chinese treaty ports. This section examines the changing nature of colonial recruiting, and its eventual demise, during the first two decades of the twentieth century.

The Indian government was always reluctant to place stringent limits on colonial recruitment. As fellow Britons with a stake in an empire in which they all took pride, the officials of that government could not easily spurn the requests for soldiers of their colonial colleagues. The availability of Indian soldiers and police for service in its far-flung territories contributed, they all agreed, to the empire's power and effectiveness. The Indian authorities saw too in the opportunity for overseas service a way to "enhance the popularity of the Indian Army by giving highly paid openings to well conducted men of adventurous spirit."[43] But the disparities of pay and consequent fears of depletion remained. The African colonies, as we have seen, offered ordinary sepoys eighteen rupees a month with rations and a bonus at the end of a tour, compared to the army's seven rupees with rations to be paid for out of this sum, leaving a take-home pay of under four rupees. The Hong Kong Regiment, at fifteen rupees and rations, offered somewhat less to its sepoy volunteers than did the African contingents, but those hired privately by the various colonial Southeast Asian police forces fared even better. The Hong Kong Sikh policeman, for instance, at thirty rupees, received close to five times the pay of the ordinary army sepoy in India, while those serving in Malaya in units such as the Perak Sikhs earned from eighteen to twenty-two rupees per month. Pay rates were also substantially higher than army pay in the Burma and Singapore police, as well as in the artillery units posted to Ceylon and Mauritius.[44]

A despairing military department official, after surveying these pay scales, conceded that although the Sikh was a "homely man" who would rather serve with his regiment in India, he was "naturally eager to take work for higher pay where he could put by a nice little sum — not altogether forgetting the chances of a little fighting and other excitements at the same time." With a vast force under arms the Indian Army could not hope to match the colonial terms, but in order to offset the pay differential to some degree, the army raised its monthly base pay to nine rupees in 1895. The additional two rupees, it was hoped, "will have the effect of keeping at home many men who would not have enlisted on Rs. 7." The army further began promoting the extension to the Southeast Asian colonies of the system of recruiting already established for Africa, with its tighter controls on pay and service. But these measures offered no solution to the problem of "depletion." This anxiety was deeply embedded in the Indian official mentality by the mid-1890s. As the commander-in-chief grumbled in 1893 on behalf of the Indian Army, "it is absolutely impossible to obtain Sikhs and Punjabi Muhammadans of the old class, and it will be suicidal to admit further demands from Africa and elsewhere on our exhausted recruiting grounds."[45]

But what did "depletion" mean? And how serious was it in reality? The facts, not surprisingly, were elusive and subject to conflicting interpretation. Some of the difficulty in recruiting could be attributed to the growing prosperity of the Punjab, well on its way by the end of the century to becoming what it has remained to the present, the granary of India. As one official wrote in 1896, "the extension of canals in the Punjab has opened up vast fresh tracts of land that can be very profitably cultivated." As army service was attractive insofar as it increased the ability of discharged veterans to buy land, so too did the availability of canal irrigation deter enlistment among those who already possessed holdings liable to benefit from perennial water supplies.[46]

Over such matters, of course, the military had no control. It did, however, attempt to gauge the potential for "depletion" by calculating the numbers of Sikhs and Punjabi Muslims in military employment as a percentage of the total populations of these groups as revealed by the census. One such calculation in 1898 indicated that nearly one-tenth of the entire Sikh male population of military age, or 39,598 men of 482,500, were employed by the Indian military; of these 28,146 were Jats, 2,452 Mazbis, and the remaining 9,000 of other classes. Among Punjabi Muslims, 21,000, or some 2 percent of those eligible, were in Indian military service. On colonial service, including both volunteers from the Indian Army and those recruited independently, the government counted a total of some 5,000 men. Of these 2,554 were Sikhs (scattered from Hong Kong and Malaya to Central Africa and Uganda); 1,548 were Punjabi Muslims (serving mostly in Hong Kong and East Africa); and a further 893 of other communities were employed in Hong Kong, North Borneo, Ceylon, and Mauritius.[47]

Some officials chose to read from these numbers the message that, although other classes might continue to be recruited for colonial service, "we should not be called upon to supply Sikhs except in very small numbers." Others, especially in the military department, regarded the whole furor as "exaggerated" and pointed to the very small number of Sikhs who signed up for overseas service each year. One 1896 calculation produced an annual total of no more than one hundred; a later count of Sikh migrants to eastern Asia came up with a total of six hundred. But assessing the extent of "depletion" inevitably involved facing several troubling questions: what did it mean to be a Sikh, or more to the point, who was to be counted as a Sikh? What kinds of Sikhs were suited for military service? As we have seen, Sikhs for various reasons stood at the heart of the Indian martial races theory. Further, there was a general consensus, clearly visible in the military recruitment figures, that Jats made the best soldiers. As Curzon wrote in 1902, they are "the fighting race." The Jat Sikh was as well, so the British were convinced, of a higher social status than other Sikhs by virtue of his adherence to the defining features of the Sikh religion as laid down in the khalsa. The "value of a Jat Sikh," then, was twofold: it lay in the fact that he was a khalsa Sikh and in the fact that he belongs to a "naturally hardy, independent, and robust race."[48]

Much in this construction of the ideal of the Jat Sikh was, as many British officials were themselves aware, an exercise in self-delusion. Those close to the recruitment process realized that the Indian Army itself played an important role in maintaining Sikhism by its enforcement of the rules and rituals associated with the khalsa. As Col. B. Duff bluntly put it in 1902, "that religion [Sikhism] only retains its vitality on account of our demand for Sikhs as soldiers. If we ceased enlisting Sikhs, that religion would absolutely die out in a few generations." Consequently, any short-fall in the numbers of Sikhs signing up for military service could be countered simply by creating more Sikhs. In 1900, Duff noted, one regimental commander, recruiting non-Jat Lobanas, "enlisted them first and made them Sikhs afterwards." "The more Sikhs we employ in India," he continued, "the more Sikhs there will be in the country. . . . Even the demand for Sikhs in the Far East has the same tendency. So long as it pays to be a Sikh, so long Sikhs will increase and multiply." The "small drain" of Sikhs to colonial service could never be "in any way injurious to us." Of course, not everyone agreed with this sanguine analysis. As A. P. Palmer wrote in reply, "By taking short Sikhs, Lobanas, Brahmin Sikhs, etc., we have lately tapped a fresh source of supply, but the proper stamp cannot be held to the unlimited extent that Colonel Duff would seem to imply. There is a limit to fecundity."[49]

One way out of the depletion dilemma, then, was to increase the recruitment of non-Jat Sikhs and restrict that of Jats. As one official vigorously argued, "A Sikh is a Sikh, whether he be Jat, Khatri, or Muzbee." For colonial recruitment, however, especially that in Southeast Asia, where men presented themselves at local depots, there was a further difficulty. As we have seen, colonial officials had difficulty telling one Sikh, or even one Indian, from another. Hence to restrict their recruiting to certain classes, A. H. Bingley noted, "would be very difficult to enforce. To them [the colonial authorities] all upcountry natives are Sikhs, and they would never appreciate the difference between a Jat and a Lobana or a Khamboh or a Kalal. They simply take the finest looking men that offer themselves for enlistment and neither know nor care what class they belong to." Echoing Duff, Bingley further pointed out that, once recruited, such men might well in time become "real Sikhs," for there was "nothing to prevent them becoming so, as indeed they do when they join corps such as the Malay States Guides."[50]

This controversy, whatever its larger implications, did not slow the recruitment of Sikhs for colonial service in the years around the turn of the century. In 1898, as we have seen, the government authorized a contingent of four hundred Sikhs for Uganda. As each tour of duty came to an end, the African contingents were regularly resupplied with Indian troopers. On 1 January 1902, the forces of all three protectorates — Nyasaland, East Africa, and Uganda — were amalgamated to form the King's African Rifles, under the command of an Indian officer, Lt. Col. W. H. Manning, who had come over to Africa with the 1893 Central African contingent. The Sikhs of the old Central African contingent were attached to whichever battalion was on garrison duty in Nyasaland, while the Indian contingents in the other protectorates together formed a separate Indian battalion (the 5th Battalion King's African Rifles, or 5 KAR) as one of five making up the new force. On several occasions in the years after 1900, as discussed in chapter 3, Sikhs from these contingents, often in company with troops sent from India, joined in the campaigns against the so-called Mad Mullah of Somaliland. In 1905, after the suppression of this uprising, a separate contingent of four hundred Punjabi Muslims was raised in India for service especially in Somaliland as part of a new 6 KAR.

Meanwhile, far away in Southeast Asia, another controversy was brewing. This time the focus of British anxiety was not just that, by leaving the country, Sikhs were "draining" India of potential troops but that, by taking service with foreign powers, they posed a threat to Britain's empire itself. As most British colonies in Southeast Asia recruited their police from among those who presented themselves locally, and as there was always an ample supply of applicants, by the 1890s, not surprisingly, the Straits authorities were reporting "increasing numbers of Sikhs" moving on, as disappointed job seekers, from the colony to Sumatra, Borneo, and Siam. By 1902 Sikhs were reported taking service with the Siamese at Bangkok, with the French in Tonkin, and with the Germans in Kaiuchou. Indeed, a few Sikhs were even spotted heading for Russian Asia, where they found employment at Port Arthur and on the Manchurian Railway.[51]

The British police commissioner in Siam, who had in his own force some 177 Indians, including 10 Sikhs, was unmoved by this Sikh migration. The "few" he knew of in foreign employ were mostly in Java, he reported, and the remainder were employed by the Chinese in Swatow. All were watchmen who came from the United Provinces and were incorrectly known as Sikhs. Issues of fairness were also involved. The adjutant-general, A. H. Bingley, committed to the principle that Indians should be free to "carry their services to the best market," argued that "the savings which these Punjabi emigrants remit to their homes in India must add much to the prosperity of their villages, and constitute an indirect, but very substantial, gain to India."[52]

Nevertheless, the fears aroused by an unfettered military emigration fed on themselves. As Curzon wrote in 1903, unleashing his imagination, "We may have at any time to fight one or other of these [continental European] powers, perhaps more than one in combination. I think it is a most serious thing that we should possibly be confronted by our Indian subjects whose brothers and cousins and kinsmen are in the ranks of the Indian Army. If men are to be enlisted from India to fight against us, the solidarity of India as a political factor in the East is gone; and I would take any steps however strong to prevent so ruinous a consummation." Indeed, Britain's very success in mobilizing thousands of Indian troops to fight abroad, visibly demonstrated during the suppression of the Boxer rebellion in China, had, so the British conceived, aroused the envy of their rivals, who now sought Indians for themselves, so that what had formerly been a minor "evil" had now become a "growing one."[53]

An array of measures was put forward to shore up the British Empire against this imaginary threat. A principal one was the classification of Punjabis in the Straits Settlements, through which much of this eastward migration took place, as members of "agricultural classes." They could then be brought under the 1883 Indian Emigration Act, which regulated the employment of "labourers" overseas and restricted their movement to an enumerated list of colonial destinations. Of course, as several critics pointed out, in Malaya Sikhs were rarely employed in agricultural labor, and they were "well able to take care of themselves"; hence they did not require the elaborate mechanism for their "protection" appropriate for indentured Indian laborers. Still, alleging that most Sikh migrants had been at one time, in the Punjab, engaged in agricultural labor, the Straits government in 1905 placed them, with all other Punjabis, under the restrictive rules of the Straits Indian Immigration Ordinance.[54]

More far-reaching was a proposal to end local recruitment altogether. Under this scheme, the Southeast Asian colonies would be required to follow the practice established for Africa in which the military authorities controlled recruiting and the recruit's term of service ended with repatriation back to India. Unlike the African arrangement, however, this proposal did not involve taking Sikh soldiers from their regiments, but simply making the army's recruiting agencies in India the sole entry point for those seeking police and military service outside India. There would then no longer be any occasion for Sikhs to wander through the Far East in search of employment, while those whose terms of service had expired would be safely back in India, out of reach of foreign recruiters. In 1903 and again in 1905 the Indian government insisted that "the surest means of arresting this flow of fighting men" was to enforce recruitment in India with compulsory repatriation. On occasion, the Indian authorities even claimed that such repatriation was in the interests of the men themselves. As Kitchener, the commander-in-chief, wrote patronizingly in 1904, "it will save them from the risk of being left out of work, and perhaps destitute, in a distant country."⁵⁵ Of course, the only interests truly served by this proposal would be those of the British themselves.

Such schemes evoked little enthusiasm in the colonies. As the governor of Hong Kong reported in 1908, after a year's trial the colony had spent some 8,152 rupees on recruitment in India, while there had been during this time "no decrease at all" in the number of those who offered themselves locally. It was, he concluded, "of no practical value for this Government to refuse to enlist men locally so long as hundreds of eligible recruits reach the colony and seek employment on the railway or in private capacities such as watchmen." Swettenham in the Straits Settlements concurred. There was no point, he said, in upsetting a system that had worked well "for a good many years" in favor of one that was more costly and less efficient. Further, he pointed out, repatriation was no boon to the Indian policemen, many of whom, encouraged to bring their families, had made their homes in Malaya during their years of service and hence had no desire to leave upon its termination.⁵⁶ Through the early years of the twentieth century, indeed, Malaya experienced a steady growth in its Sikh population.

The Chinese Treaty Ports posed a special problem. There, restrictive regulations threatened what had prompted the proposal in the first place — the security of the British Empire. In Shanghai, for instance, in 1903, some 40 percent of the international population was British, and the municipality employed two hundred Sikhs in its police force. Seventy percent of these, mostly from Lahore district, had previously served in the Indian Army. In addition, there were 180 Sikhs employed as watchmen by private firms and individuals, and a further 40 in search of work. If municipalities and other employers were forced to resort to the expensive hiring of police in India, the Foreign Office worried, they might well not employ Indians at all, but residents of other countries instead, "to the possible detriment of British interests."[57] The loss of Indian police in such cities as Shanghai, that is, could adversely affect Britain's predominance in China. Indeed, as the political situation within China deteriorated, the provision of a "sufficient" Sikh police force to protect the foreign settlements became ever more urgent. A 1905 Shanghai riot, which shook the European community, impelled the foreign-controlled Municipal Council, unwilling to rely on Chinese constables in a contest with their own people, to request an increase in the Indian branch of the police from 250 to 1,000, with the men to be volunteers from the Indian Army.[58]

Following the usual agitated discussion over whether Sikhs or some other community should be supplied, the Indian Army agreed to supply the necessary men. Even the skeptical Duff admitted that "we have undertaken an obligation to British administrations and cannot now repudiate it." In the end, however, the negotiations collapsed over the question of discipline. The Indian government insisted that these troops must be kept under military discipline, as was the case with the Indian contingents in Africa, by embodying the Indian Articles of War in the Shanghai Police Code. The British authorities in China, by contrast, anxious not to give the Chinese or the other European powers cause for suspicion, wished to make clear that this was "strictly a police force, not a small standing army that does police work." Hence, they wanted the civil courts of the Shanghai International Settlement to exercise jurisdiction over the disciplining of the force. In May 1907 the Indian government, disgruntled, withdrew its offer. Ordinary recruitment in Shanghai, together with one batch of 120 men recruited in India in 1906, sufficed to bring the Indian portion of the force up to some 500 by 1908. (The force also included 800 Chinese and 120 Europeans.)[59]

In 1909 the Indian government, confronted with continuing hostile responses from the colonial authorities, abandoned the effort to regulate the migration of Sikhs and other Punjabis seeking military employment.[60] But by the end of the first decade of the new century, the character of Sikh migration was fast changing. Increasingly, Sikhs sought more attractive arenas for overseas employment than that provided by colonial police work. Above all, they were drawn to the alluring shores of British Columbia, California, and Australia, where they took up employment in lumbering, agriculture, and similar pursuits. The Indian government did not in principle object to such migration and did not attempt to prohibit it by legislation. In these white settler–dominated states, however, the Sikhs promptly ran afoul of their racially exclusionary legislation, which forced them back into India, most notably in the famous *Komagatu Maru* incident in 1914, when some three hundred Sikhs tried unsuccessfully to land in Vancouver. Such treatment helped generate discontent among Sikhs, especially in Canada and the United States, where the Ghadr Party established itself as a focus for anti-British activity.

From their side, the British had begun rethinking their exclusive reliance on Sikh manpower for colonial policing. In addition to their ever present worries over depletion of the army's recruiting grounds, by the early twentieth century the British found the style and manner of the Sikh policeman ever less attractive. Initially, as we have seen, what the British saw as Sikh arrogance toward other races, especially in eastern Asia, was at worst an annoyance and may even have enhanced their appeal. As this "arrogance" grew, however, its disagreeable features became ever more apparent. As the Indian government wrote in 1908, on behalf of a proposal to widen the base of recruitment for the African contingents, "The political effect of allowing the Sikh to imagine that he is indispensable has been unfortunate, and the high rates of pay he receives abroad has made him discontented at home and inclined to grumble and be troublesome, while imbuing him and the Punjabi Musalman with an exaggerated idea of their own superiority to other classes."[61]

In September 1906 over half the Indian constables in Shanghai struck work for higher wages. While this incident was not politically motivated, it anticipated the kinds of difficulties that the British could expect in the future. In the short term, the Shanghai strike, as the British minister in Peking wrote, emphasized "the necessity of exercising great circumspection in making further increases in the Sikh Police Force." In the discussions regarding the supply of troops to China, one Indian officer even argued that "from a political point of view we might do well not to encourage soldiers of the Indian Army to go abroad and mix with the heterogeneous and democratic crowds in our colonies and elsewhere."[62] While the army might be able to damp down unrest among soldiers kept in barracks in India, and even to secure their loyalty by such measures as the award of land grants in canal colonies, overseas experience, in part perhaps because of the high pay and heightened expectations it brought with it, could well generate a sense of nationalist resentment at colonial rule. The streets of the great Asian cities were far from the dusty parade grounds of India.

But to reduce the army's dependence on Sikhs, in favor of a more balanced class composition, the Indian military had finally to confront the hoary martial races theory. This Indian officialdom was now increasingly willing to do. As the commanding officer at Peshawar wrote in 1907, "the practice of calling for volunteers [for colonial service] from certain classes of men only is invidious, and is regarded as a slight by those excluded, while other classes, like Sikhs, get an exaggerated idea of their superiority." Stretching but not abandoning the martial races idea, the Indian government in 1908 proposed opening up colonial service to Rajputana Rajputs and Jats from all provinces. The Jat Sikh had, of course, long formed the ideal soldier, so inclusion of other Jats involved but a small step; and Rajputs had won praise as "trustworthy" and "well liked" for their service in the Boxer rebellion. By a "judicious selection" of volunteers from these two groups, the governor-general argued, "we shall obtain a more extended training ground for our fighting material." More to the point perhaps, such recruitment would "increase the fighting strength of those classes which we know to be most loyal to the British Government." "Loyalty," in sum, as well as "martial spirit," now mattered.[63]

The secretary of state in London, in reply, saw no reason to stop short with merely these two additional classes. So in 1909 a vastly extended list of eligible communities was promulgated, including U.P. Rajputs, Hindustani Muslims, Deccani Marathas and Muslims, Konkani Marathas, and Dogras. In effect, colonial service was now opened up to every class in the Indian Army with the exception of Madrasis, Gurkhas, and Pathans. The exclusion of these three groups involved suitably tortuous reasoning. Madrasis, long disparaged as insufficiently martial, were simply dismissed as not "suitable for service in African contingents." Gurkhas were allegedly "not suited to the African climate," but they had in fact never been supplied to colonial contingents. In part, presumably, this was because the restrictions on their use imposed by the Nepal *darbar* made such recruitment impracticable. Pathans amply fitted the ideal of a martial race; in the Boxer campaign they were reputed to have "kept the Chinese in holy fear." But they had to be excluded on political grounds. To send them abroad "would result in an eventual increase of the fighting strength of the border tribes by a considerable number of well trained soldiers possessing ample money for the purchase of arms."[64]

In the immediate term these changes had little effect. In 1910, when the Indian government sought to replace a time-expired Sikh contingent in Uganda with one composed of U.P. Rajputs, the local authorities, with the Colonial Office, vigorously protested. Rajputs, they both insisted, could not stand the African climate, while their high-caste Hindu "scruples" over food and cooking would "seriously handicap" them on active duty. Grudgingly, the Indian government accepted a compromise in which the new Uganda contingent was split equally between Sikhs and Rajputs, at one hundred each.[65]

The Nyasaland government was equally adamant in its opposition to any change in the composition of its Sikh contingent. As the commanding officer Lt. P. C. H. Vincent wrote, if successive contingents were to be formed of different caste groups, varying caste prejudices, inexplicable to the Africans, would have to be accommodated, and extra expense would accrue to the government. Above all, the introduction of Muslims into the protectorate forces should be avoided. "The Moslem faith," Vincent argued, "is gaining ground in this Protectorate with rapid strides, and it would appear inexpedient to aid this movement by bringing Contingents to this country composed of Mahommedan Sepoys who might make common cause with the Tribes of the country inclined to Mahommedanism." Nyasaland was allowed to retain its Sikhs.[66]

Nevertheless, an era was coming to an end. For some years the East African governments had been gradually reducing the size of their Indian contingents on grounds of expense. By 1908 the Nyasaland contingent consisted of only two Indian NCOs and one hundred sepoys, while the special Indian force (6 KAR) of Punjabi Muslims raised for service in Somaliland had been reduced by half, from four hundred to two hundred men, with the reduction in force made up by enrolling Somali companies. As time went by, with frontier campaigning and African risings largely things of the past, the Indian contingents were used primarily for garrison and guard duty. Under such circumstances, the conviction grew up among the officers of the KAR that these units were immobile, "cumbersome," and not worth the expense of maintaining them — estimated at 13,000 pounds sterling a year in Uganda alone. The intention of the Indian government to replace Sikhs with mixed forces drawn from across India was perhaps the last straw. In 1912, expressing confidence in the reliability of their African troops, the Nyasaland and Uganda governments determined at last to do without an Indian force.[67] Ironically, the governor who ordered the withdrawal from Nyasaland was W. H. Manning, now Brig.-Gen. Sir William Manning, who as a young officer had accompanied the 1893 contingent from India. The last Nyasaland contingent left Zomba for India in December 1912, almost exactly twenty years after the first had arrived; while the last Uganda contingent was withdrawn two months later, in February 1913, and replaced by a new company of Baganda. The

140 Punjabi Muslims who made up the Indian contingent in the more unsettled Somaliland Protectorate remained in place.

In Southeast Asia as well, the days of predominantly Indian police forces were fast running out. During the years of the Great War, although the British enlisted vast numbers of Indians to fight for the empire, both Sikh and Muslim resentment at British colonialism still found ample soil in which to flourish. Muslim discontent, which flared up in a 1915 mutiny in Singapore, was fueled in part by opposition to the British war on the Ottoman Empire, while the Sikhs, pressed by intense military recruiting campaigns and more generally by the hardships of wartime existence, sought inspiration in the revolutionary rhetoric of the Ghadr Party, and subsequently in Gandhi's call for resistance.[68] Frightened, the British resorted to military coercion, most brutally in the infamous 1919 Amritsar massacre. Outside India, these events raised fresh doubts about the reliability of Sikh and Muslim police. In 1919, Walker's crack Sikh force, the Malay States Guides, was abolished. Increasingly in the years that followed, the colonial authorities encouraged Malays to join the police and military forces of the country. In so doing, the British initiated a process of accommodating and sustaining a growing Malay nationalism. Although Sikh immigration to Malaya did continue, during the interwar years the newcomers sought opportunities in commerce and entrepreneurship rather than in government service.[69]

Change came more slowly in eastern Asia. As China collapsed into a chaotic civil war, the British, precariously perched along its rim in vulnerable trading ports, anxiously sought the reassurance provided by an Indian force. At the outbreak of the Second World War in 1939, Indians still formed some 35 percent of the Hong Kong police. Still, the disruptions of the war, and then in 1947 Indian independence, set in motion a slow process of attrition that brought all recruitment of Indians for colonial police service to an end by the 1960s.[70]

CHAPTER 5

"Hard Hands and Sound Healthy Bodies"

Recruiting "Coolies" for Natal

Central to the successful working of the Victorian empire was the employment of indentured Indian laborers in colonies around the globe. Over nearly a century, from the 1830s to the 1920s, more than 1.3 million Indians left their homeland under contracts of indenture that bound them in most cases to work for a minimum of five years. The destinations to which these laborers were sent spanned the globe. Half a million went to the Indian Ocean islands of Mauritius and Reunion; over 400,000 labored in British Guiana and the British West Indies, with an additional 100,000 dispatched to French and Dutch colonies in the Caribbean; 150,000 indentured Indians went to Natal in South Africa; and some 60,000 to Fiji in the Pacific Ocean. A further 30,000 over a brief period at the turn of the twentieth century were employed in East Africa.[1]

Many of these laborers initially took the place of freed slaves on plantations in Mauritius and the West Indies. During the later nineteenth century the growing demand for sugar spurred the expansion of indentured labor recruitment and encouraged its spread to new regions such as Natal and Fiji. This unprecedented worldwide recruitment of Indian laborers, organized and controlled jointly by the imperial, Indian, and colonial governments, makes strikingly visible the central role of India within the British Empire. By its sheer size and scope, the system of indentured labor recruitment stands apart from the other streams of migration and influence — of imperial connections — examined in this study. Indian soldiers and policemen may have helped sustain the fabric of empire; but the willing arms and backs of hundreds of thousands of Indian laborers alone

136

enabled the empire, and by extension Britain itself, to prosper. Further, as an enduring legacy that has remained up to the present, indenture left behind communities of Indians in those countries where their ancestors toiled in the cane fields.

The indentured labor system has been the subject of much study and, especially since the 1970s, has given us a rich corpus of scholarship. Inspired by Hugh Tinker's pioneering *A New System of Slavery* (1974), most of the existing studies have examined two principal aspects of the indenture enterprise: the administrative structure set up to regulate it, together with the ongoing debates in Victorian Britain over the feasibility and morality of indenture; and the treatment of Indian workers as they traveled from India to the colonies and then labored on sugar plantations.[2] Some recent works have further assessed on the basis of ship lists the caste and regional backgrounds of emigrants.[3] As a result we possess substantial information about the individuals who were recruited, including for some even their height and family status. Efforts have been made as well to correlate socioeconomic well-being, and the cycles of prosperity and scarcity in Indian agriculture, with the propensity to migrate.

Despite the contributions of this scholarship, the collection and dispatch of laborers in India has received little attention. At best, as in Brij Lal's *Girmitiyas: The Origin of the Fiji Indians,* we have descriptions of the administrative structure through which emigrants were processed for shipment. At the apex of this structure, following a number of revelations of abuse and maltreatment in the early days of the system, were "protectors" responsible to the imperial authorities. To these men, posted in the Indian ports and in the colonies, fell the task of ensuring that intending emigrants were healthy and left India of their own free will, and that once they were in the colony of their indenture, they were treated according to a set of regulations that ensured fair and equitable treatment. Beneath this umbrella of "protection" were emigration agencies established by each of the sugar colonies, in Calcutta and Madras, to oversee recruitment. These agencies supervised "upcountry" subagents who in their turn employed recruiters hired locally to sign up potential emigrants. These recruits were then sent down to the port, where they boarded ships for their new colonial "homes." How far indenture involved the abduction and deception of innocents, and how far it provided opportunities willingly grasped on the part of desperately poor Indians — the subject of an enduring and intense debate — cannot be resolved on the basis of available documentation, and I do not endeavor to do so here.

In this chapter, as far as the available evidence permits, I look closely at the recruiting activities, as they took place on the ground in India, of the South African colony of Natal between 1860 and 1911. Natal is not unique, though it has distinctive characteristics, but it does provide a convenient lens through which to assess such questions as, How were colonial recruiters selected, remunerated, and disciplined? What criteria did they in turn use to decide whom to recruit for indentured labor in the colony? Which castes and regions of India were favored, which disfavored, and why? How successful were Natal's recruiters in fulfilling the colony's objectives, and how does Natal compare in its recruiting operation with other comparable colonies such as Mauritius and Fiji? In sum, this essay seeks to bring to life, not the intending emigrant, but Natal's staff of recruiters as individuals trying to fill quotas and earn money. Throughout, the aim is to understand the practices and perceptions that informed the day-to-day working of indentured labor recruitment.

Blacks, Boers, Englishmen, and Indians

In 1860, as Natal turned toward India for its supply of labor, it was following in the footsteps of Mauritius and the colonies of the West Indies. For these other colonies the recruitment of Indians had provided an alternative source of labor to that of slaves, who after emancipation in 1833 disdained, whenever they could, the backbreaking work of cutting cane. Yet Natal, on its part, had never possessed a slave economy; and unlike the thinly settled Caribbean islands, Natal contained a substantial black African population. Hence, before one can usefully address Natal's "coolie" recruitment, one needs to ask why Natal solicited Indian labor in the first place.

Natal had been annexed to the British Empire in 1843, largely to keep that strategic coastal territory out of the hands of the Boers who were streaming into interior South Africa following the Great Trek of 1835. The colony nevertheless had little to offer British settlers, who formed by the 1850s a white community of some 10,000. Devastated by Shaka's wars, the colony was then home to some 120,000 to 150,000 Africans; outside its boundaries, in the as yet unsubjugated areas of Zululand, resided perhaps a quarter of a million more Africans. At first glance, there might appear to have been ample labor for whatever enterprises the Natal colonists chose to develop. In fact, there was almost none.

Throughout the 1840s and 1850s vast tracts of land, thinly populated since Shaka's time, remained largely unoccupied and were at once laid claim to by Natal's earliest British settlers. By 1849, nearly two million acres of land had been divided among a mere 360 claimants. A decade later, fifteen men controlled some 700,000 acres; and in 1860 they were joined by the Natal Land and Colonisation Company, with its mammoth holdings of half a million acres. For such landholders, direct capitalist farming was out of the question. Most, indeed, were speculators whose limited capital was wholly tied up in the purchase of land and who sought a return in its later appreciation in value as the colony prospered. In the meantime, these men turned to the extraction of rents from African tenants as the most attractive way of securing some return on their investments. They had no interest in measures designed to force Africans off the land and into labor relationships.[4]

During the same years, the colonial government was inaugurating a system of paternalist "indirect rule" for those Africans who remained outside the market economy. Under Theophilus Shepstone, as described in chapter 1 above, the government set aside native reserves in Natal totaling two million acres in which chiefly authority was affirmed and white settlement prohibited. Though inadequate to maintain twentieth-century populations, these reserves were expressly made large enough at the time to avoid, in Shepstone's words, "so crowding the Kaffirs as to compel them to leave their location and seek work." Hence those Africans who settled in the reserves could resume traditional subsistence agriculture and meet their tax obligations by cultivating commercial crops on part of their land. Indeed, with only a small and largely urban white population, Natal's African cultivators prospered from a ready market for their crops in the towns.

Under these circumstances, between the reserves and the tenancies available on Crown and speculators' lands, Africans in Natal had little incentive to undertake wage labor for white planters. From the outset, therefore, the white farmers had railed against the system of native reserves. One Natal newspaper listed what was required: "the breaking up of the locations; a readjustment of native taxation; the cautious but firm discouragement of the heathen customs that bind the Kaffir to an indolent and licentious life; a more comprehensive and stringent magisterial surveillance," and so on. But none of this was practical politics. So, inspired by the example of Mauritius, where Indian labor had reversed the decline of its sugar industry since 1843, Natal's planters decided that the salvation of their fledgling economy lay in sugar cultivation and in the importation of indentured Indian laborers. The prospect of prosperity at last lay before this impoverished British colony.[5]

Despite this enthusiasm, Natal faced several disadvantages as it sought to take advantage of the booming mid-Victorian market for sugar. Natal's mild subtropical climate, first of all, enforced longer growing seasons and lower yields than were available in hotter, moister, fully tropical lands. Secondly, nearby Mauritius — though it provided a model and a source of talent, for many of Natal's planters and their technical staff came from that island — also provided its upstart rival, in an era of free trade, with stiff competition both in export markets and in South Africa itself. Nor was the local market, before the development of the Rand gold mines in the 1890s, at all expansive. Further, Natal had to contend with severe fluctuations in the sugar markets. A depression in the mid-1860s led to a six-year halt in the importation of Indian labor, and a sharp fall in the world price of sugar in 1884 precipitated declines in acreage and in Indian immigration that were not made good until the early 1890s. Sugar, nevertheless, sustained by Indian labor, remained from the 1860s onward the mainstay of the Natal economy.

It is essential that readers be aware at the outset of the source materials consulted for this essay. It is largely based on letter books in the KwaZulu Natal Archives, Pietermaritzburg, that contain copies of day-to-day correspondence between the Natal emigration agents in Calcutta and Madras, their superiors in Durban, and their subagents scattered throughout interior India.[6] Although this archive makes this study possible, its omissions restrict it in significant ways. Above all, for northern India, only the outgoing letters from the Calcutta agent to the upcountry subagents, not the subagents' replies, have been preserved; and the archive contains no letters between the subagents and the village-level recruiters whom they employed. For southern India we possess none of the internal correspondence between the main recruiting agency, Parry & Co., and its subagents in the interior. Hence, at the lowest level, much must be inferred and much cannot be known at all. Despite its wealth of data on policy matters, the government of India's emigration proceedings pay little attention to the recruitment procedures of individual colonies. A few special investigative reports, however, among them most notably George Grierson's *Report on Colonial Emigration from the Bengal Presidency* (Calcutta, 1883), offer useful insights and will be cited as appropriate.

The Early Years, 1860–1880

To inaugurate Natal's indentured labor recruitment, W. M. Collins, the colony's postmaster general, appointed as special agent, set out for India in early 1860. Not surprisingly, on the way he stopped off at Mauritius. There, as he wrote back to the Natal colonial secretary, he toured several of the island's sugar estates and so "had the opportunity of personally inspecting the system upon which the general treatment of Indian labourers is conducted at Mauritius." With the letter he enclosed a number of Mauritian forms and documents relating to the treatment of Indian immigrants. From Mauritius, Collins went on first to Madras and then to Calcutta. In each place he appointed an emigration agent to take charge of coolie recruitment (as it was then called) for the colony. The Madras agent was Henry Burton. Already acting as agent for Mauritius, Trinidad, and British Guiana, Burton simply added responsibility for Natal to his work for these other colonies. For each adult coolie shipped to Natal, Burton was to receive a personal remuneration of three rupees. His recruiters were to receive four rupees for each adult. In Calcutta, Collins appointed Hunt Marriott, since 1858 the emigration agent for British Guiana, as Natal's agent as well.[7] As we shall see, even as they reduced each colony's expenses, these overlapping responsibilities were to prove a continuing source of friction.

Emigration commenced almost at once. The first emigrant ship, the *Truro*, left Madras in October 1860 with 342 individuals on board and dropped anchor in Durban on November 16. The *Belvedere*, with 310 passengers from Calcutta, arrived shortly thereafter.[8] During the subsequent five years up to 1866, a total of some 5,400 indentured Indians arrived in Natal. Indian immigration then came to a temporary halt. Subsequently, complaints of mistreatment by the first batch of returned Indians in 1871, after the completion of their ten-year indenture contract, provoked an overhaul of the system. This included appointment of a Protector of Indian Immigrants in Natal and an Indian Immigration Trust Board. In 1874 indentured emigration from India to Natal recommenced under these new arrangements.[9]

We may begin by looking at the operation in northern India. Although that region supplied only one-third of Natal's immigrants, it is better documented in the archival records. As the old Natal agency had been closed down in 1866, the Colonial Office, with the concurrence of the Natal government, in 1874 appointed H. A. Firth, emigration agent for British Guiana, to act as emigration agent in Calcutta for Natal as well. With the prospect of renewed emigration, Firth at once requested his subagents upcountry to collect recruits. According to the government's regulations, each batch of one hundred emigrants had to include forty women. Hence, as Firth told his subagents, whenever men were sent without the proper proportion of females, they would be returned. "I can pay only," he wrote further, "for those who are shipped and all expenses of whatever nature must be borne by you for recruiting, registration, license fees, brass badges, printed forms, railway fares, and for the cost of returning rejected coolies to their homes. Two thirds of the amount agreed on for each adult I will pay three days after arrival in this [Calcutta] depot, and the balance three days after embarkation."[10] The rates of remuneration requested by the different subagents varied between sixteen and twenty rupees per adult male, with usually an additional two-rupee bonus payable for females.

Firth's subagents, following customary practice for colonial recruitment in northern India, were mostly appointed to districts in the eastern Gangetic plain, from Lucknow to Bihar. The initial appointees, the areas where they were to recruit, and the number of emigrants each was to send down annually to Calcutta were as follows:

D. H. R. Moses	Ghazipur	250
Nursingh Pershad Chatterjee	Ghazipur	100
Munshi Muzaffar Ali	Faizabad	250
Babu Gopal Chander Mookerjee	Jamalpur	75
Babu Triluckonauth Nandy	Dinapur	100
Messrs. Andrews and Hindry	Calcutta	200
R. Hendry	Bankipur	200
Ramjaum Khan	Unao	150
Awazali	Lucknow	150
A. Reuben	Gorakhpur	50

In May two additional individuals were added to the list of subagents:

| James W. Lowther | Mirzapur |
| Babu Chander Cant Chatterjee | Benares |

During May and June, as recruiting proceeded, Firth kept in close touch with his subagents. Sometimes he simply urged them on, as when he told Muzaffar Ali on May 13, "I hope you will be able to send me plenty of coolies." The major problem was that of poaching. Twice, Reuben complained that D. H. R. Moses was recruiting in the district assigned to him, that of Gorakhpur. By June Muzaffar Ali had also begun to complain about Moses's activities, alleging that Moses had hired away one of his recruiters. Sternly, Firth told Moses such proceedings were "quite improper and irregular" and ordered him to cease employing other agents' recruiters and to stay out of their districts. Things could go wrong even in Calcutta itself. As an exasperated Firth wrote to Gopal Chander Mookerjee on May 21, "Your chuprassee [escort] it appears allowed five men of your last challan [batch] to go to the Bazaar in Calcutta just after their arrival here. Three of these men have not since returned, and I certainly shall not pay for them." By the end of June the subagents were told to stop sending emigrants, as the funds available to reimburse them — some 3,800 pounds — had been exhausted. During the course of that year some 4,310 Indians, by far the largest number to that date, arrived in Natal from Calcutta.

By 1876, despite an increase in the rate of commission, now ranging from twenty-five to thirty rupees per adult, the number of emigrants dispatched from Calcutta had begun to lag behind the colony's requirements. That year saw a mere 754 arrivals, and the next 1,089. (For year-by-year figures, see the appendix, pp. 163–64.) As a result, F. Colepeper, clerk in the Natal Protector's office, was sent to India to see what could be done to improve recruiting. What Colepeper saw was not encouraging. "It is astonishing," he wrote in dismay, "to see the number of chimnies smoking day and night in Calcutta and its vicinity. The Hoogly begins to resemble the Thames." As a result, he said, "it has become a common practice with coolies to allow themselves to be recruited merely in order to get to Calcutta," where they then "desert at the first opportunity." In the interior, despite the extension of recruiting operations so far inland that railway fares of up to twelve rupees were being paid to send recruits to Calcutta, overseas emigration was deterred by the "immense impetus given to cultivation and the employment of labour by the railways, irrigation and other public works, and [by] the abundance and cheapness of the various food grains of late." In addition, there was the competition provided by the tea gardens of Darjeeling and Assam, whose demand for labor "is practically unlimited."[11] At no time, as Natal was only beginning to discover in 1877, were colonial recruiters ever able to disregard the powerful attractions of such nearby destinations as Assam and Calcutta itself.

To deal with this problem Colepeper put forward a number of recommendations. They included a further increase in recruiters' pay, a possible reduction in the term of indenture to eight years from ten, and holding out to potential recruits the ease of obtaining a plot of ground for cultivation in Natal at the end of the period of indenture. He further urged an end to the joint recruiting agency with British Guiana. This arrangement suited both colonies, for recruiting could take place for Natal during the first half of the year, when West Indian recruitment was prohibited, and thus the recruiting staff kept fully employed. Nevertheless, in Colepeper's view, this union was an "unholy alliance," the "most expensive way in which we could have attempted not to gain our end." Colepeper preferred establishing an independent Natal agency or, if that were deemed too expensive, a joint operation with Mauritius under which, unlike that with Guiana, Natal would no longer be restricted to a limited recruiting season each year. In a further report the following year, James Caldwell reiterated the advantages to be secured from a joint agency with Mauritius. The problem lay, as he saw it, with the upcountry recruiters, who "dictated terms to the agents in Calcutta by playing one [colony's] agency against another to enhance their prices."[12] The Natal government instead determined to reduce costs by closing down the Calcutta agency altogether in favor of a single office in Madras.

After two years with few new immigrants arriving from northern India — none in 1879 and 505 in 1880 — Natal decided to reopen its Calcutta agency. The old arrangement with British Guiana was re-established, and H. A. Firth resumed his position as emigration agent for both colonies. Firth argued on behalf of the joint scheme that there was "ample time" in the interval between the annual recruiting seasons for the West Indies to get some four ships a year off to Natal, and that it would be far more economical to use "my recruiters," who are "at hand ready to take up the work at once whenever Demerara [Guiana] closes," rather than to recruit a fresh staff. The Natal authorities also found another argument persuasive. "It is not desirable," the Indian Immigration Trust Board noted, "to confine the importation of labour to one agency alone, on the grounds that to prevent combination amongst the labourers on the estates, it would seem expedient to have a mixture of Indians, viz., Bengalees and Madrasees."[13] The imperatives of "divide and rule" and of economy conveniently went hand in hand in support of Firth's proposal.

Opportunities and Obstacles

Before resuming large-scale recruitment for Natal, Firth sent one of his Calcutta staff, Khetta Mohan Chatterjee, on a tour of the emigration depots of northern India. Chatterjee's daily inspection reports of these depots, where emigrants were collected before being sent to Calcutta, give us a glimpse of the ongoing process of coolie recruitment. After spending a few days at Bankipur and Dinapur in Bihar, he went on to Allahabad. There he found only six males in the depot, and the subagent full of excuses. The agent said, Chatterjee recounted, that "he would exert his best and urge on his recruiters, but the cheapness of living at present, owing to the abundance of crops, is a great drawback to the supply of a large number" of emigrants. With depots for Trinidad, Jamaica, and Natal, situated side by side, each supplying no more than twenty recruits a month, Chatterjee left Allahabad convinced that "affairs are at present very gloomy here." Two days later, moving rapidly upcountry, he found himself at Meerut. Asked to wait, in the "excessive cold" of a North Indian winter, until the local subagent Ilahibux returned from accompanying some coolies to Calcutta, Chatterjee refused. "I shall not undertake to travel 38 miles where there is no railway communication [to Bulandshahr] merely to help him in collecting half a dozen more people, at the sacrifice of my health." Returning by way of Cawnpore, Lucknow, and Benares, Chatterjee found everywhere unfavorable recruiting prospects due to the cheapness of grain and great competition from other colonial agencies. From Benares, for instance, he reported that "Mr. D. Moses, who is recruiting for Jamaica, has five depots here; Mr. Joshua for Trinidad two depots; and the French subagent has a depot also, besides our own."[14]

While some subagents remained in place from the 1870s, employed by British Guiana during the intervening years, the resumption of Natal recruitment also involved the hiring of new subagents and substantial shuffling of posts. The opening of the 1882 season was, for instance, announced by circular notice sent to the following individuals:

J. R. Moses	Allahabad
Nursingh Prasad Chatterjee	Ghazipur
Shaikh Ghoorah	Buxar (Baksar)
Meer Abbas	Lucknow
Babu Birbul	Cawnpore
Ahmed Khan	Faizabad
E. M. Emerson	Benares
Nobin Chunder Roy	Baliaghatta
Babu Kandhyalal	Benares
Babu Premchand Bannerjee	Dinapur
Deeplall Singh	Bankipur

The intense competition among agencies, with the animosities and poaching of recruits that resulted, spurred a move to tap new areas outside the established recruiting grounds in the eastern Gangetic plain. This region, comprising Bihar and the easternmost districts of what became the United Provinces, had long drawn colonial recruiters because its dense rural population and deep poverty increased the likelihood of successful recruitment.[15] While moving outside this region was attractive in principle, it threw up obstacles that could not easily be overcome. Firth encouraged plans to set up a subagency at Agra, but he was less enthusiastic about moving north and west into the Upper Doab and Punjab. He warned Emerson, for instance, in March 1882 not to recruit toward the Punjab "because women cannot be had there." The following year he reiterated this warning in a letter to his newly appointed Meerut subagent, Kunj Behari. "I beg you not to recruit at Amballah because women are very scarce at that place and I have always found the men to be very troublesome." Kunj Behari paid no attention and opened recruiting at Amballa. Firth sternly told him, "Having done so you must accept the consequences. These Punjabees give no end of trouble and create discontent amongst the other peaceable coolies in the depot." Part of the problem arose from their description by the British as a martial race and their subsequent recruitment for military and police service. They were, as Firth wrote, "quite unfit for field labour" as they "expect to be employed as soldiers or policemen."[16] Similar concerns had caused the Natal government in 1874 to abandon a plan to form a contingent of Sikh Pioneers for military service and road making in the colony. As W. M. Mcleod wrote at the time, "I feared that the Sikhs enlisted as Pioneers would not consent to perpetual road-making, and would not consider occasional drilling as military service."[17]

In the case of other regions, not Natal or its recruiting officers but the government of India posed obstacles to recruitment. One such prohibited group was Nepalis. Initially, as Firth wrote to Deeplall Singh in 1883, "I believe plenty of Nepaulese are to be met with at Durbhunga and Muzufferpore. These people are so very much stronger than other coolies that I am anxious to get as many as possible." He had even secured a female recruiter, who "intends to recruit only Nepaulese, especially women, and speaks their language fluently." Anxious to preserve its supply of Gurkhas for the military, the Indian government refused to permit such recruitment. Again and again into the 1890s, the emigration agent had to remind recruiters that they were not to enlist Nepalis. Nor did the Natal recruiters have any better success with a proposed recruiting center at Kurseong in the north Bengal hills. The officiating emigration agent wrote to Durban in 1884, "The Lieutenant Governor of Bengal has prohibited me from recruiting coolies from the Kurseong and Darjeeling districts where the climate is cool all the year round, as he says that the tea estates in the neighbourhood are already suffering from a scarcity of labour."[18]

More contentious was the matter of recruitment from the Ganjam district along the coast south of Orissa. This district, though it lay within the Madras Presidency, was easily accessible from Calcutta by sea. Hence in

1882 Firth awarded licenses to eleven recruiters there. By the following season these men were busily "engaged in various villages in the interior of the District, where owing to the distress which at present prevails there are plenty of labourers eager to emigrate." He anticipated that half of the twelve hundred coolies requisitioned by Natal for 1883 would be secured from Ganjam and that these "would form a most valuable acquisition to the labour force of the Colony and being in families are more likely to become permanent settlers." But the Indian authorities insisted that recruitment from the Madras Presidency must take place through the agencies located in that presidency, and so with the end of the 1883 season, they put a stop to this operation.[19]

Interior Central India still remained open, and this encouraged Natal's recruiters to move in that direction as well. From 1882 recruiters were working in Jabalpur, and the following year Firth urged R. Moses to set up a recruiting station in Bilaspur under the direction of his son Jacob. The distance from Calcutta, however, enforced higher payments to recruiters — three rupees additional per head for Jabalpur over Allahabad, and a further one rupee for Bilaspur — and so made substantial recruitment in these thinly peopled tracts impractical. Hence, by the end of the 1880s, Natal's subagencies were confined almost exclusively to the traditional recruiting grounds of Bihar and the eastern districts of the United Provinces. An attempt at the turn of the century to revisit the Central Provinces produced no better result. As the emigration agent wrote to the Immigration Trust Board in 1904, "The principal subagent at Raipur in the Central Provinces sends barely a dozen emigrants at a time, and those at Jabalpur, Hoshangabad, and Bilaspur are doing absolutely nothing."[20] Fiji, it might be noted, impelled by the same imperatives, did no better in its efforts to recruit in the Punjab and Central Provinces; and it too was shut out of Nepal.

Objections were continually raised, usually from Natal itself, to the recruitment of certain categories of individuals. Among these the most prominent were Brahmins and Muslims. Brahmins, as Firth wrote to all the subagents in March 1883, "are constantly giving trouble in the depot, so on no account whatever must you send any more Brahmins. They also give much trouble in the Colony and are strongly objected to." Equally problematic was the recruitment of Muslims. Although Muslims had been included among the emigrants from the time of the first voyages of the *Truro* and *Belvedere,* as time went on, opposition to their recruitment began to surface in Natal. In 1889, when Muzaffar Ali at Faizabad asked permission to send "two Mahomedan married couples who are strong healthy agricultural labourers," the emigration agent, now R. W. Mitchell, reluctantly refused. The "instructions from the Colony," he said, "are positive. . . . I cannot act." Rather disingenuously, however, a few days later when R. Moses inquired about taking on some Muslim women, Mitchell replied, "nothing is said about sex. I fancy you may send a few Mahomedan women but no men."[21] In 1893 the emigration agent again reminded his subagents, as he set out their recruiting quotas for the coming season, that "Natal will take Thakoors and Chettris [Kshatriya — traditional warrior castes] but no Musalmans." By 1896 Mitchell's informal exemption of Muslim women from this prohibition had become official. "Mohamedan female emigrants can be accepted," the emigration agent now told his subagents, "if they have *hard hands* and have *worked as labourers*." More generally, agents were instructed, "you may pass all females of eighteen and over no matter whether Mohamedan or of other than the lowest caste, *provided* they have reasonably hard hands and are not beggars, devotees, or dancing girls."[22] Finally, in 1903, anxious to enlarge the emigrant pool, the Natal government relented and gave Mitchell permission to allow "Musalmans to be recruited, of the *labouring class* only, men who have hard hands and have worked always in the fields."

The wide range of prohibited categories — of castes, communities, and regions — did not please the recruiters in India. Such restrictions, after all, made their work that much more difficult. After receiving instructions from Natal, for instance, that "no residents of towns are to be recruited on any account," Mitchell immediately protested to Durban that a desirable immigrant is "usually one who has succeeded in rising above the ordinary tiller of the soil and owes his robust habit of body to better food, shelter from the weather, and the less laborious life of a gatekeeper, messenger, or body servant."[23] Despite their common interest in seeing the indenture system flourish, inevitably the recruiters' interests were not the same as those of Natal's planters. The one wanted to meet his annual quota of emigrants as quickly and as economically as possible; the other wanted individuals whose caste, gender, and residential background offered the strongest assurance that they would, or so the planting community thought, set energetically to work upon arrival.

Patience was most sorely tried, on both sides, when so-called "ineffectives" were sent back from Natal, for here a substantial expenditure of time and money was at stake. Acknowledging to the Protector in Natal that "I can fully understand how annoying it is" to receive unfit men, still, Mitchell insisted, the proportion of "useless" emigrants was very small. As regards those returned from the ship *Sophia Jackson* in 1885, he wrote, "I find the pot maker is a 'Kahar,' one of the best labouring castes; the man marked 'Brahmin' who never worked is a Thakur and in this caste many excellent labourers exist. The two beggars certainly should not have been shipped, but when you see two sturdy men, and beggars are unusually so, with hard hands produced at the local recruiter's by a judicious course of wood chopping, one is apt to overlook the question of caste."[24]

These self-imposed restrictions took visible shape over the years in a marked reduction in the numbers of Brahmin and Muslim recruits. Caste data compiled by Surendra Bhana show a decline in the numbers of Muslims as a percentage of Natal's North Indian migrant stream, from a high of 19 percent in the early 1880s to no more than 3 percent annually by the end of the century. Brahmins, never more than 4 percent of the North Indian total in the earliest years of recruitment, fell away to 1 percent or less as time went on.[25] Still, given the colony's labor requirements, a rigorous prohibition could never be sustained. Other colonies, as we shall see, had no better success in restricting undesirable high-caste and Muslim recruitment.

Agents, Subagents, Recruiters: The System in Operation

As time went on, the staffing and operation of Natal's Calcutta recruiting agency became increasingly regularized. Mitchell, as emigration agent, remained in charge of the office, shared with British Guiana (Demerara), from 1884 until the termination of indentured recruitment in 1911. A few subagents likewise were employed for long uninterrupted terms in areas where emigrants were most readily available, and these individuals did much of the colony's work. About these individuals we possess some, though mostly scattered and fragmentary, information. Although local Hindus were widely employed as well, Muslims, Jews, and educated Bengali *bhadralok* seem to have been disproportionately represented among Natal's north Indian subagents. Some subagents rose through the ranks from initial employment as ordinary recruiters. Those who succeeded in doing so, as Grierson noted, were men "superior in intelligence and honesty to the average recruiter" and had as well, "while recruiter, managed to save some money," for some capital was required to set up a subagency. Sheikh Ghoorah, for instance, subagent at Baksar (Bihar) in the 1880s, impressed Grierson as "a good example" of the subagent who had "risen by ability and superior honesty from the ranks of recruiters." Ghoorah, Grierson reported, was born in Demerara. He returned to

India as a boy with his mother in 1858, only to return to Demerara under indenture in 1861 with her and his uncle. There he learned English and served as a hospital assistant. On his mother's death in 1872 he came back to India once again and settled at Baksar, where he was taken on first as recruiter, then as subagent, for Natal and Guiana.[26]

Not infrequently, family connections served to tie individuals effectively to the recruiting operation. Muzaffar Ali, for instance, taken on as Faizabad subagent when emigration resumed in 1874, remained, with an extended interruption during the early 1880s, on the Natal register until 1901. His son Mohamed Sarfaraz Ali then took over the post. This change, however, was not wholly successful, for Sarfaraz was subjected to repeated criticism for a variety of offenses, among them working on behalf of Fiji instead of Natal, employing debarred recruiters, and claiming as his own emigrants recruited for other subagents. Most striking perhaps was the case of the Moses family, whose members played a central role in Natal recruiting for some forty years. Sometimes on his own account and sometimes together with one of his three sons, R. Moses headed the Ghazipur subagency throughout the 1880s and 1890s. The eldest son, David H. R. Moses, who began recruiting at Ghazipur in 1874, operated a subagency at Benares during much of the 1880s and worked at Calcutta from 1892 to 1894. The second son, Jacob, set up a subagency at Allahabad in 1881 and in 1883 moved on to try his hand at recruiting in Bilaspur. Although the emigration agent wrote to the father, "I think it can be worked if only your son Jacob will exercise a little courage and determination," that agency had in the end to be abandoned. Subsequently, Jacob appears to have worked as a recruiter under his father. The third son, M. E. R. Moses, held a recruiting license in Ghazipur during the mid-1890s and managed his father's business affairs. On his father's retirement in 1903, M. E. R. Moses succeeded to the charge of the Ghazipur agency. As Mitchell wrote, approving the appointment, "I hope you will make as efficient a subagent [as your father]."

Despite their employment on a regular long-term basis, Natal's subagents continued to participate in the abuses commonly associated with labor recruitment. Of these, the most prominent were those of poaching emigrants from territories assigned to other subagents and surreptitious recruiting for colonial agencies other than Natal. Complaints of poaching never ceased, but for men such as Mitchell, anxious to keep up a steady flow of emigrants from Calcutta to Natal, the most exasperating practice was the diversion of recruits to other colonies. Such practices, or the threat of them, were of course attractive to subagents because they enhanced the local agent's income and, with it, his bargaining leverage.

Among the worst offenders were Muzaffar Ali and his son at Faizabad. In 1899 Mitchell discovered that Muzaffar was sending recruits to the Surinam agency at a rate of some 250 in a month. This was a matter of some consequence, for Muzaffar, whom Mitchell sometimes referred to as his "head subagent," regularly supplied Natal more emigrants than did anyone else. Mitchell was, he acknowledged, "unfortunately quite powerless to punish him in any way." So he resorted to scolding him like a schoolmaster with an errant child. "This sort of thing cannot go on. . . . You are tempted by the high commission offered by the Surinam agency to desert an agency for which you have worked for years past. Have you no sense of shame to act in this manner?" When Muzaffar protested his innocence, Mitchell retorted angrily that "I know all that goes on so you may save yourself the trouble of trying to throw dust in my eyes." Informing the Protector in Natal of this incident, Mitchell acknowledged that "I could of course increase my commission and so obtain the coolies he is now supplying elsewhere, but it would not be advisable to do so, as I find that once the commission to a contractor is increased, it is impossible to reduce it again."[27] Matters did not improve when Sarfaraz Ali took charge. In 1902 Mitchell chided Sarfaraz, "This is one of the worst lots of people you have ever sent me. It is quite clear to me that owing to the higher rates Fiji gives you are making over all the best people to them! If you don't want to work for Natal why don't you say so, and be done with it?" On this occasion, however, Mitchell had to concede defeat. Two days later he informed the Natal subagents that they would all henceforth receive Fiji rates.[28]

Of course more than one could play this game. Muzaffar Ali was himself victim as often as victor in the ongoing scramble for "coolies." In the midst of the controversy over the diversion of emigrants to Surinam, Muzaffar Ali complained bitterly that the subagent Ezekial Solomon had been recruiting in the districts reserved for him; and that Solomon had, in particular, "secretly removed" a female recruit, originally registered by him at Faizabad, to Solomon's Bahraich depot, where he had her reregistered. Like Mitchell, Muzaffar too was at the mercy of his underlings. Three of his own recruiters, posted at Cawnpore, he complained to Mitchell, had "been supplying coolies collected by them to Jamaica and they have not given him a single coolie since the last two months."[29]

Among the abuses associated with indentured labor recruitment, undoubtedly one of the most common was mistreatment of intending emigrants. It is not my intention here to assess how intending emigrants fared at the subagents' depots or on the subsequent journey to Calcutta. Evidence is, in any case, scanty. Grierson for one praised the arrangements in several Natal depots, including those of Sheikh Ghoorah at Baksar and Deep Lall Singh at Bankipur. Of the latter, he said, "The building is a commodious one, and has ample accommodation, with a well in the court-yard. . . . The building was clean and tidy . . . [with the emigrants] given each day as much uncooked food as they can eat." Of the journey to Calcutta, he asserted that the emigrants get "sufficient clothing to keep them warm and decent," with "ample railway accommodation, reserved compartments, one to every eight coolies." Grierson did admit, however, that some depots were "worse than this description."[30]

The recruiting staff had, of course, little interest in taking notice of instances of mistreatment. When on occasion protests did surface, however, Mitchell at least felt obliged to investigate them, if only to avoid getting into trouble with the Indian government. When one "Mungroo, a carpenter by trade," complained on arrival in Calcutta in December 1892 that the recruiter who had accompanied him had "kept back his tool chest and a small lotah [brass container] valued at Rs. 8.8.0 on the plea that they could not go on the train with him," Mitchell wrote D. H. R. Moses, asking him as the subagent in charge to inquire into the matter. Complaints by emigrants, Mitchell noted, "are almost invariably true, and if the man does not get satisfaction at once I shall bring him before the protector, in which case an investigation will be conducted at Benares. In the meantime the man cannot embark, and you are deprived of the commission." Moses managed to recover only a few of the man's tools; the recruiter, he was told, should make good the difference, some seven rupees, and should further be penalized a month's wages, another seven rupees, as some compensation for Mungroo's inability to embark on the ship for which his passage had been booked.[31] Another incident in 1900 involved four emigrants recruited in Cawnpore, who complained of being robbed of a total of Rs. 10.13.0; in addition, the one female member of the group claimed that she had been beaten and separated from her family. The woman was sent back at the Cawnpore subagent's expense and the district magistrate notified, for, as Mitchell wrote, "it is impossible such frequent complaints, the like of which come from no other sub-agents, can be without foundation in fact."[32]

The success of the recruiting operation depended ultimately on those who went out into the villages to sign up men and women for labor in Natal. About these village-level recruiters we know very little. They were hired and paid by the subagents, to whom they were responsible. Before commencing work, however, they had to secure recruiting licenses from the local district magistrates. These had to be renewed annually and were occasionally denied, or even withdrawn after issuance. Most frequently such cancellations involved recruiters caught working for another colonial agency when licensed to recruit only for Natal. More serious was the cancellation in 1895 of the license issued to Wazir Ali, one of Muzaffar Ali's recruiters, who was "reported to be a notorious badmash [crook] and to use the depot as a gambling hall." The most active subagents, employed year after year, usually employed the largest number of recruiters. Even with the cancellation of Wazir Ali's license, in 1895 Muzaffar Ali still received recruiting licenses for himself and fifteen others. In 1889 he had had twenty-three recruiters in his employ; in 1896 he employed thirty-four; while in 1902 his son Sarfaraz Ali had some forty recruiters working for him. Not surprisingly, R. Moses at Ghazipur and D. H. R. Moses at Benares also employed annually recruiters ranging in number from fifteen to thirty. Men like Sheikh Ghoorah at Baksar made do with ten to fifteen recruiters but were asked to send down to Calcutta proportionately fewer emigrants.

These local or village-level recruiters were often disproportionately Muslim. Brij Lal's data, for Benares district in the 1880s, indicates that Muslims comprised some 40 percent of that district's recruiters for all colonies, well in excess of their share of the population.[33] Similar proportions existed for Natal's recruiters. Of Muzaffar Ali's twenty-three Faizabad recruiters in 1889, for instance, fifteen were Muslims. R. Moses that same year employed ten Hindus and seven Muslims, while his son D. H. R. Moses had six Muslims and nine Hindus on the rolls. In 1896 Muzaffar Ali's thirty-four recruiters included twenty-one Muslims; while R. Moses that year employed eighteen Muslims of a total thirty-two and Babu Behari Lal fifteen of thirty-nine. A wide variety of castes nevertheless appeared as registered recruiters. Indeed, Grierson described them as men "of all castes." Many, he wrote, "have been recruiting all their life, but others have been shopkeepers, peons, domestic servants, shawl or cloth-sellers, or even labourers." The range of previous occupations is vividly apparent in Grierson's listing of four of Sheikh Ghoorah's men. One, formerly an orderly peon to a European zamindar (landlord), had been recruiting for eight years when interviewed; a second had been a servant to a merchant; a third had been a market weighman before taking up recruiting; and the fourth was an emigrant who had returned three years before from Mauritius.[34]

Natal's recruiters rarely included returned emigrants, nor did recruiters for the most part have personal experience of the colonies for which they recruited. Sheikh Ghoorah himself was an obvious exception. Grierson attributed his taking up recruiting to his "personal regard" for the European agent, whom he had known in Demerara. Grierson also recounted the extraordinary case of Jhumman Khan, who worked as a recruiter for Mauritius for eight years and then recruited himself. After five years in Mauritius, he returned to India and began recruiting again. The situation of Mauritius, however, is somewhat exceptional and will be taken up later. More common was Natal's disastrous experiment with returnee recruiting. In 1883 the Protector in Durban sent two Indians — Sumshoodin and Vencatachellum — back to India, where they were informed of the recruiting regulations, offered £1.10 monthly as salary plus railway fare and commission, and sent off to recruit in six Madras districts. They announced their presence in each village by beat of tom-tom, and read out the recruitment notice, only to return to Madras discouraged after touring Chingleput alone. They complained, the Madras agent reported, "that they were unable to collect any coolly [sic]" and had "no mind to waste government money by fruitless trials" in other districts. They returned to Natal on the first ship out of Madras.[35] In Grierson's view, it was not the employment of returnees as recruiters but their presence in the locality that most effectively facilitated recruitment. In Shahabad (Bihar), where there was "a healthy inflow of returned emigrants," emigration was so popular, he argued, that potential migrants searched out recruiters. A successful returnee, that is, might inspire others to emigrate, but he himself would be "too rich" to undertake the unrewarding task of actual recruiting.[36]

It is well known that success in recruitment, for the most part, had less to do with the number or energy of the recruiters than with the state of the seasons in India. Years of scarcity produced an outpouring of potential emigrants, while years of plenty brought recruiting nearly to a halt. Sometimes, as a result, the Natal agency correspondence took on a rather macabre quality. In 1903, for instance, Mitchell wrote to his subagent in Raipur, "I see the scarcity is much increased in Raipur, so you should easily get large numbers of migrants." Or, two years later: "At Benares the principal subagent assured me that emigrants would be plentiful in another month at the farthest, owing to the destruction of the crops by the late frost." Mitchell was not altogether happy about this conjuncture of dearth and laborers. As he reported sadly to the Natal Immigration Board in 1905, "It is no pleasure to any one that 'famine pine in empty stall where herds were wont to be'; all the same the Indian peasant will not emigrate though living on the verge of an empty stomach, unless pressed by want."[37]

In times of plenty, to keep up emigrant numbers, Mitchell was driven to increase the rates offered to subagents and to increase the number of staff. Neither of these expedients, however, in his view, was wholly successful. Higher fees, he pointed out in 1903 to a Natal desperate for Indian laborers, only encouraged fraud on the part of the recruiters, who pocketed "the extra money without doing much in return for it," while the employment of reliable subagents was "an exceptionally difficult matter, as the most capable men are not by any means the most reliable." So long as harvests remained "bountiful," with an "abnormal cheapness of food," matters did not improve. In 1904 Mitchell wrote to Natal, "I am employing three times as many subagents as I did a few years ago, but the results are not encouraging. I have offered an extra ten rupees per statute adult embarked, but the large increase in the rate has made very little difference in the supply of emigrants."[38]

Part of the anxiety over keeping up emigrant numbers arose from the substantial fixed costs, especially in Calcutta and at the upcountry depots, that had to be met no matter how many individuals were sent to Natal. In 1902, for instance, Mitchell reported the following items of expenditure:[39]

Office and depot charges —	
Agent's salary	Rs. 7,500
establishment	6,101
rent	3,600
blankets & clothes	2,525
depot surgeon	2,138
hospital	2,692
total	29,074
Cost of rations in depot	7,785
Charges for collection of emigrants —	
commissions to recruiters	Rs. 73,271
subagents' salaries	1,600
fees for emigrants shipped	8,721
medical exams	4,033
total	87,907
Charges for despatch —	
clothing for voyage	Rs. 10,316
tin ware	1,046
blankets	5,629
total	18,333

As the Calcutta agency that year sent off 2,770 adults, Mitchell calculated the cost per adult at Rs. 11.7 against office expenses, Rs. 32 for collection,

Rs. 3.6 for rations, and Rs. 4.11 for dispatch, making a total of Rs. 51.8.0 cost for each adult dispatched.

South India

The system of recruiting in southern India, which provided the bulk of Natal's laborers, differed substantially from that in the north. Initially, the agency at Madras was established on the same basis as that at Calcutta. Henry Burton, who had set up the agency in 1860, was followed as emigration agent in 1878, after resumption of emigration, by George Hope Ross, formerly chief sanitary officer of the Madras municipality. Determined to keep costs down, Ross dispensed with paid contractors and recruiters. Instead, "constituting himself his own contractor and recruiter, [he] moved daily among the people and encouraged them to enlist." He proudly reported that in his first six shipments he thereby saved Natal some 20,000 rupees on commissions. This was, however, not a very efficient way to conduct a large-scale recruiting operation spread across a number of districts. As the number of emigrants underwent a steady decline into the early 1880s, Ross, desperate, entered into a contract with a local merchant, who guaranteed a quarterly shipload of 300 to 350 emigrants. The contractor engaged recruiters, and the number of emigrants embarked for Natal turned upward. In the first nine months of the 1883 recruiting year more emigrants were dispatched than in either of the two previous full years. The Natal authorities were still not satisfied. In October 1883 they terminated Ross's employment and awarded the recruiting contract to the agency house of Messrs. Parry & Co.[40]

As a large commercial firm handling many lines of business, Parry's was at once better and worse suited for emigration work than an individual agent. As the *Natal Mercury* newspaper noted apprehensively when the appointment was first announced, "A mercantile firm of long standing and repute possesses a certain amount of prestige of value in the commercial world, but it is almost certain that in assuming the functions of an emigration agent its large business transactions will be a distracting element. The heads of a leading local mercantile firm . . . are hardly likely to bring to this work the undivided attention which a gentleman selected from among a number of applicants for the post could give." Parry's retorted that no individual agent "could hope to bring the same power to bear on recruiting that we can, as he has not branches of his business in each of the different districts."[41]

At the outset, to avoid disruption, Parry's kept on the same contractor, P. Balasoondrum Moodilly, whom Ross had engaged during his last year in office. Soon, however, dissatisfied, the company "swept away all the old recruiting arrangements" and started afresh on its own. Dividing the presidency into a number of subdivisions, it appointed in each one an agent, in almost all cases a European, with a remuneration ranging from five rupees per adult shipped, in the northern districts, to two rupees, for those near Madras and on the railway line. These agents in turn supervised some 140 recruiters; these were reimbursed at the rate of ten rupees for each adult male embarked and eight rupees for females. Parry's urged Natal not to send recruiters from the colony, for the local recruiters, jealous of such rivals, would "try to put every obstacle" in their way and so prevent them from getting emigrants, as had happened with the two hapless recruiters sent over in 1883. By the end of 1884 Parry's proudly claimed that the new arrangement had begun to bear fruit, with the shipping of some eighteen hundred adults in seven months. Pleased, the Natal Immigration Trust Board chairman noted that the new Madras agents were supplying immigrants at a substantially lower cost than their Calcutta counterparts.[42]

Under Parry's management, criticism was leveled primarily at the remuneration and behavior of recruiters. Parry's practice was to advance one-third of the commission due to the recruiter when a "coolie" was admitted into the depot. This advance would enable the recruiter to continue working while arrangements were made for the shipment of those collected. Once a coolie was passed as medically fit and had embarked, the recruiter would then be paid the remaining two-thirds of his commission. These funds were retained until sailing to cover the not infrequent rejection of intending emigrants, who would then have to be returned to their home districts at the recruiter's expense. The recruiter was similarly held responsible for recruits who disappeared from the depot before sailing. Although this delay in payment helped prevent loss to the agency, it had the effect, as one Natal observer charged, of encouraging recruiters in need of funds to hand over recruits to the Mauritius agency, which offered a lower commission but paid in cash on the spot. Outside observers were frequently critical as well of the "energy" recruiters put into their work. "Many of them," one wrote, "do not seem to be very keen on the job." Another caustically asserted that 95 percent of intending emigrants presented themselves to the recruiter at the subdepot. As a result "the recruiters never stir out of the town where he [sic] has his subdepot situated. It is much easier work for them to sit in the verandahs of their subdepots, and wait for the coolies to come . . . rather than tramp the country asking people if they would like to hear the terms offered for emigrants to Natal."[43]

As was true in northern India, some districts in the south, most notably North and South Arcot, produced more emigrant laborers than others. Some years too were more productive than others. (For the annual figures see the appendix, pp. 163–64.) Similarly, the recruiters for Parry's encountered many of the same obstacles, and took advantage of the same opportunities, as did their brethren to the north. Reporting in 1899, for instance, on the prospects for the far northern districts of the presidency around Vizagapatnam, Parry's told Natal, "The East coast railway is practically completed, and in consequence a large number of labourers are thrown out of employment and these people, when other work fails, are favourably disposed towards emigration. These districts too were formerly drained by Assam who now will take only khonds (or hillmen) because as a result of living in malarious districts they are able to stand the feverish climate of Assam."[44]

In the winter of 1907–08, in the waning days of indentured labor recruitment, yet while demand for coolies remained strong in South Africa, A. R. Denning from Natal toured some three thousand miles throughout southern India. He visited some 115 subdepots, and interviewed 176 recruiters. Denning's report provides therefore a last glimpse into the recruiting of Indians for Natal. Already, nationalist opposition to such recruitment was visibly and forcibly making its presence felt. Recruiters, Denning wrote, "are opposed by the influence of the swadeshi [self-rule] and Congress movements and have to spend money on all sides. They are also discarded by others as, in a manner, receivers of blood money. In many recruiting centres the swadeshi movement is opposing the work of the recruiters as much as possible. I have myself experienced the Swadeshi spirit shown in two or three instances." Denning singled out the Kistna and Godavari districts as centers of "swadeshi action."[45]

Messrs. Parry & Co. still held charge of the overall operation, but recruiting activities were in the hands of a number of subagents. Among these were Messrs. Simson Bros., who acted as subagents for a large tract that included Rajamundry, Cocananda (Godavari), and Vizagapatnam. An Englishman, Mr. Clark, looked after the emigration work on Simson's behalf, although, as Denning noted, "many of the recruiters in these localities were selected by Mr. V. M. Rajah Mudaliar, who started depots here some years ago." North Arcot and part of South Arcot were under the charge of P. N. Jumbulinga Mudaliar, "a reliable and influential man," who was also a municipal councillor at Vellore. R. K. Srinivasan, "an energetic influential young man" had charge of Nellore; T. Hart, in Bezwada and Guntur, was "hard working" but had "a difficult district to deal with." Commission payments to recruiters had now risen to forty-five rupees per adult. Three years later, in a desperate final bid for emigrants, rates were further raised to fifty rupees for men and eighty-five rupees for women. In 1911, after fifty years, and the shipment of over 152,000 Indians, indentured labor recruitment for Natal came to an end — the victim of intense nationalist hostility in India, together with the increasing availability of free Indian and black African labor in Natal.

The Larger Frame: Contrasts and Similarities

With half a dozen colonies jostling each other for laborers, one must ask whether and how the Natal recruiting operation differed from that of other colonies. In the absence of study of local records, which can alone provide this kind of information, it is hard to assess in detail the recruiting patterns of the various colonies. Exceptional is the work of Marina Carter, whose *Servants, Sirdars, and Settlers* provides a close study of recruitment for Mauritius and of life in the colony in the mid-nineteenth century. To be sure, the years she examined, from 1834 to 1874, overlap only slightly with the period studied here. Nevertheless, she has identified as a "distinct feature" of Mauritian recruiting the use of time-expired laborers (returnees) in place of the practice of commercial contracting. Such a recruiting strategy, Carter argues, in which "old Mauritius men" were given money to go into the interior, often returning to their own home areas, enabled the colony to secure entire kin groups as migrants, and at the same time eased the not uncommon apprehension felt by potential migrants as to their fate in an unknown land across the sea. Returnee recruiting, she concludes, "helped to maintain the popularity of Mauritius, overriding the market mechanism in labour procurement."[46] As we have seen, returnee recruiting was rarely employed for Natal in either northern or southern India. Part of the reason for the more successful employment of this system for Mauritius, surely, is to be found in that island's comparative closeness to India. This made possible easy movement between the two, which, together with the early introduction of indentured labor in 1834, made the island familiar to Indians contemplating overseas migration. Parry's, for instance, after its first year of operation in Madras, prided itself on having "far exceeded Mauritius with all its popularity and long standing."[47]

Natal nevertheless shared with other colonies, including Mauritius,

fundamental elements in its system of indentured recruitment. The work-
ings of supply and demand affected all equally. All colonies found it easier to secure emigrants during seasons of Indian scarcity, which drove supply; and all were equally subject to the fluctuations of the world economy,
which drove demand. Always, the critical determinant in labor recruitment
was colonial demand, and this in turn was set by the world demand for
sugar. When sugar prices were depressed, plantation owners required less
labor. Such fluctuations in demand created problems for the recruiting
agencies in India. Not only were they often hard pressed to find recruits
when demand rose, but they also found it difficult to contract their operations when demand fell. No sooner, for instance, had Parry & Co. set up
its new recruiting operation in South India than Natal, citing the depressed state of the sugar market, told it to cut back. Protesting, Parry's
replied that "an order such as your letter contains means that we must
destroy what we have created. . . . Once we disperse our recruiters . . . we
shall in the first instance break faith more or less with them . . . and to
reorganize once more should your wants increase again will be most difficult." Self-interestedly, they suggested that instead of contracting their own
operations, the Calcutta agency be closed down altogether.[48]

The Indian government, furthermore, established the framework
within which all colonial recruiters were obliged to operate. With minor
variations over time, the Indian authorities remained committed to the
encouragement of indentured emigration. Such emigration would, in
their view, help relieve crowding in overpopulated districts in India; it
would offer opportunities for economic advancement for the individual
Indian migrant; and of course, it would help alleviate the labor shortages
faced by colonial planters during a period of generally increasing demand
for sugar.[49] Despite the close ties that existed between them, it is important not to regard the Indian authorities as captives of the colonies, much
less of their planting communities. The periodic stoppages of indentured
migration when complaints of abuse arose, as in Mauritius in 1839 and
Natal in 1871, are evidence of a continuing concern for the welfare of
migrants.

The system of Protectors too, both in the Indian ports and in the
colonies, standing between planters and "coolies," enshrined the principle that the British Empire was responsible for securing its subjects from
abuse. How much protection these "Protectors" actually afforded emigrants is, to be sure, a matter of contention. A certain degree of skepti-
cism is no doubt appropriate, especially once emigrants had been placed
on plantations in the colonies. Abuse by overseers and planters,

unchecked by any continuing scrutiny, was a common feature of indentured life on the colonial plantation. Still, the Protectors took care not to identify their interests directly with those of the colonial planters. As the lieutenant-governor of Bengal wrote in 1861 with regard to those posted at the Indian ports, "The Protector should initiate no action. His authority should be limited to the checking of any abuse: to seeing that the laws and regulations in force are properly observed; and to securing the coolies from deception or violence. . . . The [Emigration] Agent should see to the interests of the colonies; and the Protector to those of the coolie."[50] Whatever its failings, this regulatory system, linking India and the colonies under the umbrella of the British Empire, stands in sharp contrast to the wholly commercial recruitment of Chinese by British agencies and others for overseas labor.

As they established regulations for indentured emigration, the Indian authorities took care to keep their own interests in view. As we have seen, they declined to permit recruitment of Nepali Gurkhas, whom they wanted as potential soldiers. They endeavored to steer colonial recruiters away from tracts specially favored by recruiters for domestic industries such as the Assamese tea plantations. Apart from occasional intervals, the entire Bombay Presidency was kept closed to colonial recruiting. This was done in response to the demands of local Indian industrialists who won the support of the provincial government for their insistence that "the labouring population of the presidency is not sufficient for its wants" and hence should not be encouraged to emigrate. Protectors adamantly refused to judge the suitability of intending emigrants for agricultural labor, confining their examination to questions of health and fitness for travel. Local district magistrates, too, on their own initiative sometimes blocked recruiting operations by harassing recruiters. As Mitchell reported to Natal in 1903, "Where the magistrate is opposed on principle to emigration out of India, as some of the younger and less experienced are, it is quite hopeless to attempt collecting emigrants in the district as the recruiters are certain to be run in by the police."

Colonial recruiters shared with each other and with most officials in India a set of racial and ethnic stereotypes that shaped patterns of recruitment. Certain caste and regional groupings, above all those of high caste, were universally disfavored, while others, especially those of lower agricultural and artisanal castes, were sought out. The preference for these latter castes was based on the presumption that, as people used to manual labor in the fields in India, they were more willing to undertake such work overseas and were fit for it. Mitchell described the preferred emigrant in a letter of instructions to his traveling agent Babu Benoy Krishna Gupta. Himself a member of an "unsuitable" higher caste, Gupta was to tour the various Natal subdepots and "to see that no emigrants are recruited except such as belong to the agricultural castes, with hard hands, sound healthy bodies, ample chests, and muscular limbs." Although the heights of migrants were always carefully recorded, height as such played no role in determining who was fit for indentured recruitment, and there is no reference to it in the Natal agency correspondence.[51]

Throughout these various directives to recruiters, a tension always existed between caste status and individual physique. We have seen how ambivalent the Natal authorities were about accepting Brahmins and Muslims. Similar anxieties accompanied the recruitment of high-caste groups such as Rajputs. As Mitchell wrote to his subagent Behari Lal in 1901, "I will take the thakurs you have already recruited if they are *paka labourers* but don't collect any more if you can get lower castes." Yet on the ground, as recruiters scrambled for migrants, such prescriptions often gave way. Marina Carter's case study of migrants from Calcutta to Mauritius, for instance, is headed by Muslims and untouchable Chamars and includes among its top ten caste groupings both Rajputs and Brahmins. The roster of U.P. migrants to Fiji from 1891 to 1911 was headed by Muslims at 15 percent, followed by Chamars at 13 percent; but Rajputs and allied castes made up 10 percent of the total, while Brahmins contributed 3.7 percent. As the study's author, Brij Lal, noted, there was a broad correlation between the numerical strength of these groups in the U.P. population and their contribution to the emigrant stream. Surendra Bhana's study of ships' registers of indentured emigrants to Natal over the forty-year period from 1860 to 1902 shows roughly similar results. From Calcutta, the leading caste groups were untouchable Chamars (15.8 percent) and agriculturist Ahirs (12.2 percent), but Muslims represented some 5.5 percent of emigrants, and the Rajput/Thakur/Chattri grouping some 8 percent.[52] In the final analysis, bodies, especially those with "hard hands," mattered more than caste taboos.

A regulated indentured labor migration, then, marked out visibly, in the bodies of those recruited, the centrality of India within the British imperial system. The interconnections of the empire provided a way of at once facilitating and, in principle, protecting emigrants, while India provided a reservoir of individuals willing to take up the opportunities they saw or hoped they would find in British colonies overseas. Had India not been part of the British Empire, recruitment of labor for colonial plantations would have been random, less organized, with the provision of fewer protections for migrants; in sum more comparable to that from China. It might also have enforced a more widespread recourse in the colonies to the employment of indigenous peoples, from Zulus to former slaves, and at a higher cost. With India as an imperial center, British colonies across the tropical world could be assured of a reliable and economical supply of plantation labor. The British, on their part, could assure themselves that, by regulating this migratory traffic, they had fulfilled their obligations as imperial rulers, while Indian diaspora populations — from the West Indies and South Africa to Mauritius and Fiji — stand to this day as a living testimony to British Indian "coolie" recruitment.

Appendix

INDENTURED LABOR RECRUITMENT TO NATAL

The following figures have been compiled from reports of the governments of India and of Natal. Small discrepancies in the numbers reported exist within these reports and between them and other compilations such as that based on ships' lists in Surendra Bhana, *Indentured Indian Emigrants to Natal, 1860–1902.*

Year	Calcutta	Madras	Total
1860	312	601	913
1861	240	359	599
1862	0	0	0
1863	0	668	668
1864	384	1,857	2,241
1865	0	984	984
1866	0	864	864
1867–73	—	—	—
1874	4,310	0	4,310
1875	2,057	0	2,057
1876	754	0	754
1877	1,089	1,173	2,262
1878	1,722	3,576	5,278
1879	0	1,116	1,116
1880	505	1,168	1,673
1881	1,703	909	2,612
1882	872	753	1,625

(continued)

Year	Calcutta	Madras	Total
1883	1,457	947	2,404
1884	1,337	1,626	2,963
1885	389	850	1,239
1886	0	227	227
1887	0	941	941
1888	0	942	942
1889	699	2,670	3,369
1890	1,108	3,432	4,540
1891 (6 mo.)	1,912	537	2,449
1891–92	1,043	2,140	3,183
1892–93	588	2,293	2,881
1893–94	1,095	1,538	2,633
1894–95	1,722	1,728	3,450
1895 (6 mo.)	0	982	982
1896	1,974	1,977	3,951
1897	2,922	3,129	6,051
1898	1,863	4,076	5,939
1899–1900	1,570	5,169	6,739
1901	816	6,199	7,015
1902	2,119	4,373	6,492
1903	2,312	2,804	5,116
1904	n.a.	n.a.	7,691
1905	n.a.	n.a.	7,914
1906	3,855	7,786	11,641
1907	474	6,012	6,486
1908	823	2,351	3,174
1909	0	2,487	2,487
1910	n.a.	n.a.	5,858
1911	2,714	2,928	5,642
Grand Total	50,716	101,468	152,184

CHAPTER 6

India in East Africa

Cruising along the coast of East Africa in 1873, charged with a mission to end the slave trade in the region, a startled Sir Bartle Frere, former governor of Bombay, discovered, as he wrote to the foreign secretary in London, that "all trade passes through Indian hands; African, Arab, and European, all use an Indian agent or banian to manage the details of buying and selling, and without the intervention of an Indian either as capitalist or petty trader, very little business is done. They occupy every place where there is trade. At Zanzibar they have the command of the Custom-houses along nearly 1,000 miles of coast." This "silent occupation of this coast," Frere wrote in some bafflement, "has been going on for forty years, but I had no idea, till I came here, how complete their monopoly has become." Nor was this Indian predominance confined to East Africa alone. "Along nearly 6,000 miles of sea coast," wrote Frere in a subsequent report, "in Africa and its islands, and nearly the same extent in Asia, the Indian trader is, if not the monopolist, the most influential, permanent, and all-pervading element of the commercial community." Indeed, he concluded, "for some of the Indian trading classes, trade in East Africa seems to have the same charms as colonizing for some of our own countrymen at home."[1] Two decades later, as British control was being extended into interior East Africa, Sir Harry Johnston, from his position first in Nyasaland and later in Uganda, spoke for many officials when he saw in East Africa a land fit for colonization by Indians or, as he called it, "an America for the Hindu," a land where Indian immigrants might freely settle to pursue whatever occupation they chose.[2]

This chapter explores the role India and Indians played in the colonization of East Africa. My aim here is not to recount the history of the Indian community in East Africa, but rather to show how East Africa became, in the early decades of colonialism, almost an extension of India itself.[3] The chapter examines two little-studied but critical aspects of the Indianization of East Africa. One is the fitful and ambivalent British encouragement of Johnston's vision of this new colony as an "America for the Hindu." The second, a close examination of the construction of the Uganda Railway, demonstrates how the building of that strategically important rail line, to quote Johnston again, involved "the driving of a wedge of India" right across East Africa to the shores of Lake Victoria.

An "America for the Hindu": Indian Settlers in East Africa

Indian trade along the East African coast long antedated the coming of the British. Since the discovery of the monsoon in antiquity, Indians, with Arabs and others, had long plied their dhows along the coasts and across the waters of the Indian Ocean. The modern growth of Indian trade with East Africa was, however, prompted by the nearly simultaneous early-nineteenth-century creation of an Omani commercial empire along the East African coast, signaled by the relocation of the Muscat sultanate from Oman to Zanzibar in 1840, and the establishment of the Pax Britannica in India and across the Indian Ocean. Together, these provided the security within which trade could flourish across a vast area of the globe.[4] The midcentury growth of the Indian trading community was striking. Frere in 1873 commented that few Indian houses could "boast an antiquity of more than forty years," whereas during the preceding forty years "the great Indian immigration to this coast has gone on at a constantly increasing rate." In the single year of 1872, he reported, some 250 traders arrived in Zanzibar alone. Estimates of the total number of Indians in the Zanzibar dominions in those years ranged upward from four thousand.

Again and again throughout his report, as if unwilling to accept what he saw before him, Frere returned to the topic of the Indian control of the goods that moved along East Africa's coast. Nor was it simply a matter of petty trade. "Throughout the Zanzibar coast-line . . . all banking and mortgage business passes through Indian hands. Hardly a loan can be negotiated, a mortgage effected, or a bill cashed without Indian agency." For the most part, although they financed the trade with the interior, the

Indians left to Arabs, or more commonly, local Swahili Muslims, the task of bringing manacled slaves and tusks of ivory down to the coast. Nor did the Indian merchants ever cut their ties with India. Commonly, as Frere wrote, the new arrival, after a brief period of apprenticeship in some older firm, "when he has made a little money, generally returns home to marry, to make fresh business connections, and then comes back to Africa to repeat, on a larger scale, the same process." Despite the longevity of their business connections with the coast, few of the individual traders in these early years saw Africa as their permanent residence. Frere wryly commented that they "seem to have as little idea of settling or adopting the country for their own as a young Englishman in Hong Kong."

Those who took advantage of these opportunities were, for the most part, from what Frere called the "four or five of the great trading classes of Western India." Most originated in, and in many cases had their trading headquarters in, the province of Gujarat, above all the regions of Kathiawar and Kutch. Inhabitants of a sea-girt nearly desert peninsula who often started out with limited capital, Kutchis quickly came to dominate East African trade. The Hindu Bhatias, who controlled some of the oldest East African firms, were, in Frere's view, "probably the most important by wealth and influence at Zanzibar." A Bhatia firm farmed the customs at Zanzibar for the sultan for half a century from 1835 to 1886. The Khojas, Ismaili Muslim followers of the Aga Khan, had also a long history of trade across the western Indian Ocean; with the Muslim Memons and Bohras, they ranged up and down the coast and, so Frere reported, "generally monopolize all that the Hindoo Bhattias and Banians do not possess of the trade in cloth and cotton goods, ironmongery, cutlery, china, and small wares." The assets of some of these firms were, not surprisingly, substantial. The leading Bhatia firm had nearly half a million pounds sterling invested in loans and mortgages in East Africa, and these were so extensive that, Frere was told, "few of the larger Arab estates in Zanzibar are unencumbered by mortgages to Indian capitalists, and a large proportion are so deeply mortgaged as virtually to belong to the Indian mortgagee."[5]

Not only did Indian merchants control East Africa's trade, but much of that trade took place with India. During the first several decades of the nineteenth century, this involved the importation of hand-loom Indian textiles in exchange for ivory. By midcentury much of the ivory was re-exported from Bombay to Europe, while the industrial revolution precipitated a dramatic decline in Indian textile exports. In East Africa, however, the United States, not Britain, took advantage of the new market for machine-made cloth. By 1859 exports of American cotton goods to Zanzibar were two-and-a-half times in value those of Britain. The American Civil War dealt this trade a devastating blow and opened up opportunities alike for Britain and for India. Frederic Holmwood, the British consul in Zanzibar, in a talk to the Manchester Chamber of Commerce in 1885, sought to encourage English manufacturers to take an interest in the East African market. In so doing, however, he made clear the extent to which Zanzibar's Indian-run trade inevitably benefited Indian markets and Indian goods. Nearly half of Zanzibar's imports, for instance, came from India; and while much of this consisted of British goods re-exported from Bombay, with the beginning of an Indian textile industry from the later 1870s, "cottons of Indian manufacture have seriously interfered with our goods." This was a product, he asserted, of the fact that "the comparatively flimsy material which the rising manufacturing industry of India is now producing can be sold at little more than half the cost of the heavier and more durable fabrics of Manchester and Massachusetts."[6]

The establishment of the Zanzibar consulate in 1841 under the direction of the Bombay government gave political substance to the growing commercial links between East Africa and India. From the mid-1840s the British Indians in Zanzibar began to claim the protection of the British consul, although they frequently resisted British attempts to force them to emancipate their slaves and refrain from slave trading. By 1873 Indians under British protection had to disavow slavery. Those who refused to do so accepted the sultan's protection and became known as the "Sultan's Hindees." These men, some 350 in 1869, were for the most part petty shopkeepers who "have all become more or less Arabized."[7] Ties were further strengthened in the 1870s with the establishment of a British Indian post office in Zanzibar and the start of regular steamer service between Bombay and Zanzibar by the British India Steam Navigation Company. In 1883 control of the Zanzibar agency was transferred to the British Foreign Office. Despite the ending of this legal connection, on the eve of the scramble for Africa, insofar as the British exercised influence over East Africa, they did so from India, and their claims took visible shape through the thousands of British Indian subjects who lived and traded in the region.

The first steps toward the partition of East Africa were taken by Bismarck's Germany. In 1884 the enterprising Karl Peters set off upcountry with the aim of securing the hinterland of Zanzibar for Germany. Two years later, the British government acquiesced in Germany's claim to what later became Tanganyika, but at the same time delimited the northern boundary of that colony in such a way as to secure for itself a vast tract of land that would subsequently become British East Africa and later the colonies of Kenya and Uganda. Reluctant to accept responsibility for either the island of Zanzibar — still nominally independent — or the areas it had now accepted as a British sphere of influence, the British government, as we have seen, turned over governance of its territory to the Imperial British East Africa Company, founded in 1888 by Sir William Mackinnon (1823–1893). A committed imperialist, Mackinnon anticipated that the trading profits from East Africa, once the interior was opened up by railways, would secure both the interests of the empire and his own fortune. In the end, it took but little more than five years for this fantasy to unravel and to bring the company down with it.[8]

The formation of the Imperial British East Africa Company, far from ending the ties between India and East Africa, served only to strengthen them. Mackinnon, like so many enterprising Scots, went out to India as a youth, where in 1847 he joined a friend, Robert Mackenzie, in a mercantile company engaged in general trade. Within a decade Mackinnon had founded the British India Steam Navigation Company; and through its fleet of some one hundred vessels he succeeded in making himself by the 1870s master of the carrying trade throughout the Indian Ocean. Mackinnon's base in India shaped the African empire building to which he devoted his later years. His Indian connections, above all, were critical to his early successes in East Africa. Mackinnon had close ties with Bartle Frere, a career member of the Indian Civil Service, whom he had first met when Frere was governor of Bombay (1862–67) and who supported, from Bombay, London, and later as governor of the Cape, the extension of Mackinnon's steamship lines throughout the Indian Ocean. As one writer has commented, although Mackinnon "sought the assistance of a variety of public figures, his fortunes were most closely linked to official circles in India, and in particular to the proconsular figure of Sir Henry Bartle Frere."[9] Charles Euan-Smith too, consul general at Zanzibar during the critical years of the negotiations with Germany, had served in the Indian Army, accompanied Frere on his 1873 mission, and served as political officer in Hyderabad and Muscat; throughout, Mackinnon lent him money, served as his patron, and sought, not always successfully, favors from him for his ventures in East Africa.

In 1888, as his East Africa company's charter was being negotiated in London, Mackinnon sent his business associate and fellow Scot George S. Mackenzie to East Africa to scout out the territory where the company intended to operate. The prospects were not encouraging. In November,

Mackenzie reported to London that the company urgently needed at once in Africa a staff of eleven Europeans, together with superintending carpenters, plumbers, blacksmiths, and masons. Given the fact that "no labour or appliances of any kind [are] available on the spot, it is a question whether it would not be better if these were introduced from India." Alike in Muscat and in Zanzibar, the sultans had long employed Baluchi mercenaries as a military force. These men, Mackenzie said, were "worse than useless." He recommended instead the employment of a complete company of Native Indian sappers. But, concerned that the appearance of an Indian force on African soil might arouse a "feeling of suspicion," he proposed that the sappers avoid bringing their uniforms and come instead in the guise of "ordinary labourers." Put into the company's uniform and "drilled quietly," they would then "appear as part of our own local levies." Ignorant of the extent of tsetse fly in East Africa, he further requested to have sent from India "two or three bullock carts" to facilitate carriage.[10]

Further difficulties arose from the fact that much of the coastline where the IBEA Company sought to establish bases had been occupied by the Germans. Here the confrontation took the unlikely shape of a tussle over the control of postal services for Indian residents. As Mackenzie wrote to the company's agent at Lamu, "I hear the Germans are striving to insist upon British Indians using German stamps. You will of course make it quite public it is unnecessary their doing so, and that Indian stamps will carry their letters as heretofore." Indians were told to bring their letters to the consulate, where they would be put on board a company ship and then posted at the first port where Indian stamps could be obtained.[11] In the end the company secured the right to establish its own post offices, and after 1890 the Germans were confined to the area south of the 1886 line of demarcation. The company proceeded to set up its headquarters in the British sphere at Mombasa, where, Mackenzie reported with pleasure, "a large number of Indians and others have come up here from Zanzibar with the intention of establishing themselves." The transfer to Mombasa signaled the end not only of Zanzibar city's commercial predominance but also of the Omani empire as the predominant power along the East African coast.

The Indian mercantile community saw in this expansion of British authority an opportunity it was not slow to take advantage of. Contracts with the company for the supply of goods and even laborers were highly profitable ventures; at the same time, the company's establishment of outposts — first along the coast from Mombasa north to Witu and Lamu, and subsequently into the interior — drew Indian traders and merchants along in their wake. By 1897 there were some one thousand Indian traders, shopkeepers, clerks, and the like in Mombasa city alone. Several of these men amassed immense wealth and so became prominent in the social and political life of early Kenya. One or two instances may give some indication of the scale of mercantile activity on the part of these Indian pioneers. Allidina Vishram, a Kutchi Ismaili, organizing caravans to Uganda in advance of the railway, made himself indispensable as a supplier of goods to the small traders, or *dukawallahs* (from *dukan,* "shop"), whose shops were scattered across the countryside, and to government officers as well. As one official later recounted, "He opened a store at nearly every Government station, and in the early days was of the greatest assistance to Government in many ways, such as transport, purchase of local produce, etc."[12]

With the spread of Indian firms into the interior came the growth of an economy based on the Indian rupee as the medium of exchange. As the administrator A. H. Hardinge wrote, "previous to 1898 the Government kept stores of trade goods" — strings of beads, lengths of cloth, and the like — that "formed the entire medium of exchange with the natives." With the opening of Indian bazaars, the government "began to close down their stores, and payment began to be made in rupees and pice; and now station trade goods are unknown." Africans had no choice but to familiarize themselves with this new currency. At Machakos, for instance, with the opening of shops by two Indian traders, Hardinge reported, "the rupee currency is beginning to be understood and used by the Wakamba as a medium of exchange."[13]

Ordinary Indians of a wide variety of backgrounds also began to crowd aboard ships to Africa by the mid-1890s. "The people are flocking to Africa," the Protector of Emigrants in Bombay reported in September 1896, "of their own free will, at their own expense. . . . Many have embarked for Mombasa in the hope of finding work on the Uganda Railway, or in connection with the trade and wants that will spring up with the railway construction." Within one month, he counted 1,449 people leaving for East African ports. The total for the year 1895–96, of 6,908, was more than twice the number of the preceding year. The passengers on board one of these ships, questioned by the Protector, included, among others, thirty-two masons and tile turners from Kutch, sixty laborers from villages in Gujarat, three Khojas and four Hindu tailors from Rajkot, and sixteen Brahmins, who intended to "follow whatever suitable business offers."[14]

The movement of Indian traders and artisans into East Africa inevitably raised the question of whether Indian agricultural "colonization" ought to be encouraged as well. For the early administrators, Indian settlers on the land were an essential element in the development of Britain's new African possessions. During the course of his 1888 tour, G. S. Mackenzie, suggesting a trial cultivation of indigo, expressed the hope that favorable reports of such a trial might "induce Indian capital to take up lands in our district." Frederic Holmwood, recently retired as consul-general in Zanzibar, in that same year offered his vision of what Indian settlers might accomplish. With most Britons of the time, Holmwood had but little expectation that the indigenous Africans could successfully take up the task of developing the continent's resources. Their "aversion if not inability for sustained work" made it "hopeless to expect" any assistance from them. Indians, by contrast, were experienced agriculturists.

In place of the stereotypes that saw Indians only as grasping traders and ineffectual "babus," Holmwood held out a vision of them as "peculiarly loyal," "law abiding," and in general fully capable of taking advantage of the "ample garden ground for personal cultivation, as well as pasturage for household flocks and milch cows" that, in his view, East Africa offered. Indeed, he went on, "the want of population existing almost throughout the fertile and healthy upland regions between the coast and the great lakes of Central Africa" offers "the very opening that India seeks, and the space available is so vast both in these uplands and in those beyond the lakes that this opening will continuously extend itself from year to year as British enterprise develops what is practically a new continent." There was, he said, "ample scope for the settlement of the Zamindar class as well as of the Rayat [peasant] classes." Even the Indians' "physique" would soon improve as they abandoned the overcrowded humid districts of Bengal and Madras for the "salubrity" of East Africa.[15]

Similar opinions were voiced by Charles Euan-Smith, Holmwood's successor as consul-general, and by Frederick Lugard. Most sanguine, however, was surely H. H. (Harry) Johnston (1868–1927), commissioner of British Central Africa (later Nyasaland) from 1891 to 1896 and special commissioner in Uganda from 1899 to 1901. As he sought Sikh soldiers for Central Africa, he also saw opportunities in Africa for a wide range of Indian occupational groups. Reflecting in 1894 on the first three years of his administration, Johnston recounted that there was not, when he arrived, "a single Indian in British Central Africa except for a doubtful Goanese. . . . Now there is quite a colony of Banyans on the Lower Shire, at Port Herald and elsewhere. . . . There are now Banyans settled at Chiromo, and higher upriver still at Tshikwawa. There is a Banyan going to establish a store at Blantyre." Further, he wrote, the administration "has introduced from India Indian cooks, carpenters, and various other artisans, and they have been found most useful." Indian cooks were especially "indispensable." The African native, he said, speaking no doubt from heartfelt experience of disappointment, "very rarely makes a satisfactory cook . . . he is dirty and clumsy. These cooks from India can really turn out meals which would not disgrace a professed cook in England." Indians, it might be noted, were not the only British subjects who found new opportunities in remote Central Africa. In a list of Europeans resident in Central Africa in 1894, the 69 English, 5 Welsh, 6 Irish, 6 Australians, and 11 South Africans were vastly outnumbered by a total of some 130 Scots. Like Indians, Scots contributed more to the empire than is often recognized.[16]

In 1895 Johnston went on to argue in favor of settling Indian agriculturists in Central Africa. Not only would their agricultural skills enrich the colony, but by giving "lessons" in cultivation, the Indians could become "valuable teachers of the Negro." Practitioners of a "wasteful" slash-and-burn agriculture, native Africans, in Johnston's view, possessed only a "quite elementary" knowledge of agriculture. "It is therefore my hope, with the prudent introduction of Indian colonists in small numbers, that they might serve on the one hand to instruct the natives as to higher modes of agriculture than their present thriftless procedure, and on the other to carry out field work, which is an impossibility to the European, both for climatic reasons and because it only pays the European settler to act as a general supervisor in this country." Johnston proposed, as an "experiment," bringing over some twenty-five families "of sturdy cultivators" from western India. With funds from the government and from planters, he would pay their passages, outfit them with tools, and supply free rations until they were self-supporting; each family would be allotted thirty acres of land free of charge. The first of several such proposals, as we shall see, Johnston's scheme met with a cool response from the Colonial Office, with the result that, even though he spoke with a number of possible settlers during an 1895 tour of India, "I had no funds at my disposal with which to pay their preliminary expenses, and they themselves were people mostly without money."[17]

Sustaining Johnston's enthusiasm for Indian colonization was a racial hierarchy that placed the European at the top, the Indian in the middle, and the African at the bottom. As a middleman who could "fill up the gap between the two extremes" of white and black, the Indian could develop the territories that lay between those suitable for settlement by the others. "Let the negroes," as he put it, "occupy (as they prefer to do) the very hot and low lying districts; let the Indian immigrants settle on the tropical but less unhealthy plateaux; and let the white man confine his settlements to the exceptionally high mountains or uplands of 5,000 feet or more in altitude." These intermediary areas were, further, "to a large extent uninhabited" yet offered "attractive conditions of fertile soil and good water supply." Indeed, he insisted, eastern and central Africa were "far more suitable as a second home for the Indian race than the West Indies, British Guiana or North Australia, because the vegetation, climate, soil, and other conditions of tropical Africa are so remarkably similar to those which prevail in India, so much so that the Indian scarcely feels in a strange land."[18]

This racial hierarchy, with its placement of the Indian in the middle, also offered, Johnston believed, a unique opportunity for the civilizing of Africa. Not only could the Indian be a "teacher" to the African, but he could also initiate a salutary process of racial improvement. Though Johnston accepted the conventional late-Victorian pieties about the capabilities of the various races, he went beyond most of his contemporaries in his conviction that race mixing, of an appropriate sort, could have positive as well as negative outcomes. What the Negro urgently required, Johnston argued, to rise above his "current level of culture" was "the admixture of a superior type of man." This the white man could not supply because the black and white races were "too widely separated in type to produce a satisfactory hybrid." The only hope for the Negro lay in "coalescing with some yellow race." To be sure, he acknowledged, an Arab-Negro intermixture had taken place on the eastern coast of Africa and in the Sudan. But the Arab "would appear to have certain inherent vices and defects of disposition which he transmits to his descendants. Although of very fine physical type, the Swahili is rather recalcitrant to European civilization. On the whole, I think the admixture of yellow that the negro requires should come from India. . . . The mixture of the two races would give the Indian the physical development which he lacks, and he in his turn would transmit to his half negro offspring the industry, ambition, and aspiration towards a civilized life which the negro so markedly lacks." Indians, therefore, while not occupying so high a position on the scale of "civilization" as the European, still ranked among the "civilized" peoples of the globe, and so could — because of both their cultural and racial characteristics — help share the "white man's burden" in Africa. In the meantime, Johnston concluded, "we must at present devote ourselves to reclaiming Africa from the unintelligent rule of Nature by educating the Black man and introducing the yellow man, and establishing ourselves in sufficient numbers in the more healthy districts so that we may direct these operations *in situ*."[19]

Despite Johnston's enthusiasms, Indians did not at once rush to take up cultivation in Central Africa. Indeed, many of the Indians the Protector saw boarding ships in Bombay in 1896 intended to bypass eastern Africa altogether, proceeding onward instead to South Africa. Interviews with Indians on board one Africa-bound ship, for instance, revealed that of some 286 passengers, 270 were bound for Natal and the Transvaal. Never simply pawns of British officials set on arranging the distribution of labor around the globe, Indian emigrants had their own preferences. The anxious Protector, worried about the political discrimination Indians faced in South Africa, found that this did not deter intending migrants. "Politically," he wrote, "the Indians may have a bad time of it in that region, but they are, I am informed, making money and are thriving." Individuals, asked what they proposed to do in South Africa, spoke of such enterprises as hawking goods, tailoring, and shopkeeping — occupations favored as well by those who stopped in East Africa. Decisive in the choice of South Africa as a destination, however, was the lure of that country's fast-growing economy, sustained by the gold-mining industry, together with the region's substantial Indian population. As several intending migrants told the Protector, he reported, "countrymen of theirs are already there and are doing well; they received letters from them asking them to come, that money was to be made in the place."[20]

No racial barriers to Indian settlement existed in the new British territories of East and Central Africa, but of course, as a region newly opened to settlement, it did not have the pull of a prosperous area with an established migrant community. Appeals to the government of India for assistance in directing the migrant flow to East Africa were unavailing. Despite an admitted interest in "finding new employment for the surplus labour of the country," the Indian government adamantly refused to help finance emigration apart from that of indentured labor on contract. All Indians, it pointed out, "indeed the whole population of British India," were free "to go wherever they liked" as long as they did so at their own expense. Indeed, the Indian authorities optimistically expected that South Africa's increasingly rigid racial restrictions on Indian employment there might encourage prospective settlers, as Johnston put it, to "give British Central Africa a trial." At the same time, the colonial secretary warned Indians who might seek to move southward from Central into South Africa that the imperial government would not be able to "support their claims for social and political equality in the older colonies."[21]

After 1896 the extension of the rail line into the African interior further encouraged the British desire to see Indian "colonists" settled on the land. The railway also, of course, in opening up opportunities throughout the region, made Indian settlement in East Africa more attractive. From his position as commissioner in Uganda, once again calling East Africa the "America of the Hindu," Johnston in 1901 took up the cudgels afresh on behalf of Indian settlement. Not only, he insisted, did "Indian trade, enterprise and emigration require a suitable outlet," but it was a "political necessity that a portion (and happily it is the richest portion) of East Africa should be open to Indian enterprise under the British flag."[22] Clearly, for Johnston, the wider the opportunities available to Indians in East Africa, the more they might be reconciled to continued colonial rule at home. In similar fashion, the successive commissioners in charge of East Africa during these years, Sir A. Hardinge and Sir C. Eliot, looked forward to extensive Indian settlement. "Every encouragement," Hardinge wrote in 1900, should be given to Indian applicants for plots of land in Ukamba province, in the hope that they might "form the nucleus of an industrious Indian colony." Eliot, citing the suitability of the soil and water "near the river Tsavo and also near Nairobi and in the Rift Valley," in 1901 saw no reason why, "as Indian traders penetrated into the most distant and dangerous parts" of the protectorate, "agriculturists should not in time be induced to do the same."[23]

As the government of India remained adamantly opposed to any state subsidy for immigration from India, those to whom the British turned as the most likely settlers were those already in East Africa, above all those on short-term employment contracts. Col. T. Gracey, wrote, for instance, that "it might be found desirable to offer inducements to some of the natives of India, who are now working on the railway, many of whom are fair examples of Mussulman Punjabi cultivators, to bring over their wives and children and settle." In similar fashion, Gen. W. H. Manning, following many "very favorable" conversations with native officers of the Sikh contingent, proposed that members of the "hardy races of the Punjab" be offered grants of land at favorable rates on completion of their service. These settlers, in return for their land, would be made liable for military service in East Africa, thus saving the expense of recruiting more men from India. At the same time, as "good farmers" they could "eventually produce an export trade possibly in food-stuffs, cotton, and other commercial products." A. S. Rogers, after talking with a number of the Sikh and Punjabi Muslim members of the Uganda military contingent, reported that there were among them "a number of very desirable agriculturists who are quite willing to settle down and take up land in this country as an experiment, provided that they receive assistance from government" until the experiment was proven a success. The terms suggested echoed those Johnston had recommended for Central Africa in 1895. These included, in addition to a grant of land free of taxes for three years, passages for themselves and their families from the Punjab, a pair of oxen and a cow, seeds and implements, and food to feed themselves until the first crop was harvested. Rogers recommended settling some two hundred families in the first instance.[24]

Before any of these schemes could be brought to fruition, however, senior officials in the protectorate government had begun to back away from their larger implications. Almost everywhere some "obstacle" or another presented itself. Several railway officials suggested settlement along the railway west of Nairobi. Others, however, pointed out that this was a Kikuyu area and the Kikuyu were "treacherous." Hence, as the railway police superintendent reported, "there would be constant trouble between the Waikikuyu and the Indians, and the former, having no regard for law, would undoubtedly murder the Indians, who would be unable to protect themselves."[25]

Most skeptical, perhaps, was the protectorate's commissioner, Sir C. Eliot. Initially, in September 1901, he contented himself with challenging the optimistic expectations of his subordinates. He doubted, he wrote to the Colonial Office, that among the Indian railway workers would be found many "Punjabi cultivators," and he further pointed out that agriculture in the Punjab depended almost entirely on irrigation, which was nonexistent in East Africa. The following January, in a dispatch that would resonate down the years to come, Eliot ruled out Indian settlement in the highland areas north of Nairobi. "Believing as I do," he wrote, "that the East Africa highlands are for the most part a white man's country, and hoping that they will be taken up by white colonists in the near future, I doubt the expediency of settling large bodies of Indians in them, as even in Mombasa there is considerable friction between the European and Indian traders." He suggested that Indian settlers be restricted to the coastal districts, where tobacco, cotton, and rice could be grown, and to the western districts toward Lake Victoria. These latter, he said, though "hot and damp," were "well adapted both for the agricultural methods and the constitutions of coolies."[26]

The reservation of the "White Highlands" for European settlement was to be a fatal blow to the hopes of any substantial Indian agricultural colonization in East Africa. But it cannot be imagined as wholly unexpected. So far back as Holmwood's 1888 report, which spoke of "two colonizations" — Indian and European — proceeding side by side, the notion of East Africa as an "America for the Hindu" had always had to make space for white settlers as well. Even the enthusiastic Johnston argued that Indian colonization was necessary in large part because the climate made white settlement impracticable in "the greater part of the territories we have acquired or are about to acquire in tropical Africa." The continent's mountainous regions, by contrast, such as those in eastern Uganda, where the land lay above five to six thousand feet in elevation, he pronounced "admirably suited to a white man's country."[27]

Hence, the grandiose visions of Indian colonization rapidly collapsed into one settlement perched above the shores of Lake Victoria at Kibos. Of the cultivation by Indians of vast tracts of uninhabited but fertile land, there was to be none. The Kibos settlement originated in 1902 with the award to a half-dozen Indians of small plots of land in a swampy area six miles from the lake. The settlement was soon put under the charge of D. D. Waller, a lowly assistant treasurer in the protectorate government. An official with experience of India, Waller endeavored, as best he could, to develop this fledgling community. The initial settlers were mainly time-expired coolies from the now completed Uganda Railway who had set up small vegetable gardens and begun some experiments with staple crops. As these ex-coolies were not members of "the agricultural class" in India, Waller recruited from among those who had come to Africa at their own expense an additional "40 to 50 experienced cultivators to settle and commence operations." By the end of 1903 the Kibos settlement spread over some 900 acres of ground, with 100 to 150 acres cleared and planted with cotton, rice, wheat, sugar cane, and other crops. Beyond the land itself, free of rent for two years, the government provided no inducements other than advances of seed and cattle. The pleased Waller reported that "the country offers such natural advantages that some of the advances made are being repaid, and all the men appear to be in good circumstances, employing native labour on their holdings." There is no doubt a certain irony in the transformation of one-time "coolie" laborers into employers of African labor. For Waller, however, this circumstance was evidence for the "civilizing" example of Indian enterprise. The Kavirondo, he wrote, "are imitating the methods of the Indian, and are growing various things, their cotton being most successful."[28] Visiting the settlement, Eliot too insisted that "not only do the Indian agriculturists prosper, but the surrounding natives successfully imitate their methods of cultivation and irrigation."[29]

So "palpable" were the advantages of Indian colonization that Waller confidently predicted that if he "were sent to India for a few months I could return with a large number of voluntary settlers." This initial burst of enthusiasm was not to be sustained. Kibos itself, with a thousand acres under cultivation by 1908, was ultimately successful as an agricultural colony. After a 1907 visit, Waller described the settlers as "building themselves better homes," "purchasing large numbers of cattle," and extending cultivation of cotton, sugar cane, chilies, and Indian corn. But, despite an immense volume of talk within the government, no effective action was ever taken to duplicate its success elsewhere. To be sure, a committee with Waller among its members recommended in 1905 the adoption of "reasonable inducements" in tax relief and grants of food and implements in order to secure the establishment of Indian communities within the areas, along the coast and near the lake, long deemed suitable for such settlement. The protectorate governor, Hayes Sadler, supported the committee's recommendations and even, clinging to the shopworn notion of Indians "affording the natives object lessons in cultivation," insisted that Indians as cultivators "will set an example of thrift and industry which the native will soon learn to follow when he realises the advantages to be gained."[30]

In the wake of this correspondence, Waller was dispatched to India in 1906 with instructions to recruit — not the two hundred families Rogers had suggested five years earlier — but a mere fifteen for settlement as cotton cultivators in Kibos and on the coast at Malindi. Waller spent several months roaming about India, to the dismay of Indian officials who felt that he sought only "samples" of cultivators from different parts of the country. In the end Waller returned to East Africa empty-handed. There existed, the acting commissioner reported, "a considerable reluctance among the families approached to emigrate except in communities," and the settlement of entire village groups would "necessitate an outlay far too large for us to contemplate." Calling Waller's tour a "failure," Hayes Sadler told the Colonial Office, "We need make no further move in this direction."[31] None was ever made.

In effect, once it was decided to reserve the highlands for white settlement, the colonial government found itself obliged to accommodate the racial sentiments of those whom it was now encouraging to settle in East Africa. Whatever men such as Eliot may have felt about questions of race, the "development of the country" was now seen as dependent upon securing a community of European settlers. Throughout 1906 and 1907, while the question of Indian settlement remained under active consideration, the colonial authorities, on the defensive, hastened to assure potential and existing white settlers that Indian immigration posed no threat to them. As the commissioner wrote in 1906, all the places marked out for Indian settlement were outside the area opened up to white settlement. Nor was there "any fear that any of the Indian immigrants of the class I should be disposed to encourage would migrate into the white area; at the most they would come to the Municipal Township's limits. There are already so many Indians in Nairobi, for instance, that with the few Indians of the agricultural class with whom we should commence the experiment, this question need hardly be taken into consideration." The settlers at Kibos, he assured the white community, had no intention of moving elsewhere. By the next year, as whites began to move into the highlands, racial lines hardened into a general hostility to Indians. The white settlers, Hayes Sadler told the Colonial Office, "want to keep the Indian, not only out of the uplands, but out of the country altogether." This spirit, he said, was "akin to that prevailing in Natal and elsewhere"; rather disingenuously he went on to explain away this hostility as being "due to the fact that the white cannot compete in the east with the Indian shopkeeper for supplies or provisions and articles in daily use, or as a petty trader."[32]

The response from the Colonial Office at home was little more sympathetic to the Indians than was that of the white settlers themselves. As was so often the case when the imperial government was confronted with racially exclusive measures in settler colonies, the colonial secretary upheld the principles of equity while winking at their violation. "It is not consonant with the views of His Majesty's Government," Elgin roundly declared in March 1908, "to impose *legal* restrictions upon any particular section of the community, but as a matter of administrative convenience grants in the upland areas should not be made to Indians."[33] Throughout this tortuous process of self-justification, only one official, J. A. L. Montgomery, East Africa's commissioner of lands, boldly confronted his colleagues with a list of what he called "facts": "(a) Indians have been in the country (notably in the Sultan's dominions) for many generations, and came long before the Europeans. (b) The Uganda Railway (the greatest factor in the development of the country) was made by Indian labour. But for such labour it would never have been constructed at all. (c) Most of the trading wealth of the country is in the hands of Indians. (d) Finally, Indians are British subjects."[34]

Yet even for Montgomery there existed "facts" of a different sort that had to be taken into account. "We must remember," he wrote in a memo on Waller's Indian tour, "that this is gradually becoming what is called a white man's country. . . . This being the case it follows that in due course this will become a self governing colony. The history of all self governing colonies in Africa teaches us that directly self-government is given restrictions are placed upon Indians." In the interests of the Indians themselves, that is, to avoid raising expectations destined to be shattered, large-scale colonization from India should be discouraged.[35] Perhaps the cruelest irony, and a major Indian grievance, was the Indians' treatment on the railway they had themselves constructed. There the British accommodation of settler prejudice led to the reservation of upper-class accommodation for Europeans alone. "The distinction is necessary," the governor H. C. Belfield wrote in 1914, "because the habits of many Indian passengers render it impossible for Europeans to take long journeys in their company with comfort or convenience." The Indian government, mindful of its domestic constituency, protested this discriminatory treatment, but to no avail.[36]

Despite this intensifying discrimination, Indian migration to British East Africa did not come to an end with the collapse of the schemes for agricultural settlement. Voluntary Indian immigration remained wholly unrestricted, and the rapidly developing economy of the region continued to draw Indians to East Africa. They came in substantial numbers as traders, merchants, clerks, artisans; and they settled in and around the urban centers, above all Mombasa and Nairobi, along the railway line, and even, as petty traders, in the zones reserved for African cultivators. Even with the line completed, in 1914 Indian railway staff numbered some two thousand, including almost all the stationmasters and the bulk of the clerks, while ex-indentured Punjabi Muslims were employed as artisans in the railway shops.

Indians also monopolized the subordinate positions in the colonial government bureaucracy. Goans, especially, seen as reliable and efficient, provided subordinate staff across a wide range of occupations, as cashiers, clerks, surveyors, typists, caterers, and the like working under European district chiefs. Parsis too, though fewer in number, held similar, and occasionally even higher, administrative positions. The Parsi Pestonjee Jamsetjee Mehta, for instance, came from India to Zanzibar in 1886 to work for the Smith Mackenzie & Co. agency house; in 1888 he followed George Mackenzie to Mombasa, where he took charge of the Mombasa customs for the Imperial British East Africa Company. He remained in the company's accounts office until its collapse and then transferred in 1895 to the protectorate service as bookkeeper and accountant; by the time of his retirement in 1907 he was head clerk in the treasury. The total number of Indians in government employ in Kenya alone at the outbreak of the war in 1914 was about one thousand. These skilled Indian employees were indispensable — indeed, as one official remarked, their presence "makes government possible" — and the numbers of Indian staff grew as the government bureaucracy expanded.[37]

Not surprisingly, the consolidation of colonial rule encouraged the old Zanzibari mercantile firms that had spread upcountry to further expand their operations. By 1910 the pioneer trader Allidina Vishram had extended his business network to encompass some thirty major branches throughout East Africa, with five hundred Indian employees, and agents operating as far afield as the Congo and Ethiopia. He then used his trading profits to diversify into real estate and the processing of local produce, establishing oil mills, a soap factory, and a cotton ginnery in Uganda, which laid the foundations of the subsequent Indian-dominated Uganda cotton industry. This investment in cotton ginning — by 1919 Allidina Vishram's fledgling ginnery of 1914 had grown, with the entry of other firms, to a total of seventeen gins — enabled the Indian mercantile community to dominate the purchase and export of Uganda cotton and to direct it to the Bombay market. By 1919 half the cotton grown in Uganda was being sold in Bombay for the use of Indian mills. These economic ties with India were reinforced by continuing social interaction. Like the early Zanzibar merchants, many still returned to get married in Gujarat, and lavished philanthropic bequests upon their native land. For many Indian traders, living encapsulated lives, East Africa was little more than an extension of Gujarat.[38]

The outbreak of the Great War, with the subsequent conquest of German East Africa in 1916, offered one last opportunity to create what had been lost in Kenya — a territory to which Indians had unimpeded access on equitable terms, free of white settler domination or other forms of racial discrimination. Tanganyika, its advocates argued, could be "a colony for India." The most ardent proponent of this idea was Sir Theodore Morison (1863–1936), one-time principal of the Aligarh College in India and member of the Council for India in London. Posted as a political officer in German East Africa as that territory was being wrested from the Germans, Morison laid out his scheme in a memorandum entitled "A Colony for India," written after he had returned to England in the spring of 1918. Morison submitted the memorandum to Edwin Montagu, Indian secretary, who in turn circulated it to the Imperial War Cabinet. Morison then, a month later, published this document in *The Nineteenth Century and After* and argued on its behalf in a letter to the *Times*.[39] The result was a storm of controversy.

Much of Morison's argument echoed ideas Harry Johnston had put forward twenty-five years before when he saw in East Africa the "America of the Hindu." German East Africa, so Morison wrote, was ideally suited to take up such a role. It was "a land crying out for population, by comparison with India hardly populated at all." The soil was of "wonderful fertility," capable of growing "anything," and the rains were "better than in India." Morison envisaged the younger sons of India's landlords leaving India "with a band of adventurous young men from their own neighborhood" to "clear the African jungle and build villages" so that "a living part of India's social life would be transplanted and would develop in a new country." Although living "hard and simple lives," they would, he imagined, in time "turn East Africa into one of the great food producing areas of the world."

Hand in hand with this vision, which critics did not hesitate to call utopian, was that of the Indian providing "object lessons" in cultivation to the African. In terms similar to those used in Johnston's time, Morison described African tillage practices as "wasteful and inefficient." Europeans could not successfully accomplish the needed transformation because European methods were too advanced, too "magical" or "mysterious" in their working, to offer "useful lessons to the negro." The rural economy of the Indian village, by contrast, was "very much more within his grasp," and so "from contact with an Indian cultivator he could get ideas which he could transplant unchanged into his own life." In sum, Indians deserved an opportunity to "play a part in civilizing the wild"; they were, once again, to be "called to share the white man's burden."

But this was not all. More was at stake than was the case in the 1890s. Along with Britain's self-governing dominions, India had rallied to the war effort. This sacrifice, Morison argued, like that of the dominions, deserved some reward. As Australia had secured territories in the South Pacific, and South Africa had won South-West Africa, so too ought India to have "a sphere of influence of her own" into which she could expand freely. Further, India deserved compensation for her citizens' exclusion, enforced by racially discriminatory legislation, from the white settler dominions. Morison proposed something in the nature of a trade-off. Indians would give up a right they cherished — that of free entry into all parts of the British Empire — in return for a "privileged position" in Tanganyika. This bargain would be sealed by awarding India administrative control, as a colonial power, over the conquered German territories in East Africa.

Similar ideas had been put forward earlier in the war by the Aga Khan; and his Ismaili community, with the other Indian traders in East Africa, were, for obvious reasons, enthusiastic supporters of Morison's scheme. So too was Montagu at the India Office anxious, in the troubled years at the end of the war, to appease Indian nationalist sentiment. As he wrote in a cabinet memo in October 1918, "I do submit with all the urgency that I can command that we shall be guilty of a grave dereliction of Imperial duty if we do not see that the Indian has some opportunity of colonization arising out of the Indian partnership in this war." But outside this small constituency the scheme was received with an icy coldness. The *Times* responded to Morison with a critical editorial the very day his letter was published. The day after Montagu's memo was circulated to the Imperial War Cabinet, Curzon as foreign secretary responded with an angry memo of his own. In biting words, he said of Montagu that the Indian secretary had "embarked on a policy of arousing the nationalist sentiment of India. He is anxious to see them enjoy responsible government. Let the class whom he hopes to produce devote some portion of their labour and energies to filling up and developing their native land before they scatter themselves on a foreign soil." Further, he charged, the Indian was not "more tolerant" but "less so" than a white man toward a "negro population." The idea beloved of the colonization enthusiasts that the Indian was somehow closer to the African, that he supplied, as Curzon put it, "a sort of physiological link or half-way house" between the races, was in his view no more than a "chimera."[40]

The presumed welfare of the African, not surprisingly, shaped much of the debate. Lord Cranworth, himself a Kenya settler, spoke for many of Morison's critics when he said that making Tanganyika an Indian colony would "constitute a betrayal of our African subjects who have fought for us." Walter Long, from the Colonial Office, reiterated Curzon's view that India had no claim on the territory as an act of justice; and given that "Africans regard Indians generally with no respect," there was no reason to hand over any territory to them to administer. Similar sentiments shaped the views of the colonial government in Nairobi. Even J. Montgomery, the sympathetic East African land commissioner of the earlier debates, insisted that the African "cordially dislikes the Indian," whom he sees as "only another coloured man no better than himself." The British alone, he insisted, could justly be entrusted with the rule of "child races."[41]

No doubt this talk had in it more than a dose of a self-serving justification for British colonialism; but it expressed as well a long-standing and widespread British hostility toward Indians of the educated and trading classes, to whom the governance of any such "Indian" colony would have to be entrusted. Then, too, the bureaucratic rivalries of Whitehall played their part; for the Colonial Office had no desire to see a new potential colony handed over to the supervision of Montagu's India Office, with the result that Morison's proposal touched off a war of contending memoranda between the two. Nor, odd though it may appear, were educated Indians invariably enthusiastic advocates of Morison's scheme. However appealing a colony of their own might be, many Indians were reluctant to renounce the idea of free movement and fair treatment throughout the empire — an ideal that had for decades reconciled Indians to participation in the imperial system — in return for the uncertain benefits of ruling an East African dependency. So far as East Africa was concerned, the securing of equal rights in Kenya mattered far more than the distant vision of a "privileged position" in Tanganyika.[42]

One might usefully speculate on how far previous experience in India may have shaped the views of British officials in these extended discussions of Indian settlement in Africa. Some of the most influential officials, of course, had had no experience of India at all. This group included, most notably, Harry Johnston, an explorer, adventurer, and occasional consul in Africa prior to service in Nyasaland; and Arthur Hardinge, a member of the foreign service who had served in Russia and the Ottoman Empire before coming to East Africa. Clearly, for these men, impressions of India and Indians had been gained in Africa and, for Johnston and Hardinge, in the 1890s — in the early years of conquest, when the support Indians could offer the empire surely favorably disposed them toward the idea of treating East Africa as the "America of the Hindu." Those who came later, such as Sir Charles Eliot, influenced above all by the decision to encourage white settlement in the highlands after 1902, as we have seen, turned slowly but decisively against the Indian cause.

The greatest enthusiasts for Indian settlement were, not surprisingly, those who had served in India. These included the officers who had come to Africa with the various Indian military contingents, as well as those, like D. D. Waller, whose official duties included work with the resident Indian population. Others, once settled in East Africa, were more ambivalent. Col. J. Montgomery (1849–1940), for instance, was the son of a Punjab governor and himself an official in the Punjab for thirty-five years. He moved to Africa only in 1906 when he took up the position of commissioner of lands. Yet, like the governor Hayes Sadler, whose sympathies were also often enlisted on the Indian side, Montgomery drew back from supporting extensive Indian colonization or awarding Indians political authority in a British colony. One might even argue that by encouraging an easy self-assurance, Indian experience may well have reinforced the notion, widespread among the official class in India at the time, that they, not the educated Indian, knew best how to rule "lesser breeds." Curzon's fierce denunciation of Montagu's reforms, and his airy dismissal of Morison's arguments as a "chimera," surely owed much to his conviction that, from his long years in the "East," he "knew" what Indians were like. And such remarks carried conviction among those less informed. For Walter Long at the Colonial Office, Curzon's description, in his 1918 memo, of Indian "racial prejudice" could "not but cause grave misgivings."

Theodore Morison's vision of German East Africa as an Indian colony was almost certainly rooted in his extensive Indian experience. Most formative, in particular, were his years at the Muhammadan Anglo-Oriental College in Aligarh. Established expressly to create a "modern" Indian Muslim elite, the college recruited an English staff who taught their Indian students European learning along with riding and sports such as football and cricket. Recruited to the faculty in 1888, Morison served as principal from 1899 to 1904. Dedicated to the idea of molding a class of educated Indians who could meet with the English on equal terms, Morison, with the other Aligarh faculty and the school's founder, Saiyyid Ahmad Khan, sought to give the college's students not the book learning of the subordinate clerk but, as one scholar described it, "the knowledge, skills, and values necessary to qualify them for public leadership."[43] Hence it is not surprising that when Tanganyika serendipitously fell into British hands, Morison saw in it an arena where his former students and other like-minded Indians could exercise the political authority they deserved. But in the political climate of the times, there was no way such a vision could be realized.

With the collapse of Morison's scheme, its advocates fell back on an idea put forward as early as 1917 by the Indian delegation at the Imperial War Conference: ensuring "free and unimpeded" Indian access to German East Africa. Montagu further advocated awarding agricultural plots in the conquered territory to demobilized Indian soldiers who had fought in the war. Equal rights of access were, at least in principle, secured by the provisions of the League of Nations mandate by which Tanganyika was handed over to Britain in 1920. Under it, rights of entry and equality of treatment were secured to the nationals of all members of the league. But of course the mandatory agreement made no provision for outside enforcement, opening the way to the kinds of administrative discrimination found in Kenya since at least 1902.

The soldier settlement scheme, as Montagu and the Indian government envisaged it, involved setting aside a substantial tract of land in Tanganyika for Indian cultivation. But even this modest proposal went

nowhere. Increasingly responsive to the views of East Africa's white settlers, the Colonial Office, claiming a solicitous regard for the interests of
the African population, adamantly opposed any "reservation" of land for
Indians. Enthusiasm within India, too, was slowly ebbing. An Indian
official, Sir Benjamin Robertson, sent on a tour of Tanganyika in 1920,
reported that, while there existed large areas of unoccupied land with
"good soil," any attempt to settle smallholders would require extensive
government subsidy and would have to contend with tsetse infestation.
"It is scarcely possible," he wrote, "to imagine the Indian without his bullock practising his traditional methods of agriculture under a system of
small holdings." At the same time, the Indian provincial authorities, when
consulted, alleged a lack of interest on the part of potential settlers.
Governed by their own preconceptions of Indian character, no matter
how much these flew in the face of the facts of Indian emigration, they
asserted simply that "the classes to which the ex-servicemen belong" are
"much too conservative to migrate to, or settle in, an unknown country
like East Africa." Except perhaps in the Punjab, "religious scruples and
attachment to their homes" would prevent agriculturists from leaving
India. Confronted with this opposition, the Indian government reluctantly abandoned the scheme in February 1921.[44]

Two years later, the Indian campaign for equal rights in Kenya came to
an embittered end. Under strong pressure from the white settler community, the imperial government abandoned any effort to secure even the
Indians' minimal demands for equality, most notably a common electoral
roll for Indians and whites and access to the highlands. Winston Churchill,
as colonial secretary, made clear the implications of this decision in a speech
in 1922. British East Africa, he said, was meant to become "a characteristically and distinctively British colony, looking forward in full fruition of
time to complete responsible self-government."[45] With Churchill's declaration Britain's East Africa territories were cut loose from the Indian moor-
ing to which they had been fastened for the preceding half century. Even
though Indians continued to settle and to prosper in East Africa during the
subsequent years, an era had come to a close.

The Uganda Railway: A "Wedge of India" Driven into the Heart of Africa

From his post in Uganda, as the 582-mile railway from the coast to the
interior was fast approaching completion, Sir Harry Johnston in 1899
described for the Foreign Office the implications of the building of this

line. It means, he said, "the driving of a wedge of India two miles broad right across East Africa from Mombasa to the Victoria Nyanza." Fifteen thousand coolies, he continued, with "some hundreds of Indian clerks, draughtsmen, mechanics and policemen, are implementing the use of the Hindustani language, and carrying the Indian Penal Code, the Indian postal system, Indian coinage, Indian clothing, right across these wastes, deserts, forests, and swamps, tenanted hitherto by wild native savages or wild beasts."[46] Extending Johnston's remarks, this section examines the building of the Uganda Railway as an Indian enterprise. To be sure, construction of the railway was financed by the British taxpayer, and the members of the railway committee in London were British nationals. But many of the senior British staff, including the managing member of the committee, came to the Uganda Railway from service in India, while the subordinate and technical staff was almost wholly Indian, as were the laborers in their thousands who wielded picks and shovels along the line. From India as well came the rules and regulations that structured railway operations, along with the locomotives that ran over its tracks. The Indian involvement with the Uganda Railway involved, that is, not just the well-known recruitment of indentured laborers. It extended to the entire project. In all that mattered, as Johnston correctly observed, the Uganda Railway was a "wedge of India," driven into the heart of Africa. Its construction gave visible shape to East Africa's position from the 1890s onward as a colony as much of British India as of Britain itself.

The construction of a railway spanning the width of Kenya, from Mombasa to Lake Victoria, had from the beginning been a key element in Britain's imperial strategy for East Africa during the scramble. A railway would, its proponents contended, make possible the ending of the East African slave trade, firmly secure British control of the headwaters of the Nile, and advance the cause of civilization throughout the interior of the continent. Mackinnon, once his Imperial British East Africa Company had been chartered, did not doubt that such a line was essential both for the commercial success of the company and for his larger mission of bringing civilization to Africa. Hence in 1891 he authorized a survey party to undertake a reconnaissance of possible routes. All the members of the party — officers, technical staff, skilled laborers, and its leader, Capt. J. R. L. Macdonald of the Royal Engineers — were recruited from India. As this was the first involvement of Indians in what was to become a vast project, it is worth observing how these men were brought together. There was no organized recruiting scheme. Rather, Capt. P. G. Twining R.E., appointed executive engineer for the expedition, undertook to

FIGURE 10. "Indian Masons at a Cutting near Voi," on the Uganda Railway, 1897. Courtesy of the Kenya Railways, Nairobi. No. 387/59.

secure its staff. As he was on leave at Simla in the Indian hills at the time of his appointment, Twining used the occasion of his travel to Bombay, en route to Mombasa, to engage the men he needed and then to bring them along with him.

At Simla itself on October 27, Twining engaged a draftsman, one Gholam Rasul. Two days later, in Rawalpindi, he engaged a surveyor, Wali Mahomed, along with one jamadar (headman) and eight Punjabi *khalassies*. On the 30th he hired a second draftsman, a second jamadar, and eleven Pathan *khalassies*. He also interviewed "two or three other men who applied for the surveyor's post, but none of them was suitable." On the 31st, the draftsman he had just hired resigned; but Twining found a replacement two days later in Mohamed Bux, "one of our Zhob valley men," whom, he said, he had "seen at the Lahore station" during a halt there. Meanwhile, his assistant Mohamed Ali, whom he had sent to Peshawar, returned with nineteen *khalassies* and two jamadars, all of whom were taken on. On November 3, now in Amballa, Twining interviewed two surveyors, but "neither of them was willing to go." In nearby Saharanpur, several other surveyors, "whom I had wired to meet me" there, "did not put in an appearance." At that point Twining left for

Bombay with two draftsmen, two jamadars, and the nineteen *khalassies* he had himself recruited. A second party, led by Wali Mohamed, followed with the other nineteen *khalassies*. Unable to secure an Indian surveyor, Twining got authorization just prior to departure for an English surveyor, one Sergeant Thomas of the Indian Public Works Department (PWD). Capt. Macdonald, traveling from England, joined the group in Aden; but he too had seen service in India. Indeed, several of the *khalassies* and jamadars Twining recruited had "previously served with Capt. Macdonald on railway survey and construction work on the Northwest Frontier of India." On arrival in Mombasa the survey party engaged some three hundred Swahili porters, cooks, and servants and then on 5 December set off into the interior. Some nine months later, on 24 September 1892, they returned after marching 4,280 miles and laying down survey lines over a distance of 2,724 miles.[47]

So far as Mackinnon was concerned, however, the entire enterprise was in vain. Always strapped for funds and teetering on the brink of bankruptcy at the best of times, the Imperial British East Africa Company was never in a position to construct a railway. Protracted negotiations with the British Treasury for a subsidy and with the Indian government for labor went nowhere. The Treasury, confronting a hostile Parliament, was unwilling to put public money into Mackinnon's profitless operation, while the Indian authorities, as we have seen, adamantly refused to make available indentured laborers to a private company without the full protective apparatus of the 1883 Emigration Act. In 1892 the company pulled out of Uganda; three years later it was liquidated. No longer could Britain avoid responsibility for the governance of East Africa. At the same time, responsibility for constructing the proposed railway necessarily fell to the British government.

After considering several bids from private contractors, the government determined to build the railway itself. In September 1895 the Uganda Railway Committee was constituted, under the Foreign Office, as the supervisory body for construction. The "Indianization" of the railway commenced at the outset and at the top. As the Managing Member responsible for the committee's day-to-day operations, the government named F. L. O'Callaghan, C.S.I., C.I.E. (1839–1909). O'Callaghan had joined the Indian PWD in 1862 as an assistant engineer and risen through the ranks, becoming by 1889 chief engineer and consulting engineer to the Government of India for state railways. After serving as secretary to government for the PWD from 1892 to 1894, he retired and returned to England. A year later he joined the Uganda committee. O'Callaghan's collaborator and the consulting engineer to the committee was Sir Alexander Rendel, K.C.I.E. (1829–1918). Rendel had been consulting engineer to the secretary of state for Indian state railways since 1872 and had designed, among other structures, the Sukkur Railway bridge over the Indus River. To O'Callaghan and Rendel fell the task of recruiting the senior staff. Within a month of the committee's formation, they had also determined that, as O'Callaghan put it in memo of September 28 regarding the railway's accounts, "the Indian system, or a modification of it, may well be introduced."[48]

Not surprisingly, O'Callaghan and Rendel lost no time in seeking out officers with Indian experience for the new railway project. O'Callaghan, for instance, recommended that "we either borrow an accounts officer from the Indian Government or try to obtain the services of one who has retired." When F. P. Quinlan, recently retired from Indian service, offered himself for the position, O'Callaghan, who had known him in India, sent him off to India to "engage a staff of accountants and clerks and take them with himself to Mombasa." W. A. Johns, an executive engineer with the Punjab Railways, was put in charge of labor recruitment in India, while George Whitehouse was appointed chief engineer, in charge of construction on the ground in Africa. A member of the Institution of Civil Engineers, Whitehouse was not in Indian government employ but had had experience in the construction of railways in India as well as in Natal, Latin America, and England itself. The locomotive superintendent, a Mr. Sandiford, was described as a man of "great Indian experience," while the senior officers of the railway police were almost all drawn from the ranks of superintendents of police in India. As the East African Indian population increased, these men had the great advantage, as Whitehouse wrote, of "a knowledge of Hindustani."

In addition to those recruited from Indian government service, a number of Europeans in India applied for positions with the railway on their own account. This often forced awkward decisions on railway officials uncertain of the qualifications of those who turned up on their doorstep. J. P. M. McInerney, for instance, a storekeeper and apprentice engineer on the Southern Punjab Railway, Whitehouse reported, "came over from India at his own cost on the chance of obtaining employment on this line, and though I do not consider his knowledge or experience warrants his being given an English appointment on sterling pay, still he is doing good work as an assistant engineer on the earthwork division"; as a result he was awarded a temporary appointment on a rupee salary but with the rank of officer. An advertisement for a traffic officer produced four applicants. Three were from India, each with ten to twelve years' service on Indian railways. But on this occasion cost trumped experience. Rejecting these men as "too expensive," Whitehouse turned instead to the fourth, a twenty-eight-year-old guard and goods checker on the Natal Railways who, "a gentleman by birth and education," possessed "sufficient knowledge of railway working to be able to carry out the simple duties now required."[49]

In addition to the railway itself, employment in the various departments of the protectorate government drew ambitious Britons from India across to East Africa. J. Montgomery, as we have seen, came from service in the Punjab to take up the post of commissioner of lands. Of more lowly status, but perhaps even more revealing for what it tells of us of the attractions of East Africa, is the career of Desmond Dalrymple Waller, whom we have already met as patron of the Kibos settlement. Born in Calcutta in 1865, Waller came from a family at the very lowest edge of respectability in British India. His father and both his paternal and maternal grandfathers were employed as clerks or examiners in the "uncovenanted" service of the Bengal government; and both his parents were born in India. Waller's paternal grandfather, Charles Waller, initially employed by a European indigo factory before joining government service, was most likely also born in India. It is a not unreasonable speculation, given their birth and occupational status, that the family's members were of mixed Indian and British stock, perhaps connected to the extended Palmer or Dalrymple clans. Not uncommonly at this time, Anglo-Indians of mixed heritage sought to shake off the "stain" of their marginal status within British India by seeking service elsewhere in the empire. Hence, if of mixed race, Waller may well have sought in East African service a way to present himself as a "pure" Englishman. From India he first went to England, where he joined a sister who was living in London. There, in 1899, at the advanced age of thirty-four, he managed to secure an appointment with the East Africa Protectorate government. He did not pass the colonial civil service examination, but rather secured a local appointment valid for service in East Africa only. The position — that of third treasury assistant — was at the very bottom of the government hierarchy, but it offered opportunities for advancement a mixed-race Waller could not hope to find in India. In 1902, turning his Indian experience to good use, he secured the post of Protector of Indian immigrants. By 1911 he had become director of transport and principal immigration officer of the protectorate. He resigned this post after no more than six or eight years, most likely to take up the life of a farmer in Kenya. Waller ultimately settled in the small Cornish village of Cawsand, where he died in 1944.[50] By the time of his death an English country gentleman, Waller had put behind him any remaining ties to his beginnings in India.

African service was not, however, always appealing to the British in India. Dr. James Cleghorn, surgeon-general with the government of India, when asked for his assistance in engaging medical staff for the railway, replied flatly that he doubted any members of the medical department would willingly go to Africa "on the terms offered." Pleading with the committee at home to sanction pay scales higher than those in force in India, Whitehouse argued that officers' allowances must "substantially compensate for the discomforts and hardships of life in Camp in an uncivilized country." In 1897 an Indian engineer brought over to evaluate the progress of the railway raised once again the question of increasing officers' pay, only to have O'Callaghan reply that "every effort had been made to obtain officers from India but they were simply not to be had and the pensioned Indian officers who had been suggested had failed to pass the medical examination."[51] The senior European staff in charge of the various departments of the railway received sterling salaries ranging downward from Whitehouse's 1,250 pounds a year to 300 to 500 for assistant storekeepers, telegraph superintendents, medical officers, and the like.

Though central to the railway's successful operation, the senior Europeans were few in number compared to the subordinate and technical staff. Almost exclusively, the individuals who served in these lower posts were Indians recruited from India. The financial compulsions sustaining such recruitment were obvious. Arguing on behalf of using the Indian system of accounts, O'Callaghan pointed out that "subordinate accountants, cashiers, clerks, etc., can be obtained in India, either Eurasians or natives, at a cheaper rate than qualified men in England, all well versed in the Indian system, and thus will have nothing to learn." But successful recruiting was not always assured. Johns warned from India in December 1895 that "a lot of railway work is opening up just now in the Punjab," so that the outlook for the hiring of surveyors, draftsmen, suboverseers, and the like was "not so promising." Two years later Whitehouse wrote anxiously to the London committee about the problem of recruiting skilled staff. "The men I am now mostly in want of," he wrote, "are clerks, signalers, and that class of subordinate, and I know of no place but India where these can be obtained." Yet, at the same time, he despaired that "it appears to be very difficult to get good men, as there seems to be a great demand for them in India."[52]

As with recruits for the colonial police forces, Indians were persuaded to sign up for service with the Uganda Railway by offers of pay at up to double the rates paid for similar work in India. Indian institutions, too, among them the Thomason Engineering College in Roorkee, which was allotted advances of money from the railway authorities for the purpose, offered assistance in recruiting. A letter from the Thomason College principal to one Hardian Singh set out the terms of employment — free passage to Africa and back, eighty rupees per month with the usual traveling allowances, and a two-year contract. The letter warned the potential recruit that "you should be well qualified in surveying, leveling, drawing, and works" and pointed out reassuringly that the African climate "is like Bombay and parts are like the North-Western Provinces."[53]

The railway pay and employment rosters illustrate the overwhelming domination of subordinate staff positions by Indians. The 1897 list, for instance, organized in accordance with the railway's divisional structure, supplies the name, salary, and date and place of engagement (whether Mombasa or India) for all individually recruited employees.[54] The individuals are not identified by regional origin or ethnic affiliation, so that someone bearing an English name could be either British or Eurasian (Anglo-Indian), while Indian regional identities involve some degree of guesswork. The chief engineer's department, at the center of the railway's operation, possessed one English head clerk at Rs. 275 per month, with two British typewriting clerks at Rs. 150 and 110. Beneath them were three Indian clerks, five draftsmen, and one tracer. The Indians were all denominated by the title "babu," and apart from two temporary appointees, all brought down salaries of Rs. 80 to 100 per month.

Similarly, in the chief accountant's department, the European employees consisted of two senior accountants lent by the government of India, at Rs. 400 and 250, with some half-dozen European or, more likely, Eurasian clerks paid from Rs. 120 to 150. The Indians on the departmental payroll, ten in number, ranged from an accountant and two cashiers, the most senior of whom was paid Rs. 250, to a half-dozen clerks paid from Rs. 80 to 120. Those departments with the highest pay scales were the locomotive division, with five English engine drivers on sterling salaries, and the maintenance division, with four permanent way inspectors, all British, paid from Rs. 250 to 300. Still, Indians held influential positions in both departments as drivers and inspectors, as well as accountants and clerks. The traffic department, along with several of the survey divisions, was wholly manned by Indians. Pay scales for the Indian staff, at least at the levels of head clerk and accountant, though lower on average, were not markedly below the salaries paid Europeans in similar positions.

As was the case with Indian employment more generally in East Africa, members of various regional and ethnic groups tended to cluster in certain departments of the railway. Clerks were predominantly either upper-caste Bengalis or Goans. Draftsmen, engine drivers, surveyors, hospital assistants, and guards, by contrast, were disproportionately Muslim. Presumably, as with the colonial sociology of India itself, Muslims were seen as better suited for the more energetic and outdoor pursuits, as distinguished from the sedentary activities appropriate to the literate and educated. It is not surprising that the members of the 1891–92 Macdonald surveying party were all Muslims from the northwest. Sikhs, eagerly sought after for the police throughout Africa, are wholly absent from the lists of employees of the railway's operating divisions. Though the few locally recruited Muslims could conceivably have been Swahilis, there is no indication of the employment of any Africans in staff positions.

Nothing better illustrates the enduring Indian imprint on the Uganda Railway than the dimensions of the track itself. In the initial discussions, gauges ranging from two feet, six inches to three feet, six inches were proposed. The latter gauge was the favorite of the imperial enthusiasts who envisaged this line as part of the famed Cape-to-Cairo scheme, which would gird the entire African continent with a unified transportation network under British control. A three foot, six inch gauge, in their view, would facilitate linkage with the Egypt-to-Sudan railway then under construction by Cromer's government at that gauge as Kitchener's forces slowly advanced on the Mahdi at Khartoum. In the end, however, a meter gauge was adopted. This was done, as one member of the railway committee, G. L. Ryder pointed out, "primarily for the sake of facilities in obtaining rolling stock from India." The line, he reminded the other members of the committee, was "being constructed on Indian methods by Indian workmen under officers with Indian experience controlled from home by a committee whose managing member is an ex-Indian official." Hence use of meter gauge — employed on nearly half the Indian lines — was appropriate, even necessary. Further, the skeptical Ryder noted, injecting a note of realism into the Cape-to-Cairo discussion, junction with the Egyptian system — whose terminus was still hundreds of miles away across deserts and jungle —"seemed too distant for the committee to attach really serious importance to the similarity of gauge."[55] Even to contemplate a rail link from Uganda to the Sudan and Egypt was surely a fantasy. But there is a certain irony as well in the fact that East Africa's railway system could never be linked to the one on which it was modeled, a railway system whose tracks came to an end, not hundreds, but a thousand miles away on the far side of a vast ocean.

In addition to adopting an Indian gauge, the Uganda Railway authorities took care to follow closely the operating procedures of the Indian lines. The railway committee's files contain such documents as the twenty-page printed pamphlet of the Bengal-Nagpur Railway entitled "Rules for Enquiring into and Reporting on Accidents." Meticulously marked in red to show desired alterations, the pamphlet was then reprinted with the same title for the use of the Uganda Railway. In similar fashion, O'Callaghan sent Rendel a copy, again marked in red to show desired alterations, of the "Schedule of Standard Dimensions in Force on all Metre Gauge Railways in India." "It seems to me," O'Callaghan wrote, "that we can hardly do better than adopt" these dimensions, which included appropriate angles for curves of track, widths of embankments, depths of ballast, and the like.[56] With the employment of Indian specifications and gauge came, not surprisingly, the use of Indian equipment. By 1897 twelve locomotives had been obtained from India, joining eight imported from Britain. To fuel its engines, coal from Wales was supplemented by the import of Indian coal, a total of 26,000 tons in 1900 and 1901 alone.

India was present too in all discussions of accounts and expenses. For the estimation of costs, Rendel suggested using the Southern Punjab Railway as a "precedent," while O'Callaghan thought the Rajputana Railway, which passed through open country with no major river crossings, offered a better comparative example. To ensure overall compliance with Indian procedures, the Indian Railway Act was put in force throughout British East Africa, where it joined an array of other Indian acts made applicable to the protectorate. Such easy copying of Indian precedents was not, however, free of complications. The decision to use the Indian system of accounts, as we have seen, was taken at the very outset. "Though capable of simplification in some respects," O'Callaghan wrote in September 1895, the Indian system "has answered well for the past thirty years, and it will in this case have the advantage of being familiar to such of the staff as may be recruited from India." But the funds to build the railway were being supplied by the British, not the Indian, government. Hence the monthly accounts had to be forwarded to the Crown agents in London, with the result that all accounts had to be prepared as well "in ordinary civil service form" and all funds converted from rupees into sterling. In its accounting procedures, as in so much else, the Uganda Railway visibly represented its hybrid status — a product of an empire at once British and Indian, yet not wholly the one or the other.

By far the greatest contribution India made to the railway was in the labor force that built it. Without the picks and shovels of thousands of "coolie" laborers, there would have been, in the conditions of late-nineteenth-century East Africa, no possibility of constructing within six years a railway line over five hundred miles long into the heart of the continent. The use of African labor was discussed, only to be rejected with scant consideration. Sir Guilford Molesworth, for instance, in an early report for the Imperial British East Africa Company, acknowledged that there "is no deficiency of population" but insisted that "the habits of the country render it doubtful whether it would be possible to hold out inducements to the aborigines to labour systematically at railway work."[57] No attempt was made to hold out any such "inducements." By the time the railway committee was set up in 1895, it was assumed as a matter of course that construction required the importation of Indian laborers. As in Natal forty years before, when Indian laborers were introduced despite the presence of a large Zulu population, the British simply took it for granted that the scattered and independent-minded tribes of the African interior could not be disciplined for arduous labor, whether of cane cutting or railway construction.

Although recourse to indentured Indian labor was by the 1890s commonplace on colonial sugar plantations, never before had the use of such labor been proposed for a large-scale public works project. Further, the proximity of East Africa to western India prompted a decision to recruit laborers from the Punjab, rather than from the usual recruiting grounds of southern and eastern India. This decision created problems for the railway authorities that were by no means easy to resolve. The Bombay Presidency, first of all, had long closed its territory to colonial recruiting to preserve its supply of labor for local industries; and while the Punjab was open, the most accessible port, that of Karachi, was within the Bombay Presidency and hence not a legally permissible site for the embarkation of indentured laborers. Furthermore, East Africa was not on the list of destinations to which laborers could be sent under indenture according to the 1883 emigration act. Hence, before any "coolies" could commence work on the railway, these legal obstacles had to be overcome, and at the same time, a recruiting structure had to be set up in an area where such recruitment had never before taken place.

As we have already seen in its negative response to the Imperial British East Africa Company's requests, the government of India opposed any indentured labor recruitment not regulated by the provisions of the 1883 act, with its array of licensed recruiters, Protectors at the ports, and so forth. The takeover of East Africa by the Crown, however, placed the

Indian government in an awkward dilemma. With the British government itself now proposing to build the railway, the Indian authorities could not so easily turn down requests for assistance. As the Indian secretary in London told the viceroy in October 1895, a month after the formation of the railway committee, the British government was "anxious" to secure Indian labor for the railway, and so urged India to "relax" the "stringency" of its emigration regulations. The government of India complied by enacting Act I of 1896, which removed the usual restrictions on recruitment when the overseas employer was the British government. The Indian government nevertheless steadfastly denied requests for labor by the sultan of Zanzibar and subsequently by British planters along the East African coast. The railway stood apart as a project of imperial importance.[58]

Lacking an established administrative structure, the recruiting operation got off to an uneven start. Several individuals, only loosely under the supervision of the railway authorities, took it upon themselves to round up laborers in the Punjab. W. A. Johns, appointed as emigration agent in November 1895 and anxious to get recruiting underway, did not bother to wait for the Indian government to act. As shipping laborers directly from Karachi to Africa was "out of the question," Johns initially proposed to have them shipped from Karachi to Bombay and then transferred to a second vessel anchored in Bombay harbor. The laborers would not to be able to go on shore, because the Bombay presidency was closed to recruitment, but Johns proposed ferrying the medical personnel out to the steamer, where they could carry out the required inspections.

Meanwhile, Johns dispatched to the Punjab a recruiter whom he had for some years employed to secure labor for the Mushkaf Bolan Railway in Baluchistan. "I am offering," he told the committee, "Rs. 15 per mensem and rations," pointing out in justification that sepoys joining the East African contingents received Rs. 18. He soon had collected some one thousand laborers. There was, of course, the small problem that recruiting "coolies" for East Africa was still illegal. "No doubt," Johns told O'Callaghan, "Uganda is prohibited, and my recruiter is without a licence; but fortified with the correspondence (in your last letter) between the secretary of state and the viceroy, he has credentials that will see him through if the men are forthcoming." Further defying the Indian government, Johns determined to ship the laborers directly from Karachi. "I think," he wrote in late December, "I have squared the Protector of Emigrants here [in Bombay] as to sailing from Karachi. . . . Anyway, it is worth chancing and once on board we will probably be all right."[59] And so the first two lots of "coolies" set sail in January 1896.

Johns's recruiting activities were complemented by those of his own recruiter, Husain Bakhsh at Lahore, acting on his own account, and by the Parsi firm of A. M. Jeevanjee & Co. at Karachi. The Indian government regarded these private Indian contractors with suspicion — in Jeevanjee's case for illegally engaging laborers in his own name instead of on behalf of the British government, and for service anywhere in East Africa rather than just on the railway. Hence after 1896 that firm was confined to supplies contractor. Still, Jeevanjee's entrepreneurial activities, first in Karachi and then in East Africa, were central to the successful functioning of the railway and subsequently to the larger development of Kenya. After a varied business career in India, Jeevanjee (1856–1939) had obtained in 1890 a contract to supply labor for the Imperial British East Africa Company, which he followed up by establishing a branch of his Karachi office at Mombasa. From here his firm entered into stevedoring, contracting, and construction work throughout East Africa. For the railway Jeevanjee not only oversaw arrangements for the shipment of laborers from Karachi but also secured contracts to supply materials and provisions, including foodstuffs for the Indian labor force. His firm further undertook the construction of government offices, railway stations, and post offices all along the line from Mombasa to Kisumu. Subsequently, when confronted with the hostility of the fledgling European settler community, Jeevanjee himself took a leading role in mobilizing Indian opinion in Kenya for equitable treatment, and for some years served on the colony's legislative council.[60]

As time went on, the Indian government set out to regularize recruiting. As Karachi was not a recognized port for emigration, throughout 1896 and 1897 emigration had to take place through Bombay, where, to the annoyance of the railway authorities, batches of emigrants were often detained. In September 1896 the government of India redrafted the employment contracts and reduced the pay offered intending laborers from fifteen to twelve rupees a month. The lower rate, it said, was "high enough to secure laborers of the desired quality." Most important, the government replaced the earlier ad hoc recruiting with an administrative structure headed by an emigration agent, initially the agency house Grindlay Groom & Co. of Bombay. As remuneration for their services they were paid four rupees per head for each "coolie" leaving India. Husain Bakhsh meanwhile remained at Lahore as head recruiting agent, while Johns went off to East Africa where he took up a position as district engineer on the railway.

In January 1898 Karachi was at last opened as a port of direct emigration for East Africa. As it was more convenient to locate the emigration agent near the recruiting grounds, the railway committee replaced the Bombay-based Grindlay Groom with Osmond Boyce, a district engineer on the railway, who in December 1897 was sent from East Africa to establish an agency at Karachi. The recruiting operation in the countryside changed over time. In the early days, as the Protector of Emigrants reported in 1901, "paid recruiters were sent into the districts, but now that the popularity of the Uganda Railway amongst the Coolies has gained ground this is found to be unnecessary." Instead, "jemadars apply to the recruiting agent [Husain Bakhsh] for work, and they are told to bring 100 men, who, if passed by the doctor, are taken on, and the Jemadar is put in charge of a gang on a monthly salary of Rs. 25. The coolies get 3 annas a day till they embark and receive one month's pay in advance."[61] Ocean transport from Bombay, where coolies had to be transshipped before 1898, and later from Karachi was entrusted to Mackinnon's British India Steam Navigation Company, which sent the laborers direct to Mombasa on chartered steamers.

With this framework in place, indentured labor recruitment grew rapidly as construction of the line was pushed forward into the interior. Indeed, the authorities in Africa often pleaded with their agents in India to secure more laborers and to send them over in batches as large as possible. By the last months of 1897 a total of some 5,000 Indian laborers had been dispatched to East Africa, where they joined some 150 Indian subordinate staff and 500 artisans. A year later, in October 1898, the railway had on its payroll some 10,000 Indian "coolies," along with a total of 859 Indian artisans. The numbers continued to rise, reaching a height of some 20,000 employed in 1901. Altogether, throughout the period from 1896 to 1902, a total of 31,983 Indian laborers were engaged for service by the railway. Of these, the not insignificant total of 6,454 were at some point invalided as unfit for work, and some 7 percent, or 2,493, died while in service.[62] Locally engaged African laborers, varying in number from 1,500 to 2,500, were also employed on the line, often for such rough tasks as clearing brush and leveling ground ahead of the Indian workers laying track.

Recruitment did not always proceed smoothly. In 1897, while recruiting operations were at their height, plague spread throughout western India. To avoid spreading contamination, the Indian government closed the ports of both Karachi and Bombay and restricted recruitment to uninfected areas of northern and eastern India. Desperate, the railway authorities scrambled to devise expedients that would permit an uninter-

FIGURE 11. "Gangs Shifting Camp at the Railhead." Photo by William D. Young. By permission of the Syndics of Cambridge University Library. RCS/Y30468I/24.

rupted flow of labor. One was simply to recruit from those regions in the east and south that remained open. These tracts were, after all, the traditional recruiting grounds for colonial planters from Fiji to the West Indies. But this scheme ran afoul of the enduring prejudice that proclaimed Punjabis to be superior to all other Indian ethnic groups. As O'Callaghan wrote in July 1897, the climate of East Africa was "unsuited" to natives of the Madras Presidency, while the restriction to Bengal, Bihar, and the eastern North-West Provinces "limits the field of recruitment to some of the poorest districts in India as regards the physique of the men, which is so important a condition for Africa, and shutting out the good recruiting grounds of the Punjab and the better parts of the North-Western Provinces." The alternative of using Chinese labor was ruled out on the grounds that treaty port migrants were the "sweepings of these towns" and liable to introduce into East Africa the "evils of race admixture."[63]

Pressure from a British government anxious to keep up the railway's labor supply induced the Indian government to reopen the Karachi port in August 1897. But to secure intending migrants from infection, the railway authorities were required to hold them in quarantine camps until they could be pronounced fit, and then to send them directly by rail to the steamer at the wharf. This in turn created other problems. In May 1898 a despairing Boyce reported that he had collected some twelve hundred men, "consisting of Mekranees [from the Makran coast], Pathans, and Peshawarees, but the spread of plague caused them to betake themselves to the fields. To induce them to return to Karachi was in itself an undertaking of some difficulty, but to further comply with the last demand made on me, viz., to have them all put into the segregation camp at Kiamari, and further to have both their persons and luggage disinfected, has been frightful work." A few weeks later, he reported, "an open fracas" took place between the sepoy camp guards and its Pathan inmates. Apparently a guard refused to let a man talk with his father through the fence, pushed him back and hit him with a stick; the two grappled, and the sentry then struck at the man with his bayonet, at which point a "general affray" broke out in which sixty intending emigrants were taken away to prison. For Boyce, reading this episode through the lens of a colonial sociology, the incident was a product of "the sustained antagonism and overbearing manner of the Hindu sepoys to our men, who were of course Mussulmen." Also, no doubt, confinement in the close quarters of a quarantine camp in a plague-infested region did not encourage equable social relations.[64]

Tempers sometimes grew short among railway officials in India as well, as they saw thousands of laborers, and hundreds of skilled staff whom they had trained, streaming out of India to Africa. One G. Winmill, locomotive superintendent for the North Western Railway in Lahore, protested this drain of personnel in stark terms. "I have," he wrote to Boyce, "a very great objection to the Uganda Railway making a recruiting ground of this line." This "exceedingly curt" letter went all the way up to the Foreign Office, which responded, in biting words of its own, that "Mr. Winmill is probably unaware that this is an Imperial work of much political importance." Still, the loss of trained staff was a matter of concern in India. When Boyce requisitioned from the North Western Railway some fifteen chargemen in the locomotive department, the railway manager replied that this request had given him "much anxiety," but "in view of the wishes of the Government that the Uganda Railway should be assisted in every way, we finally made arrangements to let the men leave." "We have," he concluded, "put ourselves to appreciable inconvenience in meeting your wishes."[65]

As recruitment was never straightforward, so too did the construction of the line not always proceed smoothly. Most famous was the encounter with the "maneaters of Tsavo," a pair of lions whose depredations entered into the popular lore of the railway. In a gripping account of this episode

the British railway official Lt. Col. J. H. Patterson described how the ram-
paging lions attacked sleeping Indian workmen in their tents and de-
voured some twenty-eight of them, in addition to a number of Africans.
Ultimately, after tracking the lions through the jungle, Patterson himself
shot and killed both of them. In appreciation, a group of workmen presented Patterson with an engraved silver bowl bearing an inscription of
gratitude over the name of the overseer Babu Purshotam Hurjee Pumar,
together with an extended Hindustani praise poem. Composed by one
Roshan Mistri of Jhelum district in the Punjab, the poem relates how the
author "came to this country of Africa, and did find it indeed a strange
land; with many rocks, mountains, and dense forests abounding in lions
and leopards"; and how "the lions fell on the workmen and destroyed
them"; and how "because of the fear of their lives the workers would sit
in their huts, the hearts full of foreboding and terror," until finally the
"brave and valiant Patterson Sahib . . . roamed about in the forests to protect us" and killed the "savage animals."[66] Other, more common disruptions also took place, among them occasional mutinous refusals to work
on the part of "coolies," threats of bodily harm directed against supervi-
sors, and desertions and deceptive practices aimed at increasing pay.

As these thousands of Indians poured into Mombasa, not only that
town but the entire line of rail took on the appearance of an Indian settlement. Arguing (unsuccessfully) for the opening of recruiting operations to private contractors, Whitehouse in August 1897 wrote that
Mombasa "is now practically the same as an Indian station, with a
Magistrate and a Judge, with the Indian Acts in force." As a result, he
insisted, "it is a very different thing for a coolie to come to Mombasa than
to go to Demerara or the West Indies, or even the Cape."[67]

Indentured recruitment was brought to an end in 1901 as the railway
reached completion; the line was opened to the lake terminus on March
3, 1903. What had this stupendous effort achieved? The railway was pro-
moted by its imperial enthusiasts as essential to secure the strategic interests of the British Empire in Africa. The Uganda Railway did little, and
at great cost, to advance this objective. On the occasion of the final confrontation with the French at Fashoda in 1898, and with the Mahdi at
Omdurman that same year, the still-incomplete railway — whose track had
barely reached the halfway point — was useless. What the railway did do,
as Johnston so cogently pointed out, was to drive a "wedge of India" into
the heart of Africa. For a time at least, the Uganda Railway made of East
Africa effectively a province of the Raj.

Conclusion

During the 1920s the web of imperial connections focused on India came undone. The collapse of this subimperial system had been foreshadowed during the years just before and during the war, but the war itself had also offered opportunities for its expansion. Hence the end came with an unexpected suddenness. By the 1930s little remained, apart from the established overseas Indian communities, to indicate that there had once existed a flourishing network of ideas, institutions, and movements of people, radiating out from India across the Indian Ocean arena. This concluding chapter assesses the nature and causes of this decline and then addresses the question of India's ambiguous position in the British Empire as both colonizer and colonized.

Decline

Loss of enthusiasm for the continued promotion of an India-centered imperial system was, by the end of the First World War, a nearly universal sentiment — among India's British rulers, the country's newly confident nationalist elite, and the rulers of Britain's colonial territories in Africa and Southeast Asia; in the Whitehall bureaucracy; and not least, among the colonized peoples among whom Indians had settled. Withdrawal of Indian police and soldiers from their posts overseas was perhaps the first sign of impending change. The Indian contingents in East Africa, part of the King's African Rifles, were disbanded just before the war in 1912 and 1913. Considerations of cost and a determination on the part of the colonial governors to employ no Indians if Sikhs were denied them, together with a growing conviction that African troops had both become sufficiently well trained and were sufficiently loyal, drove forward this redeployment. In similar fashion, the Sikh- and Indian Muslim–manned Malay States Guides, whose origins dated back nearly a half century to the first occupation of the Malay Peninsula, were abolished just after the war in 1919.

In these years, the imperial government had also to contend for the first time with the potential unreliability of Indian troops when deployed overseas. With the rise of militant nationalism in India, the favored "martial" Sikhs were often attracted to the Ghadr movement, and the equally "martial" Punjabi Muslims to the Khilafat movement. Both the Ghadr and Khilafat movements caught up their adherents in anticolonial activities centered outside India, from California to Constantinople, and so opened up to India's soldiers a larger arena than ever before in which to shape identity and action. Furthermore, this discontent, for the first time since 1857, took the shape of open mutiny. On February 15, 1915, in Singapore, four of eight companies of the Fifth Light Infantry mutinied, seized the weapons in the regimental magazine, killed their officers and a number of civilians, and then proceeded to release and arm German prisoners of war held nearby. Rallying loyal soldiers and European volunteers, the British managed to put down the uprising within a few days. Testimony at the subsequent investigation made it clear that the soldiers, Punjabi Muslims, had become uneasy at the outbreak of war with Ottoman Turkey and were responsive to preaching that presented Islam as being in danger. As one sepoy told the investigators, "About a fortnight before the outbreak I was in the regimental mosque, and I heard sepoy Manowar Ali say 'We should pray for the advancement of Islam and the victory of the forces of Islam.'" Such anxieties were facilitated by Singapore's position as a nodal point in the larger imperial system, which made it a "focus for Indian seditionists" as well as of "fanatical" Islamic activism.[1] Despite this mutiny, with its ominous portent for the future, the Indian Army fought in France, East Africa, and Mesopotamia for the empire in the First World War as it had for so many decades before. Disaffection on a massive scale took place only in the next war, once again in Singapore, when thousands of Indian soldiers taken prisoner at the fall of the city in 1942 joined Subhas Chandra Bose's Japanese-backed Indian National Army.

With the diminution of the Indian military presence overseas went the

repudiation of Indian laws and legal systems. The animus against overseas use of the Indian codes was foreshadowed in 1904 with the rejection
of codification for Southern Nigeria, followed by Lugard's enactment of
the Queensland code for the whole of Nigeria. Only after the war, however, did the Colonial Office, in part responding to settler protests, itself
begin to question the utility of using the Indian codes. Most dramatic by
far was the concerted attack on the Indian codes in East Africa. Here, by
1930 the Colonial Office, over fierce opposition alike from the local bar,
bench, and civil authorities, had forcibly overturned a system of laws that
had been in effect for fifty years and set up so-called English law in its
place. In similar fashion, the imperial authorities forced the repeal in 1919
of the Indian-based Iraq Occupied Territories Code, after a mere four
years in operation, in favor of a legal system derived from Ottoman and
Egyptian precedents.

Opportunities for Indian settlement within the empire and the opportunity for the Foreign Office bureaucrats of Simla to shape imperial strategy both dwindled rapidly after 1920. The war, with its conquest of
German- and Ottoman-controlled territories, seemingly worked to
expand, not curtail, the area open to settlement and to Indian influence.
India directed the initial campaigns in Mesopotamia, while Indian
officials urged that the newly conquered territories of Iraq and Tanganyika
be thrown open to Indian agricultural settlement, and even, in the view
of some, made over to India as colonies of its own. Such enthusiasms,
however, met with little support in Britain. Direction of the Mesopotamian campaign was taken from India after the disaster at Kut, while
administrative control of the conquered territory, initially almost wholly
in the hands of Indian officers, was transferred from the India Office to
the Colonial Office by 1921. No Indian agriculturists were ever settled in
Iraq, while the Indian secretary Montagu's plea for an Indian role in the
former German East Africa was coldly turned aside.

In Britain's established colonies, especially those with large white settler populations now become self-governing dominions, restrictions on
entry of Indians, together with denial of equal rights for Indians already
resident, grew ever more stringent as the new century progressed. Such
discrimination had been anticipated by the severe restrictions placed on
Indians in Natal when that colony received self-government in the 1890s
and by the subsequent reluctance of the imperial government to fight for
equal treatment for Indians in the negotiations that led to the Union of
South Africa in 1910. Harsh restrictions on the entry of "Orientals" into
Canada and Australia also dated from the first decade of the century. The

Indian government, responsive to its local constituency, had never sup-ported restrictions on the movement of its subjects, and even argued, if vainly, for free migration throughout the empire. Still, by 1913 it had begun taking steps actively to discourage migration to Canada. For Indians, however, the critical moment of disillusion can perhaps be said to have taken place in 1923 in Kenya. Although the imperial government had for twenty years connived at the exclusion of Indians from that colony's so-called White Highlands, Indians had still anticipated that in this colony — ruled, unlike the dominions, directly from London — their rights would be secured. Instead, the British excluded Kenya's Indians not only from the highlands but also from participation in a common elec-toral roll. There was to be no racial equality with Europeans.

Most far-reaching in its implications for India and for Indians was the ending of indentured labor recruitment in 1916. After some eighty years and the elaboration of a vast administrative apparatus, no longer was the annual departure of thousands of Indians to labor in Britain's colonial ter-ritories ever again to take place. Though Indians as individuals did con-tinue to migrate and settle overseas in the 1920s and 1930s, most notably in Malaya and in Kenya as merchants and as traders, the ending of inden-ture, combined with the restrictions on entry in the settler-ruled domin-ions, meant that the scope of opportunity for Indians was now increas-ingly confined to India itself. Whether indenture was viewed as a way out of poverty for desperately poor peasants or simply as a mask for exploita-tion and oppression, it had nevertheless tied India tightly into the larger world of the British Empire, and it did so in a way that gave India a cen-tral place in that empire.

Other, more symbolic but not inconsequential changes further announced the ending of an empire fashioned around India. In 1920 British East Africa abandoned the Indian rupee for the East African florin, equivalent in value to two British shillings, as the basic unit of its mone-tary system. Dissatisfaction with the use of the British Indian rupee had made itself felt almost from the date of the rupee's introduction by the Imperial British East Africa Company. Already in 1905, when the Indian silver rupee was made the standard East African coin, its Indian subdivi-sions of annas and pice were replaced by a decimalized subsidiary coinage. The exchange rate fluctuations of the war years, which upset the old rela-tionship between gold, silver, and the rupee, spurred consideration of a shift away from the Indian rupee. Initially, despite settler enthusiasm for a straightforward adoption of English coinage, and the gold standard along with it, the government proposed to create a separate East African rupee. Confronted with an enraged settler community that feared an artificial increase in its costs and a loss of export earnings if any tie remained to a rupee rapidly increasing in value, the government abandoned this scheme and gave East Africa instead a sterling-based "currency of its own." Although East Africa was now cut off from the Indian monetary system, the rupee lived on in ghostly form in the new florin — a silver coin similar in size and weight to the old rupee.[2]

Visible too were the transformations in architectural style. "Saracenic"-styled buildings, such as those of prewar Kuala Lumpur or J. H. Sinclair's comparable civic structures in Mombasa and Zanzibar, ceased to be built in the years after the war. The last such Saracenic structure was perhaps Sinclair's Zanzibar Peace Memorial Museum of 1925. Instead, the architecture that flourished across the empire, whether in Southeast Asia or East Africa, was that of monumental classicism — from Herbert Baker's Government House in Nairobi to Singapore's Municipal Building and Supreme Court. The empire was now to be knit together around those enduring forms in which all Britons could share as participants in an avowedly British empire.[3] India's architectural elements were to be found alone in domestic architecture, in what Abdul Sheriff calls "embellishments," as in the intricately carved balconies and delicate fretwork of Zanzibar's Stone Town dwellings, and in the form of the colonial bungalow as it spread, almost unrecognizably transformed from its Indian origins, to Southern California and even to the seaside towns of Britain.[4]

By far the longest-lasting of the Indian-derived institutions of the British Empire were its administrative structures — above all, the ideal of the district officer, ruling with disinterested impartiality, and the system of indirect rule through princes. The former found ample scope in the interwar years in Africa and in Palestine, while the latter flourished during the 1920s and 1930s as Lugard's widely hailed system of governance spread from Northern Nigeria throughout much of Africa. India's enduring imprint was of course also to be found in the established communities of Indians and their descendants — stranded, as it were, throughout lands where they found themselves all too often unwelcome.

How, we must ask, can we account for this dramatic reversal? What brought some fifty years of India's existence as an imperial center to such an abrupt end? For the British, the forces that pushed forward this transformation are perhaps not too difficult to discern. The anxieties and challenges of the unsettled interwar years inevitably enhanced a determination to make the British Empire appear truly British, with the loyal white settler dominions rallied around it, not an extension of an India where power was being shared with ever more hostile nationalists. These sentiments were further sustained by a powerful conservative constituency in Britain closely tied to settler communities overseas. Though neither Rhodesia nor Kenya secured full dominion status, the Colonial Office was unwilling to challenge the settlers' demands for a privileged position against Indian and African alike. East Africa was meant to be, as Churchill said in 1922, "a characteristically and distinctively British colony."

More important, throughout the colonial world by the 1920s, Indians simply no longer mattered for the British in the ways they had in the early years of conquest and consolidation. Trained and disciplined Indian troops were essential as the empire spread from Malaya, across Africa, and into Mesopotamia. Indian soldiers and police provided the only economical and reliable force capable of quelling insurrection and securing colonial order. By the 1920s, however, local forces, such as the now wholly African King's African Rifles, existed in sufficient number and with sufficient training to take on the task of maintaining internal security for the colonial state. In a time of settled colonial governance, Indian police could be only an embarrassment, even a liability, as the British sought to convince native peoples that colonial rule was directed to securing their interests.

Indian clerks, merchants, and even plantation laborers occupied much the same position in the colonial order. In the initial stages of empire, as its institutions were being established, the skills Indians possessed were indispensable. The colonial regime in Malaya, for instance, in the later nineteenth century could not have functioned as an effective bureaucratic state without Ceylon Tamils as clerks, and the country's export crops of coffee and rubber could not have flourished without Indian laborers. Of course, such use of Indian skills inevitably devalued the "native." Pushed aside, he was made, by contrast with the "industrious" Indian, to conform to the stereotypes of indolence and ineffectuality the British had woven about him. The "lazy native" was made lazy by the presence of Indians whose skills and abilities confined him. Nothing could be sharper than the contrast between the Malay village, with its carefully contrived subsistence agriculture, and the towns and plantations, inhabited by Indians and Chinese, that sustained the country's commercial economy.

Over time, however, Indian skills and labor were ever less necessary to keep the colonial state and economy functioning. Even indenture, as colonial authorities had begun to discover by the 1910s, was no longer essential to successful sugar cane cultivation. In 1911, five years before its empire-wide abolition, indenture was brought to an end in Natal. This act, long under consideration, evoked but little protest even among the planters. As the Natal governor wrote in 1908, "The planters appear to anticipate that greater use may gradually be made of native labour, and also that by more and more Indians reindenturing, the necessity for fresh importations will gradually decline." This transformation was sealed and a new labor force created for South Africa by the 1913 land act that drove Africans off the land as independent cultivators and into labor for whites, alike in the mines and the cane plantations.[5]

As their enthusiasm for a subimperial role for India waned, the British, to a substantial extent, effectively bowed to the mounting pressures placed on them from below. Everywhere in the empire, Indians were viewed with suspicion and disdained as rivals and competitors — by whites in South and East Africa, blacks throughout Africa, Arabs in Iraq, and Malays in Southeast Asia. By the 1920s for the British nothing was to be gained by confronting this animosity.

The decline of Indian enthusiasm for the empire is a more complicated tale. As we have seen throughout this book, many Indians — from men like Ranade, who had pronounced the growth of the empire a "gain" to the people of India, to those like Gandhi who had found remunerative employment within it — willingly participated in an empire they saw as enlarging the sphere in which Indians could flourish. Yet within the span of a few short years, and decisively by 1920, not only militant nationalists but moderates as well had lost faith in the empire. The short explanation for such a shift in sentiment, of course, is that nationalism could grow only at the expense of empire. Participation in the British Empire, in this view, was incompatible with an India that determined its own destiny. Yet, for the first twenty or even thirty years of its existence, the Indian National Congress, while never less than deeply committed to building an Indian nation, adamantly insisted on its loyalty to Crown and empire. In its many resolutions and petitions, the congress sought only an ame-lioration of India's situation within the empire, a "joint partnership on equal terms," not a break with it. Its vision was that of dominion status for India. Like the emerging Australian and Canadian nationalists of the early twentieth century who successfully accommodated themselves to a continuing existence within an empire-commonwealth that treated them as full citizens, the early congress leaders imagined a similar Indian nationalism flourishing comfortably within the British Empire.

The sources of Indian disillusionment can be found in many acts of the British Indian and imperial governments through the first two decades of the twentieth century. One surely was the increasing favoritism shown by

Britain to the white dominions. In 1907 the dominions were grouped together in a separate Dominions Division within the Colonial Office; this administrative reorganization was followed by a series of regular imperial conferences in which the dominions, but not India, were participants. Despite India's much larger population and avowed loyalty, in the twentieth century, as John Darwin has written, "British world power came to depend more and more upon partnership with the White Dominions."[6] For Indian nationalists, as a result, their country's inclusion among the self-governing dominions, despite Montagu's 1917 declaration of eventual "responsible government," seemed ever more elusive. Events from Curzon's 1905 partition of Bengal on through the 1919 Amritsar massacre served only to reinforce this sense of alienation. This history is well known and will not be rehearsed here. From the perspective of this study, what matters are those events that caught up Indians resident overseas in the larger empire. Of these, two loomed large among the concerns of India's nationalists: discriminatory treatment meted out to Indians in white settler–dominated states; and the treatment of Indian indentured laborers in the sugar colonies.

Decade after decade the legislative discrimination to which South Africa's Indians were subjected, especially as it was brought before the Indian people by men like Gandhi, aroused outrage among educated Indians. During and after the Boer War especially, as David Omissi writes, "British policy toward Indians in South Africa became something of a litmus by which Congress judged British attitudes towards Indians generally, and British perceptions of India's status within the wider Empire." For educated Indians the war in South Africa was "a test of empire."[7] Gokhale, for instance, in 1902 urged the government to adopt not the "narrower imperialism" of race, but rather "that nobler imperialism which would enable all who are included in the empire to share equally in its blessings and honours." Hence, the greater was the disappointment when the Indian Army was excluded from participation in the fighting and, even worse, when South Africa's Indians were abandoned to their fate after the war's successful conclusion. "No single question of our time," as Gokhale told the legislative council in 1910, "has evoked more bitter feelings throughout India — feelings in the presence of which the best friends of British rule have had to remain helpless — than the continued ill-treatment of Indians in South Africa."[8]

Next only to South Africa in arousing outrage in India were the conditions of labor for indentured Indians on colonial sugar plantations. By the end of the first decade of the twentieth century this discontent had taken the shape of demands for intervention by the government of India, and with it an end to indentured labor recruitment. The extended debates on indenture, complemented by commissions of inquiry established both by the Indian government and by independent nationalist political figures, which produced a complete halt to indentured recruitment in 1916, will not be reviewed here. What concerns us is why Indians sought to end indenture and what that tells us about their relationship to the imperial system.

At first glance, it might seem as though a disproportionate amount of energy was invested in the struggle over indentured labor, especially during the decade 1910–1920. Indenture, after all, given the size of India's population, did not catch up that many individuals in its net. Over the roughly eighty years during which the system functioned, from 1840 to 1920, a total of just over 1.3 million Indians went overseas as indentured laborers. Averaged on an annual basis, this would mean an intake each year of some 150,000. This of course is a substantial number of people, but an emigrant flow of that extent meant that less than one-tenth of 1 percent of India's population left the country each year. Similarly, the size of the Indian communities in the various overseas colonies, with the possible exception of Mauritius, never approached the numbers resident in even a single Indian district. At the end of the era of indenture, the Indian population of Natal, for instance, totaled 118,000, while a medium-sized Indian district such as Gonda in the United Provinces had a population of 1.5 million. Surely, one might argue, the condition of the hundreds of millions in India itself toiling in abject poverty was more deserving of attention than that of a few hundred thousand overseas.

Yet indenture did matter, and it mattered because of the way, in an era of aroused national consciousness, it exposed the inequities of colonialism. These "inequities" had existed for half a century and more, but now they captured the public imagination as they had not before. As reports filtered back to India, from Gandhi in South Africa, the sympathetic English clergyman C. F. Andrews in Fiji, and others, talk of "deception" in recruitment, of maltreatment aboard ship and on the sugar estates, indeed of the system as "radically wrong," one of "temporary slavery," resonated through the Indian press and the halls of the legislative council.[9] Much as accounts of the "middle passage" a century before had made the world aware of the horrors of slavery, so too did indenture reveal for all to see — by contrast with India itself, where much was masked or obscured — the racial hierarchies and institutionalized violence that sustained colonialism. At the same time, the destitution of the plantation laborer embarrassed an Indian elite always concerned with how their country was perceived abroad. The educated had no choice but to live with poverty at home. But abroad, in the eyes of the "civilized" world, elite Indians sought always — say, as law students in Britain — to project an image of respectability. Indenture displayed large numbers of Indians across the globe reduced as "coolies" to the lowest levels of degradation.

Beyond the exploitation of the Indian plantation worker, the shame of "immorality," of Indian women forced into prostitution and sexual servitude often at the hands of European men, most aroused popular sentiment. For Indian men in particular, to see their women treated in this fashion was humiliating. To be unable to control and protect their women undermined enduring notions of proper male behavior in Indian society. By extension, the sexual exploitation of Indian women under indenture can be seen as a form of violation, even plunder, of India itself. It deprived India of its most valued treasure, its chaste women, and sullied the purity of Mother India, Bharat Mata, herself. Of the tales that told of this degradation the most powerful perhaps, because it recounted a life under indenture, was Totaram Sanadhya's Hindi autobiography "My Twenty One Years in the Fiji Islands" (1914). Like the god Ram, in this view, the overseas Indians were exiles, their women despoiled in a way even the captive Sita had managed to avert; and the British had taken the place of the demon Ravana.[10]

With their appeals to Indian virtue and a morality shattered under indenture, such accounts could not be pushed aside. They challenged, in a way that a mere abhorrence of coerced labor could not, structures of value that sustained Indian society. Further, these accounts exposed Indians — moderate nationalists above all — to a guilty self-awareness of their own complicity in the imperial system that had brought into existence such moral degradation. The urgency and passion of the attack on indenture was perhaps a way of coming to terms with these feelings of inadequacy and betrayal.

Indenture had the further advantage that it provided a platform on which all Indians, of whatever political persuasion, together with liberal Englishmen like Andrews and even the viceroy Lord Hardinge, could join together in a common cause. Campaigning against indenture could help heal the divisive "moderate" versus "extremist" split in the Congress, while the Hindu nationalist Madan Mohan Malaviya could work with Gandhi, and both with the more secular Motilal Nehru. The inevitable conflicts that stirred Indian nationalists as they set out to construct a nation could be safely set aside and attention directed overseas. Moderates especially, as they confronted their own increasing marginalization, found in the campaign against indenture a way once again to make good a claim to leadership in the national struggle. As with the earlier attack on the "drain" of wealth to Britain, indenture was a cause that united rather than divided the Indian elite and called on the skills of petitioning and advocacy long honed by the moderates.

Not surprisingly, perhaps, the end of indenture after 1920 led to a rapid waning of interest in the plight of the overseas Indian. A few, most notably the moderate Srinivasa Sastri, endeavored to keep India's attention focused at least on the condition of Indians in South Africa. But without indenture as a rallying cry and with the nation transfixed by Gandhi's non-cooperation campaigns, overseas Indians could not help but fade from India's consciousness. In effect, the Indian communities overseas were left to look after themselves. Indeed, by the 1930s India's nationalist leaders were discouraging the ex-indentured from returning, on the grounds that they would not feel "at home" in India. The rhetoric shifted as well. From a conception of a "Greater India" — a de-territorialized nation comprised of all Indians everywhere — over time the struggle for freedom inevitably focused its efforts inward on the land of India itself. The overseas Indians, whether wealthy Gujaratis or impoverished ex-indentured laborers, "at home" nowhere, in the end became rootless cosmopolitans. One might see in their situation an anticipation of those, a half century later, who crossed the "black water" to the Gulf, or Europe, or North America, to form the NRIs (Non-Resident Indians) of the present day.

The Indian Overseas and the Web of Empire

The question remains: did Indians secure tangible benefits from their participation in the larger imperial system? Certainly, as we have seen throughout this volume, Indians never managed to secure the status they longed for — that of full citizens of an empire that treated all equally. They were always its subjects. Yet, however ambiguously, they were colonizers as well as colonized. Like the Irish perhaps, Indians have never found it easy to come to terms with their experience on both sides of the imperial equation. Hence, it is almost impossible to strike a balance of "benefits" in any definitive fashion. The numbers of those caught up in the migrations that swirled across the Indian Ocean are simply too large and their lives too varied to permit close analysis. At best we can attempt here a brief summary.

About the conditions of life and labor for indentured workers in the colonies there can be little disagreement. Despite the creation of a complex administrative apparatus and the appointment of Protectors in both the colonies and the Indian ports, British planters always subjected their indentured laborers to harsh discipline and often to personal abuse. The Indian workers were cut off from their homes and families and, except where they recreated it for themselves, from a familiar culture. Such religious solace as they received came from visiting members of such Hindu organizations as the Arya Samaj and the Sanatan Dharm.

Still, it is clear that conditions were not the same in all colonies or at all times. Rates of reindenture and return would perhaps repay closer scrutiny as clues to the attractiveness of indenture in particular times and places. Mauritius, especially, seems to have been relatively popular among those considering indenture. Marina Carter, despite making clear in several works the exploitation to which plantation laborers were subjected, has argued that Mauritius recruiting rarely involved deception or coercion. To the contrary, the island's recruiting often was carried out by time-expired laborers who returned to their home areas, where they encouraged friends and neighbors to sign up for Mauritius. Perhaps because it was close to India, with frequent traffic back and forth, Mauritius was a familiar, and thus less feared, destination than other more distant colonies. On Fiji, by contrast, the plantation regime appears to have been exceptionally harsh and brutal. Fiji's isolation in the middle of the Pacific, relatively free of outside scrutiny, together with the existence of a hostile organized native Fijian community and a monopoly of sugar procurement by the Australian Colonial Sugar Refining Company, may well have encouraged the excesses so vividly described in works such as Totaram Sanadhya's autobiography.

Were indentured laborers worse off than if they had stayed in India? Again, this question cannot be answered. One could argue that some years of indenture, followed by independent cultivation in a prospering colony, might be preferred to eking out a living as a subsistence cultivator on a tiny plot as the tenant of a grasping Indian landlord. Until well into the twentieth century, after all, Indian landlords, important pillars of the Raj, escaped government scrutiny to almost the same extent as colonial planters. Indentured returnees seem to have been concentrated at the extremes: among the destitute, on the one hand, for whom the colony held no attraction; and on the other, those with accumulated wealth sufficient to enable them to set themselves up as men of position in their old homes. In any case, some two-thirds of indentured laborers overall, despite the provision of a free passage back to India, chose to stay in the land of their indenture. Shame, and fear of losing caste status in their home villages, no doubt held many back. But there were advantages to remaining in the colony. The story of Natal's Indian community, even though subjected to continuing racial discrimination, may be suggestive.

As early as the 1880s the Natal authorities had begun to notice a tendency on the part of ex-indentured Indians to move into commercial farming. Indians, as the Protector noted in 1893, "are extending their cultivation of tobacco, beans and maize in all parts of the Colony, particularly on the coast." By 1900 Indian cultivation extended over some 38,200 acres in Natal, and Indians controlled the Durban fruit and vegetable market. Indians also predominated in skilled artisanal occupations and secured employment on the railways and in engineering works. In addition, as the Protector reported in 1887, "the demand for Indian house servants is always constant, and hotel keepers frequently apply to me, as do private residents, for cooks, waiters, dhobis, etc." Of those leaving the colony on the expiry of their indenture, two or three times as many during the 1890s sought their fortunes in the Transvaal gold fields, thereby renouncing their right to a free passage, as took up that passage and returned to India.[11]

As the new century proceeded, Natal's Indians progressively abandoned agriculture altogether for higher status and more remunerative work in the professional, commercial, and industrial sectors of the economy. In 1904 two-thirds of the Indian population of Natal was engaged in agriculture; by 1936, only one-third remained in the farm labor force, and the numbers continued their steady decline in later years. Whether the opportunities such employment made available compensated for the earlier harshness of life under indenture or the loss of ties with their homeland, not to mention racial discrimination in their new homes, cannot be ascertained. But of the increasing overall postindenture prosperity of the Indian communities in such places as Natal there can be no doubt.[12]

In addition to the indentured, many Indians were drawn overseas by the opportunities of trade and commerce. Most of these emigrants came from the established trading communities of Gujarat and Tamil Nadu and had participated in the larger trading networks of the Indian Ocean for decades if not centuries. For the most part, the British imperial order simply widened and intensified overseas Indian traders' existing commercial activities. Where traders moved into new geographical areas, they often followed in the footsteps of the resident indentured laborers, to service

FIGURE 12. Sikh community (Khalsa Diwan) of Hong Kong, 1937. Courtesy of the Sikh Temple, Hong Kong, and Gurinder Singh Mann.

those laborers' needs. Natal, for instance, was brought within the orbit of Indian trade only from the 1870s with the growth of indenture. The first merchants, known as "passenger" Indians or misleadingly as "Arabs," came to the colony from nearby Mauritius. They were soon followed by others from India itself. Unlike the merchant community of East Africa, predominantly Kutchi, that in South Africa, though still Gujarati, was composed primarily of migrants from Surat and Kathiawar. In addition to well-to-do traders, in South as in East Africa small shopkeepers and hawkers known as *dukawallahs* spread into the interior, where they initiated trade with the largely rural African population. The continued integration of these colonial trading networks is visible in the two jewelers, originally from Kathiawar, who from Natal went on to Fiji as that remote island's first Indian traders.[13]

The South African government harassed Indian traders by discriminatory legislation and heavy taxation. They were further confined in their credit dealings by the rise of international banks. Hence the Indian business community of Natal retreated in the early twentieth century to smaller-scale activities. As Padayachee and Morrell write, "Within this changing economic environment, links with London and Johannesburg overshadowed in importance links with India."[14] Still, Indian merchants prospered in the apartheid era by renouncing politics and taking advantage of the racially defined spaces that remained open to them. To an even greater extent, the less restricted Indian business community in interwar East Africa, which unlike South Africa remained open to immigration from India, prospered by expanding from petty trade into large-scale manufacturing enterprises, among them textiles, sugar, sisal processing, and cotton ginning. Even so, however, most Indians were confined to the middle roles in commerce and industry, with the overwhelming majority employed in small-scale enterprise, most notably by the 1920s the motor transport business, or as subordinate staff in larger firms. Moreover, Kenya's political system, as we have seen, effectively excluded Indians in favor of the white settler.

Despite the growth of Indian entrepreneurship in colonial Africa, one area of economic activity remained effectively closed to them — that of large-scale commercial agriculture. As we have seen, after initially encouraging Indian settlement on the land, the British reserved the productive Kenya highlands for whites and placed most of the remaining cultivable land of the colony, apart from the coastal strip, in native reserves. In the end, Indians secured for themselves only the settlement at Kibos, on the rail line some ten miles from the lake port of Kisumu. Perhaps surprisingly, given its small size, the Kibos settlement prospered from the award of plots to retired workers on the Uganda Railway. Sardar Jagat Singh, for instance, recruited in 1895 as a railway laborer, was awarded 105 acres in Kibos in 1902; he then brought over twenty Sikhs from India and arranged for each to be given twenty acres. By 1918 Jagat Singh had taken up cane cultivation and erected a flour mill. After his death in 1957, his elder son took over his thriving business.[15]

Curious myself to see what remained of this tiny Indian agricultural community one hundred years after its foundation, I ventured out to Kibos in January 2005. The railway station is derelict, and passenger traffic along the line has ceased. But some Indians remain and cane cultivation flourishes. One of the most prominent farmers is Chanan Singh, whom I visited and who today has 960 acres in cane, together with a crushing and hauling business. Chanan's father, Santa Singh, came to Kenya from Jullundur (Punjab) in 1916 as a laborer on the railway. In 1924, retiring from the railway, he received an allotment of 160 acres in Kibos. Chanan himself was born in Kibos in 1926, after his father brought over a wife from India. Over the years Santa Singh extended his holdings by purchase. In particular, he turned to advantage the fear and anxiety among

Indians that surrounded the coming of Kenyan independence in 1963. Over the course of a few years, as Chanan Singh told me, some fourteen Sikh families sold their properties and left the country. His father and then he himself, after his father's departure for India in 1972, purchased several of these, with other properties, including one from an English South African and another extensive plot held by an Ismaili. Now almost eighty years of age, Chanan Singh still presides over this extensive agricultural enterprise, employing some five hundred African workers and a few Asians, with the help of his elder son.[16]

Many Indians went overseas to serve in the military and police. Most of these men were drawn to such employment by pay scales substantially in advance of those available in the Indian Army. These men clearly benefited from India's central position in the imperial system and from the construction of Muslim and Sikh Punjabis as favored martial races. In Southeast Asia, where they were recruited on the spot, these Indians frequently stayed on, above all in Singapore and Malaya, after their retirement from the force. Further, despite the stoppage of Sikh police recruitment in 1919, as immigration from India to Malaya remained open during the interwar years, Sikhs and other Indians continued to come to Southeast Asia in search of opportunities in entrepreneurship and commerce.

Soldiers of the Indian Army, as members of a disciplined force, were required to return to India at the end of their overseas tours, whether those took the form of service in a colonial contingent or with their regiment in a formal campaign. The prospect of three years of higher pay, as we have seen, was a powerful inducement for soldiers to volunteer for colonial duty in Africa, with the aim of investing the proceeds in land on their return. For soldiers sent abroad with their regiments, overseas service was not a matter of choice, and it carried with it a substantial risk of injury or death in the service of a cause that they did not share. One can indeed argue, as India's nationalists frequently did, that these overseas campaigns enforced substantial costs in men and money on India without generating any benefits in return — that they were, in short, part of the price India paid for its colonial subjugation.

Still, service in the Indian Army secured for its soldiers benefits back in India, as soldiers' pay was invested in land, and jewels, and marriages and as retired soldiers took up residence in canal colonies specifically established for them. One source of the Punjab's enduring prosperity throughout the twentieth century is surely to be found in its situation as a vast recruiting ground for the Indian Army. One scholar speaks of a "great influx of pay and pensions" into the Punjab, especially between

1914 and 1945, on such a scale that in one district, Jhelum, the amount was equal to the rental value of all the land in the district. Further, during these same years the Punjab government allotted to military grantees a third of a million acres of irrigated Crown land. On this base, soldiers and their families erected a level of consumption the highest in rural India and an agriculture that made of the Punjab, in both India and post-1947 Pakistan, the bread basket of the subcontinent.[17]

Surveying the range of Indians who went overseas through the high colonial era, one can perhaps say that, in an imperial system not of their making and which excluded them from the best jobs and from political power, they found ways not just to survive but, for many, to prosper. Much of their success, as J. S. Mangat has written of Kenya's Indians, was due not to British encouragement but to "the enterprise with which the Indians exploited fresh avenues for economic activity and to their general economic resilience."[18] The roots of this "resilience" can be found in many elements of the Indian social order, especially the entrepreneurial skills of the extended family, which cannot be assessed here. At the same time, those skills helped make Indians into enclave communities little integrated with those among whom they lived. They thus remained into the postcolonial world vulnerable to a politics of hostility, of exclusion, and even, as in the case of Idi Amin's Uganda, of expulsion. Nevertheless, the imperial order that the British created across the Indian Ocean opened up to them, for a half century and more, a vastly enlarged arena in which, even in the face of racism and rebuffs, Indians could exercise their skills and talents.

The demise of the tottering Indian subimperial order was sealed by the successive traumas of the Great Depression and the Second World War. The worldwide depression accelerated trends toward economic nationalism and the tightening of national borders already underway at the time of the 1914–18 war. Until the 1920s the British had been committed to the free movement of peoples within the empire and to a policy of worldwide free trade. For decades they had avoided competing with their European neighbors or with the United States in the raising of protective tariff walls. From the commencement of Crown rule, India, under a system of enforced free trade, had played a key role in this system as a supplier of raw materials and importer of manufactured goods. The First World War inaugurated an era of increased surveillance of travelers, with the enforcement of passport regulations in Europe as well as India. Codified in the Indian Passport Act of 1920, such restrictions were justified on the grounds that the government should have the power to exclude "mis-chievous persons" from India. In an era of heightened nationalism that often spilled overseas, as in the Ghadr and Khilafat movements, and of imperial anxiety about "Bolshevism" and revolutionary "conspiracies," decades of unrestricted travel had to come to an end.

Restrictions on travel were soon followed by restrictions on trade. In 1931 Britain formally abandoned the gold standard, and with it free trade. Over the fierce opposition of British manufacturing interests, India was allowed to raise its own tariff barriers. At first, in the 1920s, these took the form of a "discriminating protection" awarded to major industries, first to steel and then in 1930 to cotton textiles. More wide-spread import duties soon followed. The effects of this protectionism were undercut to some extent by simultaneous imperial preferences that sought to keep the Indian market open to British goods. Still, the enact-ment of protective tariffs announced the coming of a new era. For fifty years, from the 1930s to the 1980s, India increasingly cut itself off from the world market economy. Its economic, like its political, life now focused inward, rather than outward across the sea.

The fall of Singapore and Burma to the Japanese in 1942 together delivered the final blow. As one devastated officer who joined Bose's Indian National Army put it, "I was brought up to see India through the eyes of a British officer. . . . At the back of my mind was the traditional urge of loyalty to the King." But no longer. With the surrender of the sup-posedly impregnable fort of Singapore, as Bayly and Harper write in their account of this debacle, "the entire legitimacy of the Asian empire had been shaken." Singapore's fall was followed within months by the collapse of British authority in Burma and the subsequent exodus of hundreds of thousands of Indians. Fleeing in chaotic disarray, with little or no support from the British colonial government, and leaving thousands of dead behind them, the Indians trekked back to Assam through the mud of Burma's jungle-clad hills. Weakened by disease and starvation, they strag-gled into a country little equipped to receive them, and itself on the verge of the massive 1943 Bengal famine. In Burma the Indian community had depended for its security on that of the British colonial regime. Now its members found themselves betrayed and vulnerable across Southeast Asia. British and Indian had come, as one British officer told his Indian subaltern in Singapore, to "the parting of our ways."[19] If the empire had abandoned them, the Indians who had served and prospered under it had no choice but to seek their own destiny.

Abbreviations

CAB	Cabinet papers (The National Archives, Kew)
CO	Colonial Office (When used alone, CO refers to the Colonial Office itself; with a numeral following, it identifies a file in the National Archives, Kew.)
Col. Sec.	Colonial Secretary
EAP	East Africa Protectorate
Emig.	Emigration
Est.	Establishment
Extl.	External
FMS	Federated Malay States
For.	Foreign
FO	Foreign Office (When used alone, FO refers to the Foreign Office itself; with a numeral following, it identifies a file at the National Archives, Kew)
Gen.	General
GOC	General Officer Commanding
Gov.	Governor
IBEA Co.	Imperial British East India Company
ICS	Indian Civil Service
IG	Inspector General
II	Indian Immigration Letter Books, KwaZulu Natal Archives, Pietermaritzburg

IO	India Office (London)
KAR	King's African Rifles
KW	Keep With (marginal notes accompanying a file of correspondence)
Mily.	Military
Mss. Eur.	European Manuscripts
NAI	National Archives of India, New Delhi
OIOC	Oriental and India Office Collections, British Library, London
Pol.	Political
PP	Parliamentary Papers
Progs.	Proceedings
Rev. & Ag.	Revenue and Agriculture
Sec.	Secretary
SOAS	School of Oriental and African Studies
SofS	Secretary of State
SS	Straits Settlements
SSLegCo	Legislative Council of the Straits Settlements
TNA	The National Archives (formerly Public Record Office, PRO), Kew
WO	War Office

Notes

Introduction

1. H. J. Mackinder, *The First Ascent of Mount Kenya,* quoted in Peter H. Hansen, "Vertical Boundaries, National Identities: British Mountaineering on the Frontiers of Europe and the Empire, 1868–1914," *Journal of Imperial and Commonwealth History,* 24 (1996): 56.

2. V. S. S. Sastri, "The Kenya Question," *The New Age,* 10 May 1923, pp. 19–20, cited in Robert J. Blyth, *The Empire of the Raj: India, Eastern Africa, and the Middle East, 1858–1947* (Basingstoke: Palgrave Macmillan, 2003), 126–27.

3. For a recent account see Sugata Bose, *A Hundred Horizons: The Indian Ocean in the Age of Global Empire* (Cambridge, MA: Harvard University Press, 2006), 151–70.

4. See Radhika Singha, "Exceptions to the Law and Exceptional Laws: A 'Proper' Passport for Colonial India," paper delivered at the 20th International Congress of Historical Sciences, Sydney, Australia, 3–9 July 2005. Also see Radhika Mongia, "Race, Nationality, Mobility: A History of the Passport," in Antoinette Burton, ed., *After the Imperial Turn* (Durham, NC: Duke University Press, 2003), 196–214.

5. See Sir William Willcocks, *Sixty Years in the East* (London: William Blackwood & Sons, 1935), esp. 13, 32.

6. Ibid., 171.

7. H. M. Durand, Memorandum on the External Relations of India, 17 October 1885, in For. Dept. Secret E May 1886, no. 74. See Blyth, *Empire of the Raj,* esp. ch. 1.

8. See the extensive writings of Antoinette Burton, Catherine Hall, Mrinalini Sinha, and others. Much of this is summarized in Burton, ed., *After the Imperial Turn.*

9. Tony Ballantyne, "Rereading the Archive and Opening Up the Nation-

State," in Burton, ed., *After the Imperial Turn,* 102–21, esp. 112–13. See also Tony Ballantyne, *Orientalism and Race: Aryanism in the British Empire* (Basingstoke: Palgrave Macmillan, 2002), pp. 13–17.

10. See Michael Pearson, *The Indian Ocean* (London: Routledge, 2003), ch. 7, esp. 190; and Kenneth McPherson, *The Indian Ocean* (Delhi: Oxford University Press, 1993), 4, 8.

11. For a recent study that endeavors to treat the Indian Ocean in the colonial period, see Bose, *A Hundred Horizons.* The Bose volume appeared as my own book was going to press, and so I am unable fully to take its arguments into account here.

12. J. DeVries, "The Move toward Economic Globalization: The Euro-Asian Trade, 1495–1795," and Diego Holstein, "The Multiple Origins of Globalization," papers delivered to the panel on Economic Globalization: Historical Perspectives and State of Research at the 20th International Congress of Historical Sciences, Sydney, Australia, 3–9 July 2005.

13. For a useful series of essays on the larger issues at stake, see A. G. Hopkins, ed., *Globalization in World History* (London: Pimlico, 2002). For an insistence, in my view rightly, on the persistence until the interwar years of an "interregional" Indian Ocean arena between the national and the global, see Bose, *A Hundred Horizons,* esp. 272–79.

14. Taylor cited in Nicholas D. Kristoff, "At This Rate We'll Be Global in Another Hundred Years," *New York Times,* 23 May 1999, sec. 4, p. 5.

1. Governing Colonial Peoples

1. Lauren Benton, *Law and Colonial Cultures* (Cambridge: Cambridge University Press, 2002), 3.

2. Ibid., ch. 4. See also Radhika Singha, *A Despotism of Law: Crime and Justice in Early Colonial India* (Delhi: Oxford University Press, 1998).

3. Eric Stokes, *The English Utilitarians and India* (Oxford: Clarendon Press, 1959), 224–25.

4. Ibid., p. 259.

5. Speech of 10 July 1833, in T. B. Macaulay, *Complete Works* (New York: G. P. Putnam's Sons, 1898), 11: 582. See also the similar statements by Macaulay's successor as law member, J. F. Stephen, in W. W. Hunter, *Life of Lord Mayo* (London: Smith, Elder and Co., 1876), 2: 168–69.

6. David Skuy, "Macaulay and the Indian Penal Code of 1862," *Modern Asian Studies* 32 (1998): 513–57, esp. 538–45. I am grateful to the participants in the seminar that I gave at the Nehru University in January 2005 for forcing me to sharpen my thinking on this topic.

7. Memorandum of 22 September 1868, in *Progs. SSLegCo. for 1868,* liii.

8. Memorandum by R. C. Woods, 20 October 1868, TNA CO273/22/795.

9. Speech of 31 March 1869, *Progs. SSLegCo. for 1869,* 12.

10. CO Note of 29 January 1869, CO273/22/795.

11. Speech of 31 March 1869, *Progs. SSLegCo. for 1869*, 12.

12. Memorandum of 2 April 1871, CO273/49/10169.

13. Governor SS to CO, 29 June 1870, CO273/38/8721.

14. Memorandum by colonial secretary of 29 May 1892, CO273/181/13399.

15. See residents reports collected in *Progs. SSLegCo. for 1878*, council paper No. 5, 15 March 1878.

16. Report of FMS legal adviser of 21 August 1900, CO273/262/33385. See also Emily Sadka, *The Protected Malay States, 1874–1895* (Kuala Lumpur: University of Malaya Press, 1968), 251–55.

17. Report of FMS legal adviser, 21 August 1900, CO273/262/33385.

18. Order-in-Council of 7 July 1897, OIOC LPJ/6/451, file 1381. See also TNA FO2/142.

19. See H. F. Morris and James S. Read, *Indirect Rule and the Search for Justice: Essays on East African Legal History* (Oxford: Clarendon Press, 1972), esp. 112–13.

20. Hardinge to Kimberley 25 February 1895, FO2/142/1–3; and Hardinge Report on East Africa to 1897, PP 1898, 60: 235.

21. Legislative Dept. KW of 13 April 1897, For. Dept. Extl. A September 1897, no. 48–54.

22. Hardinge to Ainsworth, 20 March 1896, FO107/50.

23. Hardinge to Kimberley, 25 March 1895, FO2/142/1–3.

24. Report on Ukamba Province from 1895 to 1905, PP 1906, 80: 149.

25. Morris and Read, *Indirect Rule*, 117.

26. Cited in ibid., 118.

27. Dispatch of 8 June 1909, cited in ibid., 119.

28. Minute by acting chief secretary of Uganda, 15 April 1927, in ibid., 125.

29. Minute by H. G. Bushe of 19 November 1923 and associated correspondence, CO533/298; W. Ormsby Gore to governor Tanganyika, 23 December 1927, CO822/3/3; Morris and Read, *Indirect Rule*, 119–25.

30. Judge high court to governor Nyasaland, 16 June 1926, CO533/631.

31. Chief justice to governor Kenya, 23 June 1925, CO822/3/3; chief secretary Uganda to governor Uganda, 15 April 1927, cited in Morris and Read, *Indirect Rule*, 124–25.

32. SofS Colonies to governors of Kenya, Uganda, and Tanganyika, 10 May 1927, CO822/3/3.

33. Minute of meeting of H. G. Bushe with George Ishmael of 18 December 1929, CO822/18/6. I am grateful to Katherine Prior for her help in tracking down this and other related Colonial Office files on East African law.

34. Morris and Read, *Indirect Rule*, 104.

35. Somaliland Order in Council of 17 October 1899, For. Dept. Extl A, August 1900, no. 20–23; Northbrook to Salisbury, 21 July 1874, quoted in Blyth, *Empire of the Raj*, 72–73.

36. Robert L. Tignor, "The 'Indianization' of the Egyptian Administration under British Rule," *American Historical Review* 68 (1963): 636–61.

37. For an account of the controversy, see H. F. Morris, "How Nigeria Got

Its Criminal Code," *Journal of African Law* 14 (1970): 137–54. Egerton served in the Straits civil service from 1883 to 1903 and in Nigeria from 1903 to 1912.

38. For general accounts see Michael Fisher, *Indirect Rule in India* (Delhi: Oxford University Press, 1991); and Barbara Ramusack, *The Indian Princes and their States,* The New Cambridge History of India, vol. 3, no. 6 (Cambridge: Cambridge University Press, 2004).

39. Fisher, *Indirect Rule,* ch. 10.

40. A. E. H. Anson to SofS Colonies, 13 June 1871, PP 1874, 45: 766; memo by J. F. A. McNair, ibid., 838.

41. Campbell to Col. Sec. SS, 24 October 1872, CO273/61; Campbell Report of 5 June 1873, CO273/74. See also R. J. Wilkinson, ed., *Papers on Malay Subjects,* Part 2 (Kuala Lumpur: Government Press, 1907), 99.

42. Kimberley to Clarke, 20 September 1873, PP 1874, 45: 659; and Minute of 31 August 1873, CO273/63.

43. Pangkor Engagement of 20 January 1874, PP 1874, 45: 704.

44. Braddell memo [n.d.], ibid., 848; Clarke to Kimberley 24 February 1874, ibid., 736.

45. Clarke to Kimberley, 24 February 1874, ibid., 739.

46. Carnarvon to Clarke, 27 May 1874, and to Jervois, 27 July 1875, PP 1875, 53: 181.

47. Stanley speech of 19 May 1874 in House of Lords, *Hansard Parliamentary Debates,* 3rd ser., vol. 219, cols. 467–77; Birch memo, n.d., PP 1874, 45: 850.

48. Col. Sec. SS to Sec. Govt. India For. Dept., 26 November 1874, and Sec. Govt. India For. Dept. to Col. Sec. SS, 8 February 1875, For. Dept. Pol. B, February 1875, no. 95–96.

49. Report of 2 April 1875, PP 1875, 53: 150–51.

50. Memo of 28 June 1875 on Speedy's report, ibid., 181–82; Stanley speech of 28 February 1876 in House of Lords, *Hansard Parliamentary Debates,* 3rd ser., vol. 227, col. 1006.

51. Jervois to Carnarvon, 16 October 1875, PP 1876, 54: 325–28, 334–35; and Carnarvon to Jervois, 10 December 1875, ibid., 362–65.

52. Jervois to Carnarvon, 10 February 1876, ibid., 685–86; and Carnarvon to Jervois, 1 June 1876, ibid., 776–78.

53. Report of assistant sec. for Native States, enclosed in Anson to Hicks Beach, 6 March 1879, PP 1878–79, 51: 422; Perak administration report for 1886, 14 May 1887, PP 1888, 73: 704.

54. Swettenham report of 26 July 1897 on "Durbar" Held at Perak, CO273/229/20303. For Curzon's 1902 durbar, see my *Ideologies of the Raj,* 196–98.

55. Margery Perham, "Introduction to the Fifth Edition," in F. D. Lugard, *The Dual Mandate in British Tropical Africa,* 5th ed. (London: Frank Cass, 1965), xxxi–xxxiii; and Margery Perham, *Lugard,* vol. 2, *The Years of Authority, 1898–1945* (London: Collins, 1960), 147–49.

56. Lugard, *Dual Mandate,* 203.

57. Hardinge to Salisbury, 10 May 1897, OIOC LPJ/6/452, file 1434; and Salisbury to Hardinge, 2 May 1898, FO107/88.

58. Tignor, "'Indianization,'" esp. 649, 659.

59. Mary A. Hollings, ed., *Life of Sir Colin Scott-Moncrieff* (London: J. Murray, 1917), 63–64, 201–3; Tignor, "'Indianization,'" 654–57; Sir Colin Scott-Moncrieff, *Note on the Nile Barrage* (Cairo: National Printing Office, 1890), p. 5. For discussion of the larger issues involved, with an account of Willcocks's career, see David Gilmartin, "Imperial Rivers: Irrigation and British Visions of Empire," in Durba Ghosh and Dane Kennedy, eds., *Decentring Empire: Britain, India, and the Transcolonial World* (New Delhi: Orient Longman, 2006), 76–103.

2. Constructing Identities

1. For general discussion, see my *Ideologies of the Raj*, esp. ch. 4; and Bernard S. Cohn, *Colonialism and Its Forms of Knowledge: The British in India* (Princeton: Princeton University Press, 1996).

2. John Crawfurd, *History of the Indian Archipelago* (Edinburgh: A. Constable and Co., 1820), 1: 46, 50, 52. See also Syed Hussain Alatas, *The Myth of the Lazy Native* (London: Frank Cass, 1977), ch. 1.

3. Frank Swettenham, *British Malaya* (London: A. Lane, 1907), ch. 7, esp. 134, 136–41; Hugh Clifford, *Malayan Monochromes* (New York: E. P. Dutton and Co., 1913), p. 120. See also Alatas, *Myth of the Lazy Native*, ch. 2; and P. C. Wicks, "Images of Malaya in the Stories of Sir Hugh Clifford," *Journal of the Malay Branch of the Royal Asiatic Society* 52 (1979): 57–72.

4. Swettenham, *British Malaya*, 134, 259, 305, 344. For the British attitude to the Bengalis, see my *Ideologies of the Raj*, 105–6, 166; and Mrinalini Sinha, *Colonial Masculinity: The "Manly Englishman" and the "Effeminate Bengali"* (Manchester: Manchester University Press, 1995).

5. Cromer to Strachey, 3 April 1906, cited in Tignor, "'Indianization,'" 658.

6. For a brief summary of these contrasting views, see my *Ideologies of the Raj*, 6–9, 72–75.

7. Clifford, "Life in the Malay Peninsula," in Paul H. Kratoska, ed., *Honourable Intentions* (Singapore: Oxford University Press, 1983), 227–56. See also Clifford, "The East Coast," in W. R. Roff, ed., *Stories by Sir Hugh Clifford* (Kuala Lumpur: Oxford University Press, 1966), 10–17.

8. Clifford, "Among the Fisher Folk," in Roff, ed., *Stories*, 190; and Clifford, *Malayan Monochromes*, 121.

9. Swettenham, *British Malaya*, 119, 232.

10. On rubber, see F. A. Stockdale, *The Royal Botanical Garden, Paradeniya, Ceylon, 1822–1922* (Colombo: H. W. Cave, 1922), esp. 45; and "Pioneers of Rubber Planting in British Malaya," *British Malaya* 1 (1927): 281–82. Biographical notices of early planters are given in *The Planter* (the journal of the Society of Planters of Malaya) from 1921 onward.

11. For an account of this migration, see Rajakrishnan Ramasamy, *Sojourners to Citizens: Sri Lanka Tamils in Malaya* (Kuala Lumpur: privately printed, 1988),

chs. 2 and 3, esp. 60–61, 70–71, 80, 86, 88–90. For Maxwell, see *Selangor Administration Report for 1890* (Kuala Lumpur: Government Press 1891), 23.

12. See Rajesh Rai, "Race and the Construction of the North-South Divide amongst Indians in Colonial Malaya and Singapore," *South Asia,* n.s., 27 (2004): 245–64.

13. Swettenham, *British Malaya,* 305; Clifford, "Life in the Malay Peninsula," in Kratoska, ed., *Honourable Intentions,* 247; Clifford, "The East Coast," in Roff, ed., *Stories,* 110–11.

14. For discussion of these enactments, see Paul Kratoska, "Ends That We Cannot Foresee: Malay Reservations in British Malaya," *Journal of Southeast Asian Studies* 14 (1983): 149–68.

15. Minute by W. A. Ellis of 21 March 1927, cited in P. Kratoska, "The Peripatetic Peasant and Land Tenure in British Malaya, *Journal of Southeast Asian Studies* 16 (1985): 16–45, esp. 29.

16. For discussion, see A. C. Milner, "Islam and Malay Kingship," *Journal of the Royal Asiatic Society* (1981): 46–70; Milner, *The Invention of Politics in Colonial Malaya* (Cambridge: Cambridge University Press, 1995), esp. 146–53, 216–19; and William Roff, *The Origins of Malay Nationalism* (New Haven: Yale University Press, 1967).

17. For discussion, see my *An Imperial Vision,* esp. 1 and ch. 3.

18. Isabella Bird, *The Golden Chersonese* (1883; reprint Kuala Lumpur: Oxford University Press, 1967), 338–39; K. Bellamy, chairman of Public Works Dept., speech at inauguration of Selangor secretariat, 2 April 1897, in *The Selangor Journal* 5 (2 April 1897): 233.

19. *Selangor Journal* 5 (19 March 1897): 219–21; Spooner speech of 2 April 1897, in ibid. (2 April 1897): 238; J. P. Rodger, *Selangor State Administration Report for 1894,* 30 April 1895, PP 1895, 70: 720. Spooner (1853–1909) served in the Ceylon survey and public works departments from 1876 to 1891. He was Selangor state engineer from 1891 to 1901 and general manager of the FMS Railways from 1901 to 1909.

20. W. Robert Foran, *Malayan Symphony* (London: Hutchinson and Co., Ltd., 1935), 83. Hubback (1871–1948) joined the FMS PWD in 1895 and served as government architect from 1900 to 1914.

21. For the parallel case of the clock tower at Mayo College, Ajmer, see my *An Imperial Vision,* 78–80.

22. For these buildings, see Gretchen Liu, ed., *In Granite and Chunam: The National Monuments of Singapore* (Singapore: Singapore Resource Library, 1997), 88–97. For the Nagore shrine, see C. A. Bayly, ed., *The Raj: India and the British, 1600–1947* (London: National Portrait Gallery, 1990), n. 452.

23. *Selangor State Administration Report for 1908* (Kuala Lumpur, 1909), 26; and *Selangor State Administration Report for 1909* (Kuala Lumpur, 1910), 31.

24. See Liu, ed. *In Granite and Chunam,* 106–13.

25. For Abu Bakar's use of "liberalism," see Milner, *Invention of Politics,* 197–216, 220–21.

26. For discussion of princely building, see my *An Imperial Vision,* ch. 4.

27. Ibid., 35–38.

28. Curzon to Cromer, 19 April 1905, OIOC, Curzon Papers, Mss. Eur. F111/621/173; Thomas R. Metcalf, "Past and Present: Toward an Aesthetics of Colonialism," in G. H. R. Tillotson, ed., *Paradigms of Indian Architecture* (Richmond, Surrey: Curzon, 1998), 12–25; Paula Sanders, "Making Cairo Medieval: Architecture, Religion and Empire in Nineteenth Century Egypt" (unpublished manuscript), ch. 2. I am grateful to Professor Sanders for allowing me to consult this work and for supplying me with copies of source materials.

29. Swettenham, *British Malaya,* 287.

3. Projecting Power

1. SofS to Viceroy, 8 November 1875, For. Dept. Pol. A, January 1876, no. 144–60A; Sec. Govt. India Mily. Dept. to Brig. J. Ross, 16 November 1875, Mily. Dept., November 1875, no. 380. For a brief account of the campaign, see Government of India, *Frontier and Overseas Expeditions from India* [1907–11] (reprint, Delhi: Government Printing Office, 1983), 6: 347–50.

2. Blyth, *Empire of the Raj,* esp. ch. 1.

3. Testimony of Sir Stafford Northcote, 7 July 1869, PP 1868–69, 6: 9; Report of the Select Committee on the Army, PP 1867–68, vol. 6.

4. Report of the Select Committee on the Army, ibid., 6: 795.

5. Final Report of the Royal Commission on the Administration of the Expenditure of India, vol. 4, PP 1900, 29: 111–14, 187.

6. G. F. MacMunn, *The Armies of India* (London: Adam and Charles Black, 1911), 2, 129. For a full account of the "martial races" ideology, see David Omissi, *The Sepoy and the Raj* (Basingstoke: Macmillan, 1994), ch. 1, esp. 23–35; and Heather Streets, *Martial Races: The Military, Race, and Masculinity in British Imperial Culture* (Manchester: Manchester University Press, 2004), esp. ch. 3. The quotations in this and the following three paragraphs are taken from Omissi and from MacMunn, ch. 5.

7. Streets, *Martial Races,* 69–75.

8. The literature on the Gurkhas, mostly by retired British officers, is extensive. For an analysis, see Lionel Caplan, "The Bravest of the Brave: Representations of the 'Gurkha' in British Military Writings," *Modern Asian Studies* 25 (1991): 571–97.

9. For the history of Gurkha recruiting, see C. J. Morris, *Handbook for the Indian Army: Gurkhas* (Delhi: Manager of Publishing, 1933; revised 1936), esp. 129; and Purushottam Banskota, *The Gurkha Connection: A History of the Gurkha Recruitment in the British Indian Army* (Jaipur: Nirala, 1994).

10. Mansfield memorandum of 15 March 1870, OIOC Mss. Eur. F/114/5 (3); Col. Burne to Quartermaster General, 16 November 1875, Mily. Dept. November 1875, no. 396. Pioneer units consisted of soldiers who also served as laborers.

11. For the prime minister's speech, and further correspondence on the *pani patya* question, see TNA FO766/11; and the discussion in Byron Farwell, *The Gurkhas* (London: A. Lane, 1984), esp. 88, 141.

12. For. Sec. to Resident Katmandu, 18 July 1920, For. & Pol. Extl. B, Octo-

ber 1920, nos. 104–8; Resident to For. Sec., 7 August 1920, and For. Sec. to Resident, 9 August 1920, For. & Pol. Extl B, October 1920, nos. 37–39. I am grateful to David Omissi for sharing this reference with me.

13. See Nadzan Haron, "Colonial Defence and British Approach to the Problems in Malaya, 1874–1918," *Modern Asian Studies* 24 (1990): 275–95, esp. 285–87.

14. Timothy H. Parsons, *The African Rank and File: Social Implications of Colonial Military Service in the King's African Rifles, 1902–1964* (Portsmouth, NH: Heinemann, 1999), esp. 14, 54–61.

15. Ibid., 56. For a full account of the Kamba, see Timothy H. Parsons, "Wakamba Warriors Are Soldiers of the Queen: The Evolution of the Kamba as a Martial Race, 1890–1970," *Ethnohistory* 46 (1999): 671–701; for an overview of martial races ideology in Africa, see Anthony H. M. Kirk-Green, "Damnosa Hereditas: Ethnic Ranking and the Martial Races Imperative in Africa," *Ethnic and Racial Studies* 3 (1980): 393–414.

16. WO to CO, 24 February 1876, TNA CO882/3/6, f. 306v.

17. Sec. Govt. India to SofS India, 23 June 1890, OIOC L/MIL/7/14768; memo by E.S.M. of 3 November 1920, L/MIL/7/14824.

18. For an account of the Indian role in the campaign, see Government of India, *Frontier and Overseas Expeditions,* vol. 6, ch. 4, pp. 25–53.

19. Ibid., ch. 5, pp. 54–64.

20. Kirk-Greene, "Damnosa Hereditas," 401. On the Uganda Rifles and the 1897 mutiny, see Government of India, *Frontier and Overseas Expeditions,* 6: 187–91.

21. Jackson to Salisbury, 26 September 1897, PP 1898, 60: 424.

22. E. G. Vaughan to commissary-general Bombay Command, 10 July 1898, L/MIL/7/12678.

23. Lt. Col. A. H. Pearson to Mily. Sec. Govt. India, 25 June 1896, L/MIL/7/12666, collection 272.

24. For an account of this campaign, see the reports included in L/MIL/7/12681; and Government of India, *Frontier and Overseas Expeditions,* vol. 6, ch. 12.

25. J. R. L. MacDonald to Salisbury, 17 January 1898, PP 1898, 60: 450; and W. A. Broome to FO, 4 August 1898, FO2/170.

26. Cave to FO, 3 July 1896, L/MIL/7/12666. On this occasion the sultan conferred the Order of the Brilliant Star of Zanzibar on the three English officers of the 24th.

27. Treasury to FO, 21 February 1896; IO to FO, 27 February 1896; and Treasury to IO, 16 March 1896, FO2/117.

28. See Government of India, *Frontier and Overseas Expeditions,* vol. 6, ch. 13.

29. For a full account of the operations in Somaliland, see ibid., chs. 7 and 8.

30. WO to FO, 18 September 1899, L/MIL/7/14504; and adjutant general to Sec. Govt. India, 3 October 1899, L/MIL/7/14507.

31. Singh, *Reversing the Gaze,* esp. diary entries of 11 August 1900, 114; and of 21 January 1901, 145.

32. Ibid., entry of 14 July 1901, 157–59.

33. Anand Yang has in preparation a collection of letters from Indian soldiers during the Boxer rebellion.

34. For the "particular care" taken in the shipping of ghee to Mombasa for the Indian troops, see Lt. Col. A. H. Pearson to Bombay Govt., 19 March 1896, L/MIL/7/12666.

35. See David Omissi, ed., *Indian Voices of the Great War: Soldiers' Letters, 1914–1918* (Basingstoke: Macmillan, 1999); and Streets, *Martial Races,* ch. 6.

36. Wilson, *Loyalties: Mesopotamia,* 111. Wilson's volume contains a full account of the campaign.

37. For information about the labor corps, I am grateful to Radhika Singha, who shared with me her unpublished paper, "Convicts, Primitives, and India's Contribution to the Great War, 1916–1920."

38. History of the Shaiba Bund Project by Maj-Gen. J. C. Rimington, September 1916, For. & Pol. Secret-War February 1917, nos. 235–66. See also Singha, "Convicts, Primitives, and India's Contribution to the Great War."

39. For information on India's provision of naval craft and technical expertise in Mesopotamia, I am indebted to Priya Satia, "Redemption on the Tigris: The Fate of Technology and Empire in World War One," unpublished paper prepared for my graduate research seminar, University of California, Berkeley, spring 1999; this paper is forthcoming in *Past and Present.*

40. George Buchanan, *The Tragedy of Mesopotamia* (London: W. Blackwood, 1938), 127, 250; and Montagu speech of 6 August 1918 in House of Commons, *Hansard Parliamentary Debates,* 3rd ser., vol. 109, cols. 1142–43.

41. A. T. Wilson to Col. C. E. Yate 28, November 1914, enclosed in Yate to Sir E. Grey, 28 January 1915, For. & Pol. Secret-War May 1915, nos. 178–303. For full discussion of the British debates over the fate of Mesopotamia see Blyth, *Empire of the Raj,* ch. 6.

42. Viceroy to SofS India, 7 December 1914, For. & Pol. Secret-War February 1915, nos. 101–19; Hardinge, "Note on Future Status of Basrah," 24 February 1915, quoted in Blyth, *Empire of the Raj,* 136; and Willcocks, *Sixty Years in the East,* 72.

43. A. H. Grant note of 18 March 1915, For. & Pol. Secret-War May 1915, nos. 178–303; KW Notes, pp. 36–37.

44. SofS to Viceroy, 9 December 1914, For. & Pol. Secret-War February 1915, nos. 101–19; Mark Sykes memo of 15 November 1915, quoted in Blyth, *Empire of the Raj,* 141.

45. Barrett to Chief of General Staff, 23 November 1914, For. & Pol. Secret-War June 1915, nos. 47–50; Barrett to Chief of General Staff, 19 December 1914, and Chief of General Staff to Barrett, 20 December 1914, For. & Pol. Secret-War March 1915, nos. 607–94.

46. Barrett to Chief of General Staff, 24 December 1914, Cox to Sec. Govt. India, 15 January 1915, Punjab Govt. to Home Dept., 27 January 1915, and Cox to Sec. Govt. India, 6 March 1915, For. & Pol. Est. A July 1915, nos. 20–64.

47. GOC Force "D" to Chief of General Staff, 12 May 1915, and Sec. Govt.

India to Cox, 15 June 1915, ibid.; Sec. Govt. India to Cox, 17 September 1915, For. & Pol. Est. B October 1915, nos. 44–48.

48. For a list of appointees in 1916, see "Basra Appointments" in 1916 For. & Pol. Index. For European office clerks and the like, see correspondence in For. & Pol. Est. B April 1916, nos. 245–70. Most European staff accepted the posts offered but requested pay increases to offset higher living expenses; these requests were usually granted.

49. See Knox to Cox, 18 March 1916, and further correspondence in For. & Pol. Est. B September 1916, nos. 66–67, and in For. & Pol. Est. B October 1916, nos. 275–307. Indian staff, like their European counterparts, requested and received substantial pay increases on taking up appointments in Mesopotamia. But not all posts were easily filled. For the difficulty encountered in procuring subassistant surgeons from India for newly opened civil dispensaries in Iraq, see For. & Pol. Est. B May 1917, nos. 210–45.

50. Gen. Sir J. Nixon to For. Sec. Govt. India, 17 November 1915, For. Sec. to Nixon, 30 November 1915, and KW by H. D. G. Law of 23 November 1915, For. & Pol. Est. B, December 1915, nos. 197–98. After his return to India, Dobbs served as chief commissioner of Baluchistan (1917–19) and Indian foreign secretary (1919–22) before returning to Iraq as high commissioner from 1923 to 1929.

51. Memo by G. D. Bell on the Administration of Justice in the Occupied Territories of Iraq, c. July 1916, For. & Pol. Secret-War June 1917, no. 155; S. G. Knox, Report on the Administration of Civil and Criminal Justice for 1915, and for 1916, For. & Pol. Secret-War February 1918, nos. 205–22.

52. S. G. Knox, Report on the Administration of Civil and Criminal Justice for 1917, For. & Pol. Secret-War October 1918, nos. 188–90.

53. KW note of 23 November 1915 by H. D. G. Law, For. & Pol. Est. B December 1915, nos. 197–98; KW notes of 12 June 1916 and 1 August 1917 by Denys Bray, For. & Pol. Secret-War February 1918, nos. 205–22, and of 12 June 1918, For. & Pol. Secret-War October 1918, nos. 188–90.

54. Viceroy to SofS, 18 October 1916, For. & Pol. Secret-War November 1917, no. 107; viceroy to SofS, 27 April 1917, For. & Pol. Secret-War June 1919, nos. 183–303; note by Hirtzel of 30 December 1916, quoted in Blyth, *Empire of the Raj,* 152.

55. SofS to viceroy, 29 March 1917, For. & Pol. Secret-War June 1919, nos. 183–303.

56. E. Bonham-Carter, Report on the Administration of Civil Justice for Baghdad Vilayet for 1918, For. & Pol. Secret-War B February 1920, nos. 291–92. The transformation was pushed forward by the fact that, after the war, many Indian officials, either by preference or because they were recalled, returned to their regular posts within India. By June 1919 the number of Indian officers serving in Iraq, from a high of fifty-eight a year before, had fallen to thirty, out of some two hundred British officials in the Iraq civil administration. See Arnold, *Mesopotamia, 1917–1920,* 156–58.

57. A. T. Wilson, Review of the Civil Administration of the Occupied Territories of Iraq, For. & Pol. Secret-War B December 1919, nos. 600–602; Bon-

ham-Carter letter of January 1919, quoted in Arnold, *Mesopotamia, 1917–1920,* 173. Knox was denied promotion to the senior position of judicial secretary on the ground that he was too tied to the Indian codes. Cox to Sec. Govt. India, 21 October 1918, For. & Pol. Secret-War June 1919, nos. 183–303.

58. Report on the Administration of Civil Justice for 1918, For. & Pol. Secret-War B February 1920, nos. 291–92; Report on the Administration of Civil Justice for 1919, For. & Pol. Extl. B October 1920, nos. 285–86.

59. Viceroy to SofS, 1 June 1916, For. & Pol. Secret-War February 1917, nos. 229–34. By 1917 the Indian government had effectively abandoned the effort to secure a "field of expansion" for Indians in Mesopotamia and looked instead to conquered German East Africa. See, e.g., viceroy to SofS, 27 April 1917, For. & Pol. Secret-War June 1919, nos. 183–303; and chapter 6, "India in East Africa."

60. WO to IO, 24 October 1919, L/MIL/7/14824; Arnold, *Mesopotamia, 1917–1920,* 239, 298.

61. Civil commissioner to IO, 10 April 1920, high commissioner to For. Sec. Govt. of India, 16 December 1920, and correspondence regarding the status of laborers recruited for service in Iraq, in For. & Pol. Secret-Extl December 1921, nos. 1–79.

62. Civil commissioner to depty commissioner police Basra, 13 May 1919, and depty commissioner police Basra to civil commissioner, 11 June 1920, ibid.

4. Recruiting Sikhs for Colonial Police and Military

1. See Norman Miners, "The Localization of the Hong Kong Police Force, 1842–1947," *Journal of Imperial and Commonwealth History* 18 (1990): 296–315.

2. For an account of Speedy's life, see John M. Gullick, "Captain Speedy of Larut," *Journal of the Malayan Branch of the Royal Asiatic Society* 26 (1953): 4–103.

3. Dist. Supt. Police Lahore to Dpty. IG-Police Lahore, 3 October 1873, and Dpty IG-Police Lahore to IG-Police Punjab, 13 October 1873, For. Dept. Pol. A, December 1873, Nos. 37–40.

4. Speedy to Commissioner Police Calcutta, 16 September 1873, For. Dept. Pol. A, April 1874, nos. 166–69.

5. Sec. Govt. Bengal to Sec. Govt. India For. Dept., 29 September 1873, ibid.

6. Colonial Secretary Straits Settlements to Sec. Govt. India, 26 November 1874, For. Dept. Mily. B July 1875, nos. 11–11A.

7. Jervois to Carnarvon, SofS Colonies, 19 August 1876, TNA CO273/84. For Swinburne's appointment, see Jervois to Carnarvon, 18 October 1876, CO273/85.

8. Adjutant General to Sec. Mily. Dept., 10 February 1875, For. Dept. Mily. B July 1875, nos. 11–11A; and KW by P.G. of 20–5-74, Home Police May 1874, nos. 48–53.

9. Emily Innes, *The Chersonese with the Gilding Off* (1885; repr. Kuala Lumpur: Oxford University Press, 1974), 2: 74; Bird, *The Golden Chersonese,* 283.

10. Speech of W. G. Gulland, 18 November 1884, *Progs. SSLegCo for 1884,*

p. B140; Hugh Clifford, *Studies in Brown Humanity* (London: G. Richards, 1898), 128. For the controversy over the relative utility of employing Chinese and Indian police in Hong Kong, see the report of the 1872 Police Commission cited in Miners, "Hong Kong Police Force," 303–05.

11. Perak Annual Report for 1884, by F. A. Swettenham, 28 March 1885, PP 1887, 58: 377.

12. J. M. Gullick, "Syers and the Selangor Police, 1875–1897," *Journal of the Malaysian Branch of the Royal Asiatic Society* 51 (1978): esp. 1–33.

13. J. P. Rodger to Col. Sec. SS, 13 October 1888, and Gov. SS to CO, 15 October 1888, CO273/155; and Pahang Annual Report for 1889, PP 1890–91, 57: 351.

14. Maj.-Gen. H. T. Jones-Vaughan to Gov. SS, 15 November 1894, CO273/199; and Perak Annual Report for 1896, 12–13.

15. "Report of a Commission Appointed to inquire into the desirability, or otherwise, of introducing Chinese as Ordinary Members of the Police Force," 16 June 1873, *Progs. SSLegCo for 1873,* cii–cvi; Memo by Maj. S. Dunlop, inspector-general police, of 15 September 1876, CO273/85; "Report of the Police Commission, 1879," *Progs. SSLegCo for 1879,* cclxxviii–cclxxx; report of inspector-general police for 1881, *Progs. SSLegCo for 1882,* 95–98.

16. Omissi, *Sepoy and the Raj,* 10–29; Streets, *Martial Races,* 93–101.

17. Note by Eric St. J. Lawson, commissioner police Siam, of 20 February 1905, For. Dept. Extl. A May 1905, nos. 175–77; Jones-Vaughan to Gov. SS, 15 November 1894, CO273/199.

18. Commissioner Central Africa to C-in-C India 8 August 1892, Mily. Dept. B May 1893, nos. 2107–46. At the time Johnston wrote, Kipling, still a young man, had only begun to gain fame in England and could hardly have been widely read in Central Africa.

19. Perak Annual Report for 1887, PP 1888, 73: 748; Swettenham to J. Chamberlain 12 August 1903, Rev. & Ag. Dept. (Emigration) A December 1904, nos. 1–2.

20. Selangor Annual Report for 1895, PP 1896, 58: 340; Jones-Vaughan to Gov. SS, 15 November 1894, CO273/199; Annual Report on Malay States Guides for 1899 by Lt.-Col. Walker, CO273/262/31573.

21. SofS India to Sec. Govt. India, 27 December 1888, For. Dept. Extl. A February 1889, nos. 100–101; Pollock to Sec. Govt. India 21 October 1889, For. Dept. Extl. A December 1889, nos. 127–28. See also the notes in For. Dept. Extl. A October 1889, nos. 10–15.

22. A. S. Rogers to IBEA Co., 26 January 1893, and IBEA Co. to Rosebery, 5 August 1893, PP 1893–94, 62: 532–33, 556; Rennell Rodd to H. M. Durand, 3 September 1893, For. Dept. Secret E January 1894, nos. 480–86.

23. Mily. Dept. KWs of 27 and 29 September 1893, and Sec. For. Dept. to R. Rodd, 27 October 1893, For. Dept. Secret E January 1894, nos. 480–86.

24. SofS India to viceroy, 23 April 1891, and Mily. Dept. KW note by E.H.H.C. of 24 April 1891, For. Dept. Extl. B May 1891, nos. 46–47.

25. Johnston to FO 10 November 1894, Rev. & Ag. Dept. (Emigration) February 1895, no. 8; KW note by E.H.H.C., 24 April 1891, For. Dept. Extl. B May 1891, nos. 46–47.

26. KW note by W.B.W. of 1 May 1891, For. Dept. Extl B May 1891, nos. 46–47; Maguire note of 8 May 1891 and WG note of 8 May 1891, For. Dept. Extl B, October 1891, no. 131.

27. Johnston to C-in-C India, 8 July 1892, Mily Dept. B May 1893, nos. 2107–46. For an account of the operations in Nyasaland, see H. Moyse-Bartlett, *The King's African Rifles* (Aldershot: Gale and Polder, 1956), 17–23.

28. Johnston to FO, 26 April 1894, FO2/66.

29. Edwards's report of 21 February 1893, FO2/117. See also Manning's report of 4 August 1893, ibid.

30. Godfrey's report of 1 October 1898, OIOC L/MIL/7/14407, collection 322. See also adj.-gen. note of 28 October 1895, Mily. Dept. February 1896, nos. 2501–67.

31. For pay and conditions of service in African contingents, see adj.-gen. note of 27 August 1895, Mily. Dept. February 1896, nos. 2501–67; C-in-C India to Johnston enclosed in Johnston to FO 12 April 1895, FO2/117. For Indian Army pay and incentives, see Omissi, *Sepoy and the Raj,* 54–61.

32. Johnston to FO, 12 April 1895, FO2/117.

33. Johnston to FO, 10 November 1894, Rev. & Ag. Dept. (Emigration) February 1895, no. 8; Report on the Administration of British Central Africa for 1896–97, by A. Sharpe, PP 1897, 62: 28; Sharpe to C-in-C India 7 May 1897, FO2/143; Report on the Administration of British Central Africa for 1897–98, by W. H. Manning, PP 1899, 63: 253–54.

34. Gov. Gen. to SofS India, 5 February 1896, Mily. Dept. February 1896, nos. 2501–67. See also reports in L/MIL/7/1442, collection 323.

35. Jackson to Salisbury, 26 September 1897, PP 1898, 60: 424; Macdonald to Salisbury, 17 January 1898, ibid., 450.

36. British So. Africa Co. to FO, 14 March 1898, and CO to FO, 14 April 1898, FO2/170.

37. For requests by Indian officers to transfer to West Africa, see the petitions in L/MIL/7/15787, 15791, and 15806. Lugard praised Willcocks as an "officer of exceptional Indian experience" in a letter to Chamberlain of 31 August 1899, L/MIL/7/15798. He subsequently criticized Willcocks's "expectation" that his frontier experience equipped him to "run the show" in West Africa. M. Perham and M. Bull, eds., *Diaries of Lord Lugard* (London: Faber and Faber, 1963), 4: 417.

38. Lugard to CO, December 1897, L/MIL/7/15788. See also A. H. M. Kirk-Greene, "Indian Troops with the West African Frontier Force," *Journal of the Society for Army Historical Research* 42 (1964): 17–20.

39. On the Ashanti campaign, see Willcocks to Chamberlain, 25 December 1900, PP 1901, 48: 557; and Moyse-Bartlett, *The King's African Rifles,* 37–40.

40. Lugard to Chamberlain, 23 April 1900, Chamberlain to Lugard, 6 June 1900, CO to IO, 21 August 1900, and Gov. Gen. to SofS India, 7 March 1901, in L/MIL/7/15798.

41. Annual Report on Northern Nigeria for 1900, PP 1902, 65: 501; Annual Report for 1905–06, PP 1907, 54: 98, 181–82.

42. Gov. N. Nigeria to CO, 27 November 1908, and CO to IO, 12 July 1909, L/MIL/7/15811.

43. Govt. of India to SofS India, 27 October 1898, Mily. Dept. December 1898, no. 1314.

44. See NAI Mily. Dept. Note no. 48 of 1896.

45. KW note by C-in-C of 4 October 1893, For. Dept. Secret E January 1894, nos. 480–86. See also Mily. Dept. Note 48 of 1896.

46. See Omissi, *Sepoy and the Raj,* 48–52; and chapter 3 of the present volume.

47. Govt. of India to SofS India, 27 October 1898, Mily. Dept. A December 1898, no. 1314. For the class composition of the Indian Army, see Omissi, *Sepoy and the Raj,* 20.

48. Curzon to Hamilton, 3 September 1902, and Mily. Dept. Note of 20 September 1902, enclosed in Curzon to Hamilton 24 September 1902, OIOC Hamilton Papers Mss. Eur. D.510/11.

49. Notes by Col. B. Duff of 23 September 1902, and A. P. Palmer of 26 September 1902, Mily Dept. B April 1903, nos. 1512–16. See also Richard G. Fox, *Lions of the Punjab* (Berkeley and Los Angeles: University of California Press, 1985), ch. 8, esp. 140–43. Duff subsequently rose to the positions of chief of staff (1906) and commander-in-chief of India (1914–16).

50. Notes by A. H. Bingley of 1 August 1902, Mily. Dept. B April 1903, nos. 1512–16; and of 28 February 1902, Rev. & Ag. Dept. (Emigration) April 1902, nos. 34–35. Khatris were commonly an educated urban caste, and Mazbis were of untouchable origin. For discussion of the difficulties the British encountered in classifying Sikhs, see Fox, *Lions of the Punjab,* 110–13.

51. Col. Sec. SS to Sec. Govt. India, 27 October 1894, Rev. & Ag. Dept. (Emigration) March 1895, no. 7; Note by A. H. Bingley of 31 March 1902, Rev. & Ag. Dept. (Emigration) April 1902, nos. 34–35.

52. Note by E. St. J. Lawson of 20 February 1905, For. Dept. Extl. A May 1905, nos. 175–77; and KW Note by W. H. Bingley of 31 March 1902, Rev. & Ag. Dept. (Emigration) April 1902, nos. 34–35.

53. Notes by Curzon of 25 February 1903, and by E. G. Barrow of 19 January 1903, Mily. Dept. B April 1903, nos. 1512–16. Curzon's phantasm did, of course, materialize some forty years later in a form unimaginable in 1903, with the formation under the Japanese of the Indian National Army.

54. Note by R. E. V. Arbuthnot of 5 March 1902, Rev. & Ag. Dept. (Emigration) April 1902, nos. 34–35; SofS India to Gov. Gen., 25 December 1903, and Sec. Govt. India to Col. Sec. SS, 14 July 1904, Rev. & Ag. Dept. (Emigration) December 1904, nos. 1–2.

55. Govt. India to SofS, 21 June 1892, Mily. Dept. July 1892, No. 338; Gov. Gen. to SofS, 9 April 1903, Mily Dept. B April 1903, nos. 1512–16; Kitchener note of 8 August 1904, enclosed in Gov. Gen. to SofS, 8 June 1905, Mily Dept. B June 1905, nos. 1450–62.

56. Gov. Hong Kong to CO, 11 February 1908, Mily. Dept. Army B July 1909, nos. 1329–32; Swettenham to Chamberlain 12 August 1903, Rev. & Ag. Dept. (Emigration) December 1904, nos. 1–2.

57. FO to IO, 4 June 1903, and Minister Peking to For. Sec., 12 September

1903, enclosing note by Sec. Shanghai Municipal Council of 31 August 1903, Rev. & Ag. Dept. (Emigration) December 1904, nos. 1–2.

58. Chairman Shanghai Municipal Council to Sec. Govt. India, 19 January 1906, Mily. Dept. Police B April 1908, nos. 1221–68.

59. Minister Peking to FO, 17 September 1906 and 13 October 1906, with enclosures and notes, and Gov. Gen. to SofS, 14 May 1907, Mily Dept. B April 1908, nos. 1221–68; Minister Peking to Sir E. Grey, 27 October 1908, Mily. Dept. B July 1909, nos. 1329–32. On the Shanghai Municipal Police, see Robert Bickers, *Empire Made Me: An Englishman Adrift in Shanghai* (New York: Columbia University Press, 2003), ch.4, esp. 64–67, 86.

60. Gov. Gen. to SofS, 1 July 1909, Mily. Dept. B July 1909, nos. 1329–32.

61. Gov. Gen. to SofS, 31 December 1908, Mily Dept. B March 1909, no. 381.

62. Minister Peking to FO, 13 October 1906, and KW note by A. R. Martin of 3 May 1907, Mily. Dept. B April 1908, nos. 1221–68.

63. GOC Peshawar to adj.-gen., 16 November 1906, and Gov. Gen. to SofS, 31 December 1908, Mily. Dept. B March 1909, no. 381. For the performance of Rajput soldiers, see Amar Singh's account of the Boxer rebellion in chapter 3, above.

64. SofS to Gov. Gen., 26 February 1909, and Gov. Gen. to SofS, 1 July 1909, Mily. Dept. B July 1909, nos. 1127–29; Gov. Gen. to SofS, 31 December 1908, Mily. Dept. B March 1909, no. 381. For an earlier though similar view of Pathan recruitment, in this case for the Uganda contingent, see C-in-C to Govt. India, 12 December 1897, in Gov. Gen. to SofS, 10 March 1897, FO2/170.

65. SofS to Gov. Gen., 5 November 1909 and 16 January 1910, and viceroy to SofS. 28 January 1910, Mily. Dept. (Army) May 1910, nos. 433–46; CO to IO, 19 January 1910, CO534/11; commander Indian contingent Uganda to adj.-gen. KAR, 3 February 1912, CO534/15.

66. Vincent to commanding officer KAR, 5 November 1909, and governor Nyasaland to CO, 24 November 1909, CO534/11.

67. Gov. Uganda to SofS Colonies, 12 January 1912, CO534/15. See also Moyse-Bartlett, *The King's African Rifles*, 158–59.

68. For the 1915 mutiny, see conclusion, below.

69. For a general account, see K. S. Sandhu, "Sikh Immigration into Malaya during the Period of British Rule," in Jerome Chen and Nicholas Tarling, eds., *Studies in the Social History of China and Southeast Asia* (Cambridge: Cambridge University Press, 1970), 335–54.

70. Miners, "Hong Kong Police Force," esp. 309–12.

5. "Hard Hands and Sound Healthy Bodies"

1. See David Northrup, *Indentured Labor in the Age of Imperialism, 1834–1923* (Cambridge: Cambridge University Press, 1995), table A.1, pp. 156–57. For East Africa, see chapter 6 of the present volume.

2. Hugh Tinker, *A New System of Slavery* (London: Oxford University Press,

1974). Among the more recent accounts are Marina Carter, *Servants, Sirdars, and Settlers: Indians in Mauritius, 1834–1874* (Delhi: Oxford University Press, 1995); K. O. Laurence, *A Question of Labour: Indentured Immigration into Trinidad and British Guiana* (London: James Curry, 1994); Brij V. Lal, *Girmitiyas: The Origins of the Fiji Indians* (Canberra: Journal of Pacific History, 1983); and Madhavi Kale, *Fragments of Empire: Capital, Slavery, and Indian Indentured Labor in the British Caribbean* (Philadelphia: University of Pennsylvania Press, 1998).

3. Surendra Bhana, *Indentured Indian Emigrants to Natal, 1860–1902* (New Delhi: Promilla, 1991).

4. H. Slater, "Land, Labour and Capital in Natal, 1860–1948," *Journal of African History* 16 (1975): 257–84; and Colin Bundy, *The Rise and Fall of the South African Peasantry* (Berkeley and Los Angeles: University of California Press, 1978), 168–82.

5. Cited in L. M. Thompson, "Indian Immigration to Natal (1860–1872)," in *Archives Yearbook for South African History*, vol. 2 (Cape Town: Publications Branch of the Director of Archives, 1952), 1–76.

6. Full footnote citations are given only for extended extracts from this correspondence.

7. Collins to Colonial Secretary, 26 April 1860; to H. Burton, 18 August 1860; to Colonial Secretary, 15 September 1860, 17 October 1860, and 5 February 1861, KwaZulu Natal Archives, East India, file 55. See also Y. S. Meer, ed., *Documents of Indentured Labour, Natal, 1851–1917* (Durban: Institute of Black Research, 1980), 48–51.

8. For the lists of passengers on these first two ships, see Meer, ed., *Documents*, 54–79.

9. For the relevant documents, including enactments and regulations in Natal, see ibid., 172, 176–77, 211–38.

10. Firth to subagents, 31 March 1874, II B/1/14. In practice the prescribed sex distribution was rarely maintained, with the percentage of males commonly reaching 65 percent. See Bhana, *Indentured Indian Emigrants to Natal*, 19–20.

11. Report on Emigration from Calcutta by F. Colepeper, 5 March 1877, II 1/3/53.

12. Memoranda by James Caldwell of 15 and 17 September 1878, ibid.

13. Indian Immigration Trust Board meeting of 19 March 1880, II 1/6/73; Firth to Protector of Immigrants Natal, 30 June 1880, II 1/7/875.

14. Khetta Mohan Chatterjee Inspection Reports, especially from Allahabad (25 December 1880), Meerut (27 December 1880), and Benares (3 January 1881), II B/1/12.

15. For the districts of origin of indentured laborers see Lance Brennan, John McDonald, and Ralph Shlomowitz, "The Geographic and Social Origins of Indian Indentured Labourers in Mauritius, Natal, Fiji, Guyana and Jamaica," *South Asia* 21, special issue (1998): 39–71, esp. 41–50. Over time the center of recruitment shifted from Bihar to the U.P., especially to the districts of Gonda and Basti.

16. Firth to Kunj Behari, 15 February 1883, 6 March 1883, and 10 March 1883, II B/1/16.

17. W. M. Macleod to Colonial Sec. Natal, 3 August 1874, in Meer, ed., *Documents,* 204–5. For discussion of reluctance to recruit Punjabis, see Lal, *Girmitiyas,* 53.

18. Firth to Deeplall, 12 February 1883; Officiating Emigration Agent to Protector Durban, 22 January 1884, II B/1/16.

19. Firth to Protector of Emigrants Calcutta, 3 March 1883, ibid.

20. Mitchell to Secretary Indian Immigration Trust Board, 23 January 1904, II A/2/1/96.

21. Mitchell to Muzaffar Ali, 11 February 1889, and to D. H. R. Moses, 16 February 1889, II B/1/18.

22. Mitchell to subagents, 3 November 1896, and to B. K. Gupta, 6 November 1896, II B/1/22.

23. Mitchell to subagents, 21 November 1895, and Protector of Immigrants Natal, 22 November 1895, II B/1/21.

24. Mitchell to Protector of Immigrants Natal, 1 June 1885, II B/1/17.

25. Bhana, *Indentured Indian Emigrants to Natal,* 77–82.

26. Grierson, *Report on Colonial Emigration from Bengal Presidency* (1883), 10, 12; and Grierson, Diary, 33, 40, OIOC, V/27/820/35.

27. Mitchell to Muzaffar Ali, 9 January and 21 January 1899; Mitchell to Protector Natal, 20 January 1899, II B/1/25.

28. Mitchell to Sarfaraz Ali, 10 March 1902, and to all subagents, 12 March 1902, II B/1/28.

29. Mitchell to Solomon, 3 December and 14 December 1898; Mitchell to Magistrate Cawnpore, 17 February 1899, II B/1/25.

30. Grierson, *Report on Colonial Emigration,* 7–9. See also the description of the subdepot in Lal, *Girmitiyas,* 27–30.

31. Mitchell to D. H. R. Moses, 5 January and 7 February 1893, II B/1/20.

32. Mitchell to B. E. Hoff, and to Magistrate Cawnpore, 5 March 1900, II B/1/26.

33. Lal, *Girmitiyas,* 23.

34. Grierson, *Report on Colonial Emigration,* 12; and Grierson, Diary, 40–41.

35. Emigration Agent Madras to Protector Natal, 21 February and 2 March 1883, with enclosure of 26 February from recruiters, II 1/12/246 & 302.

36. Grierson, *Report on Colonial Emigration,* 15; and Grierson, Diary, 9. Deeplall of Bankipur had one returnee working as recruiter under him and knew of two or three others, Grierson, Diary, 11.

37. Mitchell to Indian Immigration Trust Board, 17 April 1905, II 1/133/168; Mitchell to Indian Immigration Trust Board, 24 June 1905, II A/2/8/282. For general discussion, see Lal, *Girmitiyas,* 25–26, 55–56.

38. Mitchell to Protector Natal, 17 February 1903, and to Indian Immigration Trust Board, 23 January and 18 February 1904, II A/2/1/96.

39. Report on Calcutta Agency Expenditures for 1902, II 1/121/2272.

40. Ross to Protector Natal, 27 December 1882, II 1/12/93; Ross to Indian Immigration Trust Board, 21 July 1883 and 12 March 1884, II A/3/2. The internal correspondence of this firm with its recruiting staff and other agents in the interior is not available. Hence, even though the south supplied twice as many

Natal-bound emigrants as the north, we know much less about the recruiting operation in Southern India as compared to that through Calcutta.

41. *Natal Mercury (Durban),* 14 January 1884; Parry & Co. to Protector Natal, 20 December 1884, II 1/22/1563.

42. Parry & Co. to Protector Natal, 20 February and 1 March 1884, II 1/19/501; Parry to Protector, 18 March 1884, II 1/20/625; Parry to Protector, 20 December 1884, II 1/22/1563.

43. Parry & Co. to Protector Natal, 14 November 1892, II 1/61/145. W. R. James to Protector Natal, 16 April 1903, II 1/117/832.

44. Parry & Co. to Protector Natal, 24 April 1899, II 1/94/877.

45. A. R. Denning to Indian Immigration Trust Board, 13 February 1908, II A/2/15/54. For Indian opposition to indenture, see conclusion of the present volume.

46. Carter, *Servants, Sirdars, and Settlers,* 66-67.

47. Parry & Co. to Protector Natal, 20 December 1884, II 1/22/1563.

48. Ibid.

49. See Minute by Lieutenant-Governor Bengal of 11 September 1875, NAI Bengal Emigr. Progs. November 1875, nos. 9-19. The Indian authorities doubted that emigration on the scale envisioned would have any considerable effect in relieving Indian poverty.

50. Lieutenant Governor of Bengal Note of February 1861, cited in Carter, *Servants, Sirdars, and Settlers,* 83.

51. Mitchell to Benoy Krishna Gupta, 30 September 1896, II B/1/22. For discussion of heights of emigrants, see Lance Brennan, John McDonald, and Ralph Shlomowitz, "Toward an Anthropometric History of Indians under British Rule," *Research in Economic History* 17 (1997): 185-246. They make clear that emigrant height, though measured, was not used as a measure of physical ability, and there was no minimum height requirement (194-96).

52. Carter, *Servants, Sirdars, and Settlers,* 302; Lal, *Girmitiyas,* 69-70; Bhana, *Indentured Indian Emigrants to Natal,* 77-82; and Brennan, McDonald, and Shlomowitz, "Geographical and Social Origins of Indian Indentured Labourers," 55-66.

6. India in East Africa

1. Frere to Granville, 27 February 1873, and "Memorandum Regarding Banians or Natives of India in East Africa" of 31 March 1873, enclosure in Frere to Granville, 7 May 1873, FO881/2270.

2. Report on the Administration of the Eastern Portion of British Central Africa from 1891 to 1894, PP 1894, 57: 779; and Frere's Report on the Uganda Protectorate, 10 July 1901, PP 1901, 48: 577. The term "Hindu" is used here to include all Indians regardless of religion, rather as the term "English" was often used in those years to mean "British."

3. Several good standard histories of the Indians in East Africa exist. Espe-

cially noteworthy are J. S. Mangat, *A History of the Asians in East Africa* (Oxford: Clarendon Press, 1969); and R. J. Gregory, *India and East Africa: A History of Race Relations Within the British Empire* (Oxford: Clarendon Press, 1971).

4. For the Omani commercial empire, see Abdul Sheriff, *Slaves, Spices and Ivory in Zanzibar* (Oxford: James Curry, 1987).

5. Frere Memorandum of 31 March 1873, FO881/2270. For an account of East Africa's Indian merchants in these years, see Mangat, *History*, ch. 1; and Sheriff, *Slaves, Spices and Ivory*, esp. 65, 105–9.

6. Holmwood to Manchester Chamber of Commerce, 10 April 1885, in SOAS Mackinnon Papers, box 66, file 12. See also Sheriff, *Slaves, Spices and Ivory*, ch. 4.

7. Political Agent Zanzibar to For. Dept. Govt. of India. 12 September 1874, in For. & Pol. A December 1874, nos. 61–64.

8. For the political developments of these years, see John S. Galbraith, *Mackinnon and East Africa, 1875–1895: A Study in the "New Imperialism"* (Cambridge: Cambridge University Press, 1972).

9. See J. Forbes Munro, "Shipping Subsidies and Railway Guarantees: William Mackinnon, Eastern Africa and the Indian Ocean, 1860–93," *Journal of African History* 28 (1987): 209–30.

10. G. S. Mackenzie to Sec. IBEA Co., 23 October and 14 November 1888, SOAS Mackinnon Papers, box 63, file 1A.

11. Mackenzie to Sec. IBEA Co., 26 January 1889, and to Stuart Sandip, agent at Lamu, 28 January 1889, ibid.

12. Minute by chief secretary Uganda, 9 June 1925, cited in Mangat, *History*, 53. See also Mangat's discussion of the career of Allidina and other merchants, ibid., 49–62.

13. A. Hardinge, "Report on the Administration of the East Africa Protectorate to 1897," PP 1898, 60: 199–209.

14. Protector of Emigrants, Bombay, to Commissioner of Customs, 8 September 1896, and Memorandum by Acting Commissioner of Customs, 11 September 1896, Rev. & Ag. Dept. (Emigration) October 1896, nos. 15–16.

15. Mackenzie to Sec. IBEA Co., 25 April 1888, SOAS Mackinnon Papers, file 1A; Report by Frederic Holmwood [n.d.] in For. Dept. Secret E November 1888, nos. 192–200.

16. H. H. Johnston, Report on the Administration of the Eastern Portion of British Central Africa from 1891 to 1894, 31 March 1894, FO2/66.

17. H. H. Johnston to For. Sec., 1 June 1895, in Rev. & Ag. Dept. (Emigration) November 1895, no. 8.

18. H. H. Johnston to FO, 17 November 1894, Rev. & Ag. Dept. (Emigration) A, January 1895, no. 8.

19. Johnston report of 31 March 1894, FO2/66.

20. Protector of Emigrants to Commissioner of Customs, 21 July 1896, Rev. & Ag. Dept. (Emigration) September 1896, nos. 2–4.

21. SofS India to FO, 18 December 1894, Rev. & Ag. Dept. (Emigration) A, January 1895, no. 8; Johnston, Report on British Central Africa for 1895–96, 29

April 1896, PP 1896, 58: 429; Col. Sec. to FO, 11 September 1895, Rev. & Ag. Dept. (Emigration) November 1895, no. 8.

22. Johnston, Report on the Uganda Protectorate, 10 July 1901, PP 1901, 48: 577.

23. Hardinge to FO, 24 August 1900, LPJ/6/548, file 1743; Eliot to Lansdowne, 6 September 1901, LPJ/6/654, file 2721.

24. Col. T. Gracey, Report on Uganda Railway of 25 March 1901, PP 1901, 48: 637–38; Memo by Gen. W. H. Manning of 24 April 1902, FO2/571, and by A. S. Rogers of 11 December 1901, FO2/569.

25. See, e.g., the letters of George Whitehouse of 20 September 1901 and C. Farquhar, railway police superintendent, of 28 August 1901, FO2/569.

26. Eliot to Lansdowne, 6 September 1901 and 5 January 1902, LPJ/6/654, file 2721; see also FO2/569.

27. Johnston to FO, 17 November 1894, Rev. & Ag. Dept. (Emigration) A, January 1895, no. 8; Johnston Report on Uganda Protectorate of 10 July 1901, PP 1901, 48: 577.

28. Report [n.d.] by C. W. Hobley; and Waller to Eliot, 16 October 1903, LPJ/6/654, file 2721.

29. Annual Report on the East African Protectorate (EAP) for 1902–03, 18 April 1903, PP 1903, 45: 716.

30. Report of Indian Immigration Committee of 10 November 1905, and Commissioner EAP to CO, 21 May 1906, LPJ/6/769, file 2102; Governor EAP to SofS Colonies, 17 December 1907, PP 1908, 71: 1063. For the later growth of the Kibos settlement, where land grants continued to be made for some years, see the conclusion of the present volume.

31. Waller to acting commissioner, 8 February 1907, and Jackson to SofS Colonies, 13 February 1907, CO533/27; SofS India to Viceroy, 11 July 1906, Commerce & Industry Dept. (Emigration) August 1906, nos. 13–16; for correspondence on Waller's mission within India, see Commerce & Industry Dept. (Emigration) November 1906, nos. 12–18. See also Hayes Sadler to SofS Colonies, 17 December 1907, PP 1908, 71: 1063.

32. Commissioner EAP to CO, 21 May 1906, LPJ/6/769, file 2102; Governor EAP to SofS Colonies, 17 December 1907, PP 1908, 71: 1063.

33. SofS Colonies to Governor EAP, 19 March 1908, PP 1908, 71: 1071.

34. Commissioner of Lands to Governor [n.d., 1907], ibid. 1064.

35. Montgomery minute of 8 May 1907, enclosed in Hayes Sadler to SofS Colonies, 13 May 1907, CO533/29.

36. Governor to CO, 1 May 1914, and IO to CO, 29 July 1914, Commerce & Industry Dept. (Emigration) August 1914, no. 22.

37. For an excellent general account of the Indian position in the East African economy during these years, see Mangat, *History,* ch. 3. For Mehta, see his application for a pension of 17 December 1906, in CO533/19.

38. There are numerous studies of Indian lives and livelihood in East Africa. Most useful perhaps are the books by R. J. Gregory, especially his *South Asians in East Africa: An Economic and Social History* (Boulder, CO: Westview Press,

1993). See also, Savita Nair, "Moving Life Histories: Gujarat, East Africa, and the Indian Diaspora, 1880–2000," Ph.D. dissertation, University of Pennsylvania, 2001.

39. "A Colony for India," July 1918, in Montagu to Imperial War Cabinet, 16 July 1918, TNA CAB 24/58/5132; reprinted in *The Nineteenth Century and After* 84 (September 1918): 430–41; letter to the *Times,* 24 August 1918, 4–5.

40. Montagu memo of 18 October 1918, CAB 24/69/6028; Curzon memo of 19 October 1918, CAB 24/69/6062.

41. Cranworth to W. H. Long, 21 October 1918, CO691/18; Memo by Long on "The Indians and German East Africa," 14 November 1918, CO537/1017.

42. For accounts of the controversy, see Mangat, *History,* ch. 4; and Blyth, *Empire of the Raj,* ch. 5.

43. David Lelyveld, *Aligarh's First Generation* (Princeton: Princeton University Press, 1978), 318.

44. Note by the Representatives of India at the Imperial War Conference, 4 May 1917, CO537/995; Robertson Report of 4 August 1920, and Govt. of India to SofS India, 10 February 1921, PP 1921, 10: 1020–25.

45. Churchill's speech is quoted in Blyth, *Empire of the Raj,* 123.

46. Johnston to Salisbury, 11 October 1899, quoted in Roland Oliver, *Sir Harry Johnston and the Scramble for Africa* (London: Chatto and Windus, 1957), 293.

47. Twining to Macdonald, 4 December 1891, in SOAS Mackinnon Papers, box 63, file 1B. For a general account, see the "Railway Survey Report," PP 1893–94, 62: 105. The term *khalassie* refers to a "free" laborer, or independent contractor not under indenture.

48. Memo by F. L. O'Callaghan of 28 September 1895, CO537/50. Note that Rendel's telegraphic address was "Sukkur London." The honors awarded O'Callaghan and Rendel were the Star of India and Order of the Indian Empire. The original correspondence of the railway committee is contained in CO537, vols. 50–58. Individual citations will be given only for extended quotations.

49. Whitehouse to committee, 30 November 1896, CO537/51; and memo of 7 January 1897, CO537/52.

50. For information on Waller's life, I am indebted to Katherine Prior, who examined the genealogical and employment records held in the TNA and OIOC.

51. General Remarks on the Uganda Railway by C. W. Hodson, 28 December 1897, and committee reply, CO614/4.

52. Whitehouse to railway committee, 19 June 1897, CO537/53.

53. Letter enclosed in W. A. Johns to Whitehouse, 21 June 1896, CO537/51.

54. Lists are enclosed in Whitehouse to railway committee, 19 June 1897, CO537/53.

55. Note on railway gauge by G. L. Ryder, 24 July 1897, CO537/53. See also Final Report of the Uganda Railway Committee, 22 February 1904, PP 1904, Cmd 2164, pp. 6–9.

56. O'Callaghan to Rendel, 11 October 1897, CO537/53.

57. Final Report of the Uganda Railway Committee, 3.

58. SofS India to Govt. India, 31 October 1895, Rev. & Ag. Dept. (Emigration) July 1896, nos. 9-17. See also the correspondence in LPJ/6/430, file 1717.

59. Johns to railway committee, 6 December 1895, and Johns to O'Callaghan, 28 December 1895, CO537/50. For the Indian government's response to this irregular recruiting, see Govt. of India to SofS India, 2 June 1896, Rev. & Ag. Dept. (Emigration) July 1896, nos. 18-55.

60. For Jeevanjee, see Mangat, *History*, 53-55, 82, 103-9.

61. FO to IO, 15 June 1896; Govt. of India to SofS India, 8 September 1896; and related correspondence, CO537/51; and Report of Protector of Emigrants, Karachi, for 1900-1901, cited in Mangat, *History*, 37.

62. For the yearly statistics, see Final Report of the Uganda Railway Committee, 13.

63. Memorandum by O'Callaghan of 15 July 1897, LPJ/6/465, file 2514; and FO memo of 21 August 1897, CO537/52.

64. Boyce to O'Callaghan, 5 May 1898, and 18 May 1898, CO537/56.

65. Winwill to Boyce, 2 September 1898; FO to NW Railway Manager, 16 December 1898; and NW Railway Manager to Boyce, 17 May 1899, CO537/55.

66. J. H. Patterson, *The Man-Eaters of Tsavo* (London: Macmillan and Co., 1907), esp. 103, 106, 332-38.

67. Whitehouse to O'Callaghan, 12 August 1897, CO614/1.

Conclusion

1. For the Singapore mutiny, see *Report of the Government Inquiry in Connection with the Mutiny of the Fifth Light Infantry at Singapore* (Simla, 1915), OIOC, L/MIL/17/19/48, esp. 8-10, 25, 325. For general discussion of mutinies in the post-1858 Indian Army, see Omissi, *Sepoy and the Raj*, 131-50.

2. The files on the East African currency question are extensive. For the introduction of the Indian rupee, see FO2/956; for the postwar debates, see the CO-Treasury correspondence in TNA Treasury file 7387, T1/12283; file 29716, T1/12408; file 56010, T1/12547; and file 18357, T1/12547. I am indebted to Katherine Prior for collecting the relevant information from these files for me. East Africa subsequently shifted from a florin- to a shilling-based coinage.

3. For a brief discussion, see my *An Imperial Vision*, chs. 7 and 8. British building in India also during these years largely reverted to the use of classical forms. For a brief account of Sinclair's work, see Abdul Sheriff, *Zanzibar Stone Town: An Architectural Exploration* (Zanzibar: Galley, 2001), ch. 8.

4. Sheriff, *Zanzibar Stone Town*, ch. 4. For the spread of the bungalow form, see Anthony King, *The Bungalow* (London: Routledge and Kegan Paul, 1984).

5. Governor Natal to SofS Colonies, 8 May 1908, Commerce & Industry Dept. (Emigration) September 1908, no. 21. By the 1930s Indians comprised no more than 15 percent of Natal's cane field labor force. See also my "Indian Migration to South Africa," in Metcalf, *Forging the Raj* (Delhi: Oxford University Press, 2005), ch. 11.

6. John Darwin, "A Third British Empire? The Dominion Idea in Imperial Politics," in Judith M. Brown and W. Roger Louis, eds., *The Oxford History of the British Empire*, vol. 4, *The Twentieth Century* (Oxford: Oxford University Press, 1999), 64–87. For the Indian side, see S. R. Mehrotra, *India and the Commonwealth, 1885–1929* (London: George Allen and Unwin, 1965), esp. chs. 1 and 2.

7. Omissi, "India: Some Perceptions of Race and Empire," in D. Omissi and A. S. Thompson, eds., *The Impact of the South African War* (Basingstoke: Palgrave, 2001), ch. 11; esp. 219–20, 227.

8. Speeches of 26 March 1902 and 25 February 1910 in Imperial Legislative Council, in R. P. Patwardan and D. V. Ambedkar, eds., *Speeches and Writings of Gopal Krishna Gokhale* (Poona: Asia Publishing House, 1962), 1: 20, 293.

9. For a classic account, see Tinker, *A New System of Slavery*, chs. 8 and 9. For Andrews, see ibid., 336–38, 359–61; and Brij Lal, ed., *Crossing the Kala Pani* (Canberra: Research School of Pacific and Asian Studies, Australian National University, 1998), chs. 7 and 8.

10. For discussion, see John D. Kelly, *A Politics of Virtue: Hinduism, Sexuality, and Countercolonial Discourse in Fiji* (Chicago: University of Chicago Press, 1991), esp. 45–63. I am grateful to Rachel Sturman for sharing her thoughts on indenture with me.

11. Government of Natal, *Report of the Protector of Immigrants for 1887*, A16; *for 1889*, A65; *for 1892–93*, A34; *for 1893–94*, A15; and *for 1899*, A42 and annexure 5. For crop statistics, see Colony of Natal, *Statistical Yearbooks*.

12. For one account, see Bill Freund, *Insiders and Outsiders: The Indian Working Class of Durban 1910–1990* (Portsmouth, NH: Heinemann, 1995).

13. See Vishnu Padayachee and Robert Morrell, "Indian Merchants and Dukawallahs in the Natal Economy, 1875–1914," *Journal of Southern African Studies* 17 (1991): 71–102, esp. 74–76; and K. L. Gillion, *Fiji's Indian Migrants* (New York: Oxford University Press, 1962), 133.

14. Padayachee and Morrell, "Indian Merchants," 100–101.

15. Information taken from the exhibit "The Indian Contribution to Kenya" at the National Museum, Nairobi, January 2005. See also the family histories collected in Cynthia Salvadori, ed., *We Came in Dhows* (Nairobi: Paperchase Kenya, 1996). For Sikhs, see esp. ibid., 1: 191; 2: 168–70.

16. Author's interview with Chanan Singh, Kibos, 25 January 2005.

17. Clive Dewey, "Some Consequences of Military Expenditure in British India: The Case of the Upper Sind Sagar Doab, 1849–1947," in Dewey, ed., *Arrested Development in India* (New Delhi: Manohar, 1988), 93–169, esp. 96–117.

18. Mangat, *History of the Asians in East Africa*, 136–38.

19. Christopher Bayly and Tim Harper, *Forgotten Armies: The Fall of British Asia, 1941–1945* (Cambridge MA: Harvard University Press, 2005), 146, 154, 181–87.

Bibliography

Note: This bibliography includes the major archival sources and published primary source materials consulted for this work, together with a selection of frequently cited or centrally important recent publications. Further titles are cited, where appropriate, in the individual reference notes.

Primary Sources

NATIONAL ARCHIVES OF INDIA, NEW DELHI [NAI]

Commerce and Industry Department — Emigration Branch, 1905–20
Home Department Police Proceedings
Home, Revenue and Agriculture Department — Emigration Branch, 1879–81
Foreign Department Proceedings — External, Military, Political, Secret, 1870–1920
Foreign and Political Department Proceedings — Establishment, External, Secret-External, Secret-War, 1915–20
Military Department Proceedings — Army, Police, 1870–1910
Revenue, Agriculture and Commerce Department — Emigration Branch, 1871–78
Revenue and Agriculture Department — Emigration Branch, 1881–1905

THE NATIONAL ARCHIVES (PUBLIC RECORD OFFICE), KEW [TNA]

Cabinet papers (CAB), vol. 24
Colonial Office (CO), series 273, 533, 534, 537, 614, 691, 822, 882
Foreign Office (FO), series 2, 107, 766, 881

KWAZULU NATAL ARCHIVES, PIETERMARITZBURG
Indian Immigration (II) Letter Books

ORIENTAL AND INDIA OFFICE COLLECTIONS,
BRITISH LIBRARY, LONDON
Records Division (IOR)
Public and Judicial (L/PJ)
Military (L/MIL)

European Manuscripts Division (Mss. Eur.)
D510, F111, F114

SCHOOL OF ORIENTAL AND AFRICAN STUDIES,
UNIVERSITY OF LONDON
Papers of Sir William Mackinnon

Published Government Documents

Government of India, *Frontier and Overseas Expeditions from India* [1907–11]. Reprint, Delhi: Government Mono Type Press, 1983. Vol. 6, "Overseas Expeditions."
Government of Natal, *Reports of the Protector of Immigrants*. 1887–1899.
Grierson, George, *Report on Colonial Emigration from the Bengal Presidency*. Calcutta: privately printed, 1883. In OIOC V/27/820/35.
Hansard's Parliamentary Debates, 3rd series.
Parliamentary Papers (PP) (House of Commons). 1867–1910.
Proceedings of the Legislative Council of the Straits Settlements. [Official publication of the Straits Settlements government.] 1868–1884.

Selected Books and Articles

Alatas, Syed Hussain. *The Myth of the Lazy Native.* London: Frank Cass, 1977.
Banskota, Puroshottam. *The Gurkha Connection: A History of Gurkha Recruitment in the British Army.* Jaipur: Nirala, 1994.
Benton, Lauren. *Law and Colonial Cultures.* Cambridge: Cambridge University Press, 2002.
Bhana, Surendra. *Indentured Indian Emigrants to Natal, 1860–1902.* New Delhi: Promilla, 1991.

Bird, Isabelle. *The Golden Chersonese.* 1883. Reprint, Kuala Lumpur: Oxford University Press, 1967.

Blyth, Robert J. *The Empire of the Raj; India, Eastern Africa, and the Middle East, 1858–1947.* Basingstoke: Palgrave Macmillan, 2003.

Bose, Sugata. *A Hundred Horizons: The Indian Ocean in the Age of Global Empire.* Cambridge MA: Harvard University Press, 2006.

Burton, Antoinette, ed. *After the Imperial Turn.* Durham, NC: Duke University Press, 2003.

Carter, Marina. *Servants, Sirdars, and Settlers: Indians in Mauritius, 1834–1874.* Delhi: Oxford University Press, 1995.

Clifford, Hugh. *Malayan Monochromes.* New York: E. P. Dutton, 1913.

Ghosh, Durba, and Dane Kennedy, eds. *Decentring Empire: Britain, India, and the Transcolonial World.* New Delhi: Orient Longman, 2006.

Gullick, John M. "Captain Speedy of Larut," *Journal of the Malayan Branch of the Royal Asiatic Society* 26 (1953): 4–103.

Lal, Brij V. *Girmitiyas: The Origins of the Fiji Indians.* Canberra: Journal of Pacific History, 1983.

Lui, Gretchen, ed. *In Granite and Chunam: The National Monuments of Singapore.* Singapore: Singapore Resource Library, 1997.

MacMunn, G. F. *The Armies of India.* London: Adam and Charles Black, 1911.

Mangat, J. S. *A History of the Asians in East Africa.* Oxford: Clarendon Press, 1969.

Meer, Y. S., ed. *Documents of Indentured Labour, Natal 1851–1917.* Durban: Institute of Black Research, 1980.

Metcalf, Thomas R. *Ideologies of the Raj.* Cambridge: Cambridge University Press, 1994.

———. *An Imperial Vision: Indian Architecture and Britain's Raj.* Berkeley and Los Angeles: University of California Press, 1989.

Miners, Norman. "The Localization of the Hong Kong Police Force, 1842–1947," *Journal of Imperial and Commonwealth History* 18 (1990): 296–315.

Morris, H. S., and S. Read. *Indirect Rule and the Search for Justice: Essays on East African Legal History.* Oxford: Clarendon Press, 1972.

Moyse-Bartlett, Lt. Col. H. *The King's African Rifles.* Aldershot: Gale and Polden, 1956.

Oliver, Roland. *Sir Harry Johnston and the Scramble for Africa.* London: Chatto and Windus, 1957.

Omissi, David. *The Sepoy and the Raj.* Basingstoke: Macmillan, 1994.

Padayachee, Vishnu, and Robert Morrell. "Indian Merchants and Dukawallahs in the Natal Economy, 1875–1914," *Journal of Southern African Studies* 17 (1991): 71–102.

Parsons, Timothy H. *The African Rank and File: Social Implications of Colonial Military Service in the King's African Rifles, 1902–1964.* Portsmouth, NH: Heinemann, 1999.

Roff, W. R., ed. *Stories by Sir Hugh Clifford.* Kuala Lumpur: Oxford University Press, 1966.

Sandhu, K. S. "Sikh Immigration into Malaya during the Period of British Rule." In Jerome Chen and Nicholas Tarling, eds., *Studies in the Social History of China and Southeast Asia*. Cambridge: Cambridge University Press, 1970.

Sheriff, Abdul. *Slaves, Spices, and Ivory in Zanzibar*. Oxford: James Curry, 1987.

———. *Zanzibar Stone Town*. Zanzibar: Gallery, 2001.

Singh, Amar. *Reversing the Gaze: Amar Singh's Diary, A Colonial Subject's Narrative of Imperial India*. Edited and with commentary by Susanne Hoeber Rudolph and Lloyd Rudolph with Mohan Singh Kanota. Boulder, CO: Westview Press, 2002.

Skuy, David. "Macaulay and the Indian Penal Code of 1862," *Modern Asian Studies* 32 (1998): 513–57.

Streets, Heather. *Martial Races: The Military, Race, and Masculinity in British Imperial Culture*. Manchester: Manchester University Press, 2004.

Swettenham, Frank. *British Malaya*. London: J. Lane, 1907.

Tignor, Robert. "The 'Indianization' of the Egyptian Administration under British Rule," *American Historical Review* 68 (1963): 636–61.

Willcocks, William. *Sixty Years in the East*. London: William Blackwood & Sons, 1935.

Wilson, Arnold Talbot. *Loyalties: Mesopotamia, 1914–1917: A Personal and Historical Record*. London: Oxford University Press, H. Milford, 1930.

———. *Mesopotamia, 1917–1920: A Clash of Loyalties: A Personal and Historical Record*. London: Oxford University Press, H. Milford, 1931.

Index

Page numbers in *italic* indicate figures.

King's African Rifles (KAR), 72, 77–78,
84, 86, 87, 128, 134, 204, 209
Kipling, Rudyard, 6, 111, 117
Kitchener, H. H., 81, 99, 130
Klings, 52, 110
Knox, S. G., 96–99
Komagatu Maru incident, 132
Kuala Kangsar, 64, *65*
Kuala Lumpur: architecture in, 56, 57–60,
58, 59, 61, 62–63, *64,* 208; Chinese
immigrants in, 53
Kurds, 95
Kutch, 167, 171, 217
Kut el-Amara, 69, 90, 206

Labor, Indian: in Ceylon, 107; in East
Africa, 114; in Mesopotamia, 90–91,
101; in Nigeria, 123–24; in South Africa,
216. *See also* Indentured labor
Lahore, 103, 199, 202
Lake Victoria, 166, 177, 178, 188
Lal, Brij, 137, 162
Lamu, 114, 170
Land tenure: in Malaya, 54–55; in Natal,
138–39; in Punjab, 54, 55, 126
Larut, 39–40, 102, 103, 105
Law: common, 19, 21, 27; and indenture,
101, 197, 198; and land tenure, 54–55;
and migrant labor, 129; and military
duty, 70; and railway operating procedure, 196; rule of, 17, 32, 33; and travel
restrictions, 4, 220; and utilitarianism,
18–19. *See also* Civil law *entries;* Criminal
law *entries;* Islamic law; Legal system
entries
League of Nations, 99, 186
Legal system, Australian, 30–31, 45. *See
also* Queensland Criminal Code
Legal system, English: colonial applicabil-
ity of, 27, 28, 29, 45, 206; and common
law, 19, 21, 27; distinguished from
Indian legal system, 19, 21, 32; reform
of, 32; and rule of law, 17, 32; and
utilitarianism, 18
Legal system, French, 30
Legal system, Indian: adopted by East
Africa, 23–29; adopted by Malaya, 22–
23; adopted by Mesopotamia, 29, 97,
99; adopted by Straits Settlements, 19–
23, 30–31; and civil law, 17, 18, 26; and
civil procedure code, 18, 24, 25, 52;
codification of, 18, 27; and criminal law,

17–18; and criminal procedure code, 18,
21–22, 24, 25, 28; criticized by Colonial
Office, 27, 31–32; criticized in East
Africa, 25, 26–28; criticized in Mesopotamia, 99; criticized in Nigeria, 31;
criticized in Straits Settlements, 20–21;
distinguished from English legal system,
19, 21, 32; and Hinduism, 17, 46; and
Islam, 17, 25, 46; Macaulay's involvement in, 18–28; and Mughal Empire,
17–18; and penal code, 18–19, 21, 22, 24,
25, 27, 28, 41, 97, 188; rejected in East
Africa, 27–29, 206; and utilitarianism,
18–19
Liberalism, 54, 65–66, 213
Long, Walter, 184, 186
Low, Hugh, 22, 41–42
Lugard, Frederick, 4, 30, 31, 43, 122–24,
172, 206, 208

Maasai of East Africa, as martial race, 77–
78
Macaulay, Thomas, 2, 18–19, 28, 49, 67
Macdonald, J.R.L., 121, 188, 190
Mackenzie, George S., 169–70, 172, 181
Mackinder, Halford, 1
Mackinnon, William, 114, 169, 188, 200
MacMunn, G. F., 72, 73
"Mad Mullah" of Somaliland, 72, 85, 86,
87, 128
Madras, 54, 122, 133; indentured labor
recruitment in, 137, 140, 141, 146–47,
156–59, 201
Magdala, 103
Mahdi army, 80–81, 203
Malacca, 9, 13, 19, 62, 69, 109
Malaviya, M. M., 213
Malawi. *See* Nyasaland
Malaya: agriculture in, 50, 51, 54–55, 209;
army recruitment in, 77; census in, 53;
Ceylonese immigrants in, 47, 51–52,
209; character of inhabitants of, 47–49;
Chinese immigrants in, 36, 50–51, 53, 54,
105–6, 209; civil law in, 42; colonial
architecture in, 56–66; colonial identity
construction in, 52, 53, 54, 71, 77, 111,
209; compared to African colonies, 42,
43; consolidated into Federated Malay
States, 23, 42; durbar system in, 42;
economic structure of, 53, 54; education
in, 49; Indian laborers in, 51, 209;
Indian police in, 102–13, 130, 135, 219;

Text: 10/13 Galliard
Display: Galliard
Compositor: BookMatters, Berkeley
Indexer: Andrew Joron
Cartographer: Bill Nelson

CPSIA information can be obtained
at www.ICGtesting.com
Printed in the USA
BVOW03s1311281217
503760BV00001B/21/P

9 780520 258051